AFRICAN AMERIC
GENTRIFICATION IN WASHINGTON, D.C.

Urban Anthropology

Series Editors: Italo Pardo and Giuliana B. Prato,
University of Kent, UK

The first series of its kind to be established by a major academic press, Urban Anthropology publishes ethnographically global, original, empirically-based works of high analytical and theoretical calibre, all of which are peer reviewed.

The series publishes sole-authored and edited manuscripts that address key issues that have comparative value in the current international academic and political debates. These issues include, but are by no means limited to: the methodological challenges posed by urban field research; the role of kinship, family and social relations; the gap between citizenship and governance; the legitimacy of policy and the law; the relationships between the legal, the semi-legal and the illegal in the economic and political fields; the role of conflicting moralities across the social, cultural and political spectra; the problems raised by internal and international migration; the informal sector of the economy and its complex relationships with the formal sector and the law; the impact of the process of globalization on the local level and the significance of local dynamics in the global context; urban development, sustainability and global restructuring; conflict and competition within and between cities.

Other titles in the series

Anthropology in the City
Methodology and Theory
Edited by Italo Pardo and Giuliana B. Prato
ISBN 978–1–4094–0833–8

The New Environmentalism?
Civil Society and Corruption in the Enlarged EU
Davide Torsello
ISBN 978–1–4094–2364–5

Seeing Cities Change
Local Culture and Class
Jerome Krase
ISBN 978–1–4094–2878–7

African Americans and Gentrification in Washington, D.C.

Race, Class and Social Justice in the Nation's Capital

SABIYHA PRINCE
Independent Scholar

Routledge
Taylor & Francis Group

LONDON AND NEW YORK

First published 2014 by Ashgate Publishing

Published 2016 by Routledge
2 Park Square, Milton Park, Abingdon, Oxon OX14 4RN
711 Third Avenue, New York, NY 10017, USA

First issued in paperback 2017

Routledge is an imprint of the Taylor & Francis Group, an informa business

Copyright © 2014 Sabiyha Prince

Sabiyha Prince has asserted her right under the Copyright, Designs and Patents Act, 1988, to be identified as the author of this work.

All rights reserved. No part of this book may be reprinted or reproduced or utilised in any form or by any electronic, mechanical, or other means, now known or hereafter invented, including photocopying and recording, or in any information storage or retrieval system, without permission in writing from the publishers.

Notice:
Product or corporate names may be trademarks or registered trademarks, and are used only for identification and explanation without intent to infringe.

British Library Cataloguing in Publication Data
A catalogue record for this book is available from the British Library

The Library of Congress has cataloged the printed edition as follows:
Prince, Sabiyha, 1959–
    African Americans and gentrification in Washington, D.C. : race, class and social justice in the nation's capital / by Sabiyha Prince.
        pages cm. – (Urban anthropology)
    Includes bibliographical references and index.
    ISBN 978–1–4094–4612–5 (hardback : alk. paper)
    1. African Americans – Washington (D.C.) – Social conditions. 2. Washington (D.C.) – Race relations. 3. Washington (D.C.) –Social conditions.
    4. Gentrification – Washington (D.C.) I . Title.
    E185.93.D6P75 2013
    305.8009753–dc23   2013020852

ISBN 13: 978-0-8153-4644-9 (pbk)
ISBN 13: 978-1-4094-4612-5 (hbk)

Dedicated to the memories of Lee Folia
Verina Prince and Madeline Elizabeth Eversley

Contents

Acknowledgments

This book stems from the collective efforts of numerous individuals. The work may not be the perfection its years to completion merit but any shortcomings on these pages should, in no way, reflect negatively upon the stellar support I received from so many along the way.

I begin by acknowledging the help of my former colleagues at American University. I particularly want to thank Rachel Watkins and Brett Williams—two extraordinary scholars and friends who read and edited my work during the early stages of its writing and lent other, pivotal forms of support throughout this demanding process. I also want to thank the dozens of people who took action in response to my failed tenure bid. Your commitment to confront unfairness was an important source of encouragement for me. My spirits were bolstered by your concern and the instances where so many of you campaigned for change on this matter by organizing, Facebooking, writing letters and, even, meeting with those persons who were responsible for this disappointing decision.

My work has also keenly benefitted from the input of academics at other institutions. Anthropologists Judith King-Calnek, Arlene Davila, Lesley Gill, Faye Harrison, John Hartigan, Jane Henrici, John Jackson, Elgin Klugh, Karla Slocum, and Alaka Wali all fit this description as do my interdisciplinary cohorts Michelle Boyd, Carl and Caleen Jennings, Marie-Elena John-Smith, and Lorna Skyers who helped in a variety of capacities. Journalist-friends Julia Chance, Keith Harriston, and Geraldine Moriba-Meadows provided important supports at key points over the years. I also owe particular debts of gratitude to friend and historian-extraordinaire, Yevette Richards Jordan and Professor Leith Mullings who remains my original anthropological mentor and a continuous inspiration. Conversations with local scholars C.R. Gibbs and Mayra McQuirter assisted with the completion of this project as did a bevy of current and former graduate students worked as both teaching and research assistants during my 12-year stint at American University. These include Dr. Michelle Carnes, Dr. Michelle Chatman, Dr. Ariana Curtis, Sean Furmage, Mahri Irvine, Nikki Lane, Rafael Lainez, Barbra Lukunka, Julie Maldonando, Ashante Reese, Dr. Malinda Rhone, Kalfani Ture, and Dr. Arvenita Washington-Cherry. I also owe a great debt of gratitude to Stacey Terrell, Erika Crable Amanda Yerby, and Amanda Huron for their assistance with various aspects of this project as well as undergraduate students in D.C. inequality class and various independent studies that helped me discuss issues and work out frameworks. This latter description includes Emily Conrad, Ava Page, Jesse Sarnoff, and Drew Sunderland. Finally, Nina Shapiro-Perl took time out of her schedule to advise me on videotaping interviews with seniors in Washington, D.C.

and it is because of her efforts that I was able to produce these visual representations that will stand the test of time.

Ingrid Drake was very generous with sharing interviews she transcribed as a part of the Ivy City Oral History Project. I would like to thank her and all the women and men who shared their stories for this important community-based effort. Patrick Crowley, Fred Carter, Zein El-Amine, Netfa Freeman, Amy Hendrick, Linda Leaks, Dominic Moulden, Parisa Norouzi, Gertrude Saleh, and Anu Yadav offered key insights and opportunities leading up to this book being completed.

Wayson Jones provided much-needed support with editing and the qualitative research consultancy Dr. Asher Beckwitt was indispensable throughout the final phases of this project. The work of external reviewers was also central. These readers' feedback exposed me to new bodies of literature and helped strengthen the final draft of this manuscript.

I was also assisted by the financial support and/or research of The Fiscal Policy Institute, The Center for Community Voice at American University, The D.C. Humanities Council, and The Martin Luther King Library of Washington, D.C.

Thank you to Neil Jordan of Ashgate Publishing who has been a remarkably steady hand throughout a process that overlapped with difficult circumstances. These include the passing of my mother, aunt, and mother-in-law as well as kooky, extreme environmental conditions in the form of a hurricane, a derecho, a microburst, record heat waves and two earthquakes that left power outages and crumbling edifices in their wakes. The contributions of Celia Barlow and Carolyn Court at Ashgate Publishing have also been central to seeing this project through to fruition.

I also wish to honor the help of caregivers Carolene "Candy" Morgan, Jasmin Bose, and Athew McCalla. Their work occurred behind-the-scenes but without their important and much-valued assistance, none of this researching and writing could have been achieved. I thank them for taking care of my baby girl and mother respectively.

A booming thank you to my attorney and home-slice Lisa D. Butler for her legal-counsel and friendship. There are additional friends and collaborators whose names I have omitted although they, too, have provided crucial forms of support. I have done this to preserve their anonymity or protect myself (in case I inadvertently forget to mention someone—gulp!). Although I do not list folks by name, all of their contributions have been immeasurable. Included among the nameless are friends and neighbors who offered child care, pet care, and/or house sitting services on multiple occasions. This would have been a much more chaotic process without their helpful hands and well wishes.

Family and fellowship are the most important elements of my life. Thank you to Steve, Thandiwe, and Mariama for the silliest and most loving and supportive household a person could ever have. Thanks also to Chris Prince, Lee Prince-Fletcher, Harold Eversley, and Terry Handy for their kinship, love, and encouragement.

Last but not least, a heartfelt thank you goes out to all the current and former residents of Washington, D.C. who lent their stories to me for this book. These pages would be blank without their generosity of time and spirit. This ethnography was truly a collective effort and I am filled with a tremendous sense of gratitude for what has been so graciously shared. I hope that everyone's efforts will contribute to broadening discussions about social justice and vulnerability in relation to gentrification in the Nation's Capital today.

Introduction

I was standing amid the crowd on 14th and V Streets, NW in Washington, D.C., just a few feet from the entrance to Busboys and Poets restaurant and bookstore, when I had to quickly step out of the way to avoid getting hit by a car. A small White boy was navigating a battery-operated, Jeep a few feet ahead of a young White couple who apparently were his parents. The trio rounded the bend in a staggered fashion and attracted the attention of some of the people milling about on that balmy, spring evening. As I waited for friends and talked on my cell phone, I had to laugh and apologize to my brother who I forgot was on the other line. "Hold on a minute [pause]," I said after taking in the scene, "I'm sorry, I just had a gentrification moment."

Gentrification moments are being had in all quarters and discussed by a wide array of people. I have heard hotel clerks, hip hop artists, yoga instructors, activists, and bloggers talking or rhyming about gentrification. I have been in on conversations with African Americans as they gather around dining room tables, in church basements at the end of home-going ceremonies, or even in the restrooms of nightclubs. The most candid of these discussions are taking place in racially homogeneous environs rather than through discussions in the general public realm.[1] Predominantly Black locations or events attended by African Americans are stocked with data on African American thought and experience around gentrification.

This statement is not intended to minimize the value of more diverse settings as advantageous places to conduct ethnographic research on this topic. Spaces with varied selections of people are important and also attended to for this project but I have observed how, through exercises in civility, people erect masks to preserve order or shield acquaintances from hurt feelings during potentially-heated discussions across race/class boundaries. Without privileging one type of information or setting

---

1 The Internet offers up a daily supply of unadulterated talk on race coming from academics, credentialed and up-and-coming journalists, bloggers, and lay consumers of online news and opinion who can post comments and exchange ideas with others through an assortment of websites. There are also websites that specialize in exploring themes of race and ethnicity in the U.S. and on a more global scale. While this represents one form of public discourse, it does not approximate the dynamic of talking with different types of people directly on these subjects. The anonymity of the Web also breeds candor and bigotry. Such exchanges can supply the ethnographer with provocative and confrontational text for cultural analysis, but there are also problems with these types of samples. There is no way to verify the identities of those involved in conversations with any certainty.

over another, suffice it to say that the frankness often displayed during in-group conversations constituted essential elements to my field data.

African Americans and Gentrification in Washington, D.C. focuses on the perspectives and experiences of African Americans as they confront, interpret, and act upon contemporary urban restructuring in the form of gentrification. The Nation's Capital is the original American "Chocolate City" (CC)—a euphemistic label for urban areas with a majority African American population. When the legendary funk band Parliament-Funkadelic released "Chocolate City," their masterful ode to Washington, D.C., they did so in 1975 during a liminal period in U.S. urban history: after the uprisings of the late 1960s but before the war on drugs and neoliberalism hit with a vengeance. This was also the decade when the African American population of D.C. reached its statistical zenith at 71 percent (U.S. Census Bureau, 1970). Parliament's musical tribute was heard across the country at house parties and barbeques and over hand-held radios and large, living room stereos. The song didn't just sound good; it carried a message that was embraced in celebration of Black urban life and political self-determination. In a convergence of demographics, expressive culture, and politics, perhaps CC entered the lexicon as a signal of African American's refusal to fade into the complacency of assimilation or defeat.

Much has changed in D.C. since the 1970s. The city's African American population began a gradual decline in the very same decade. Black people in noticeable numbers headed to the surrounding suburbs in search of safety and larger, more affordable homes (Manning, 1998). These voluntary movements represent one form of migration but the latest changes are taking place under different circumstances and more quickly than many observers ever anticipated.

African Americans and Gentrification in Washington, D.C. centers the lives and standpoints of African American Washingtonians and is anchored in the work of scholars of both African American and critical urban studies. African Americans of varied socioeconomic backgrounds are the focus of this book with particular emphasis being placed on the needs of economically vulnerable populations. Racism has had detrimental effects on Blacks of different classes but the poor are the most susceptible to dislocation and other crucial adversities. This book attends to the impacts of class inequality and racism over time and ensures stories of the poor are heard alongside those of all others.

Gentrification is what occurs when communities experience an influx of capital and concomitant goods and services in locales where those resources were previously non-existent or denied. The concept was coined by urban theorist and social justice activist Ruth Glass as she witnessed the changes taking place in London during the early 1960s (1964). Descriptively, the term is meant to encompass the availability of new mortgages, home improvement loans, and funding for real estate development and new businesses. Gentrification generates a host of impacts and it also affects diverse populations differentially.

Issues of class and race factor heavily into the demographic shifts that occur through gentrification. The legacy of racism erects barriers that limit the advantages

African Americans derive from the influx of monetary and other resources that gentrification brings about. Examples of African Americans directly benefitting from this form of urban restructuring are circumscribed as evidenced by a lower volume of Black gentrification and the most predominant patterns of Black gentrification occurring in one particular neighborhood—Anacostia (Lewis, 2010).

Statistics validate what the racialized visual indicators suggest about demographic changes in the District. More than 200,000 African Americans have left D.C. since the 1970s (Manning, 1998). When I began the research for this book the Black populace stood at approximately 55 percent, which represented an 11 percent decrease since the 2000 census (U.S. Census Bureau, 2008). The non-Hispanic White population increased by 14 percent during that same period, prompting demographers to project that this trend would continue and that D.C. would cease to be majority Black by 2015 (Aizeman, 2007). However, the gears of speculation had to shift after the postulation that, given that African Americans were barely 50 percent of the city's population when the 2010 census was completed and due to the rapid pace of their outmigration up to that point, the percentage of African Americans living in this city probably fell below half by spring of 2011 (Morello and Keating, 2011; U.S. Census Bureau, 2010). It is within this hastily changing context that this book conveys the voices and life paths of African Americans who, either through birth or migration, call Washington, D.C. home.

Various sectors of societies contend with gentrification (Lees, Slater, and Wyly, 2008; Modan, 2007; Prince, 2002, 2005). By considering the perspectives and experiences of African Americans in Washington, D.C. alongside the work of scholars looking at the effects of gentrification across the country, my findings counter any misperceptions people may have about race declining in significance in U.S. life. The downward political and economic movement African Americans of varied socioeconomic strata faced because of residential segregation, housing foreclosures, unemployment, and wealth imbalances mitigates this argument and social scientists using quantitative approaches, legal studies, and qualitative data-gathering strategies continue to document the impact of racism on racial-ethnic minorities today (Cacho, 2012; Crenshaw, 1995; Fields and Fields, 2012).

Historically, race has overlapped with class and other markers of status and identity (Aguirre and Baker, 2008). While the poor have tremendous challenges to navigating a societal landscape fraught with disparities (Lin and Harris, 2008), *African Americans and Gentrification in Washington, D.C.* also incorporates the experiences and perspectives of college-educated African Americans. Research has shown that Black professionals face unique discriminatory practices despite or even because of their educational achievements and economic successes (Cose, 1993; Feagin and Sikes, 1994). They, like the poor, are also a diverse group composed of people who act in ways that are not predictably associated with their socioeconomic status (Prince, 2004).

This book elaborates on how the inequalities of race and class position are intrinsically tied to gentrification. The association between gentrification and hierarchy sparks a need to analyze the culture of supremacy or control and attending to power relations also sets the stage to account for chronological change. Grappling with the past includes considering the consequences of enslavement, struggles against Jim Crow and African Americans' experience with urban renewal. Power continues to be a relevant issue today because this history has left indelible marks upon the present and because gentrification constitutes a neoliberal strategy in the way it privileges market forces in the availability of housing in urban environments. Given this socioeconomic and historical context the focus of *African Americans and Gentrification in Washington, D.C.* moves from the past to an examination of contemporary uneven urban development. As the connection between power relations and economic hierarchies only constitutes the tip of the iceberg, this book also explores how societal inequalities can shape the contours of identity, ideology and intra-racial diversity.

A focus on power relations has concrete implications for social justice. Real people exist behind the statistics of growing inequality in Washington, D.C. and many advocates for these populations do not see gentrification as the solution for extricating people from the dire economic conditions that confront the poor daily. This debate rages at a time when anti-poverty, grassroots activists are going up against developers, politicians and their surrogates to mitigate gentrification's effects. Conflict is occurring with local governmental officials, leaders in commerce, and the beneficiaries of gentrification who have emphasized the importance of growing the city and its tax base and marketing profile. On the other side of the argument are organizers and activists advocating to increase budgetary allotments for children's education and recreation, job training, affordable housing, and other needs for working class residents. By conducting field research I learned how and why social justice advocates do not envision gentrification as the vehicle through which more equitable conditions in this city will be achieved.

African Americans and Gentrification in Washington, D.C. documents examples of gentrification increasing the vulnerability of low income residents. This book also recalls my observations of progressive residents moving toward racial reconciliation when they join forces across the boundaries of race, class and ethnicity to mitigate the harm of gentrification collectively. The specter of people working for social justice in diverse groupings offers an edifying and hopeful vision for the future of these relations. These actions present an opportunity for a sustainable change that is more viable than the commodification of multiculturalism through the *consumption of ethnicity* in restaurants and clothing stores. And while I would not describe cross-cultural collaborations as problem-free, the lessons participants of various race and class backgrounds can learn from each other holds the potential to expand the purview of individual existence in ways that are life enhancing in interesting ways.

My exploration into standpoint, hierarchy, race relations, and social justice also constitutes a study of a place—the city of Washington, D.C. Washington, D.C. has a history and a political economic configuration that makes it singular among urban areas of comparable size or geographic location and its uniqueness is not inconsequential for gentrification. In addition to being a city that borders the American north and south and is at once a provincial small town and the anchor of a global metropolitan area, Washington, D.C.'s functional and symbolic importance resonates nationally. The Nation's Capital is also noted for its dramatic gaps between the wealthy and the impoverished, indicators that have worsened in the contemporary period (Nelson and Ojha, 2012). It is run by a form of governance that diminishes local autonomy for the sake of federal imperatives. This city also has a history of Black achievement that extends beyond the period of Reconstruction (Gatewood, 1993). It is a place of paradoxes.

Washington, D.C. may seem singular among other urban centers but concentrating on this particular city is still broadly instructive. One reason is because the Nation's Capital has been an overlooked area in contemporary anthropological studies. This is ironic given its status as a federal city, a locus for rapid demographic change, and a major tourist destination. Interest in what occurs in Washington cuts across geographic boundaries and should establish D.C. cultural anthropological studies as significant additions to research on similarly transformative processes occurring across the country and around the world. *African Americans and Gentrification in Washington, D.C.* chimes in on discussions about these issues and advances our understanding of contemporary, urban change and its impact upon social relations.

Getting the Work Done

Without initially knowing it my research on D.C. began in 2005. At that time I was engaged as a humanities scholar for a community-based project organized around the performance of a one-woman play. *The Home* was written and performed by activist and playwright Zahira Kahlo[2] and presented in a style similar to the theatrical work of Anna Deavere Smith.[3] In the performance Kahlo "becomes" various District residents who were connected to the dislocation of African Americans from the public housing complex slated for demolition. The Humanities Council of Washington, D.C. awarded a grant to organize performances of *The Home* in a church, a residence for seniors, and community centers across the city. Project

---

2   Throughout this book pseudonyms are used on place of the real names for people and housing projects. I do not use false names for neighborhoods deeming the pseudonyms and changes in other identifying information sufficient for protecting the confidentiality of project participants.

3   Anna Deavere Smith is an actor/playwright who has appeared in television and film. Currently a professor at New York University, Smith is the author and sole star of Twilight: Los Angeles and Faces in the Mirror. These two plays exemplify a unique style of theatrical presentation wherein the actor plays each role. In Smith's case the cast of characters constitutes individuals who vary by gender, age, race and class and this is a setup that requires impersonation. As is also the case with Kahlo, the themes of these particular two plays also center on contemporary urban conflicts that are fraught with racial-ethnic tension http://www.annadeaveresmithworks.org/bio.

directors asked me to lead post-performance discussions with the audiences of each location about the sociocultural implications of the play. This project was initiated by the efforts of a local African American theater company and, as such, modeled an innovative approach for artists, academics, and activists to collaborate with local institutions and draw attention to social justice struggles.

Working on this community-based arts project was the impetus for me to formulate an ethnographic study of D.C. Initially, curiosity motivated me to talk with residents who came from a diverse selection of neighborhoods across the city. These conversations improved my post-performance audience engagement so I heightened my observations of these communities. Afterwards I quickly resolved to question residents about gentrification and incorporate my observations of the play at the performance and discussions after the event into a larger ethnographic project.

I arrived by car and early for each performance and walked around the neighborhoods we visited just to get a feel for the areas. Sometimes this involved bringing my two daughters along and a fruitless search for something tasty and relatively healthy to eat near the performance site. The notes I recorded after driving and walking about before the play and those resulting from the performance overall as well as the audience discussion that followed were data. The course of my research project was shaped through my involvement with *The Home*. I was introduced to new acquaintances and previously unheard-of streets. Hearing and watching the reactions of the rambunctious youth or wheelchair-bound elders, most of whom were riveted by Kahlo's depictions, resonated and set me on the path of this research project. By the following year I had begun a newly-expanded exploration into the repercussions of gentrification in the Nation's Capital.

My data were obtained through a combination of qualitative research strategies. The resources, skills, and social networks I have honed and developed as an urban ethnographer and second-generation Washingtonian have centered my approach to illuminating historical information on Black Washingtonians and capturing their views and experiences as they deal with and attempt to make sense of gentrification. As a native and current resident of this metropolitan area, I utilized my phone book, email addresses, and diverse networks of friends, family, and acquaintances to locate African American residents of various ages and class backgrounds and from different neighborhoods. Despite my close personal ties to this city, it was important that I be unacquainted with the majority of the participants in this project.

Oral history collection, participant observation, and group and individual interviews enabled me to amass information on the viewpoints and life experiences of a range of African Americans who are current and former residents of Washington, D.C. Over the course of gathering these data I talked, laughed, ate, grieved, rode the bus, attended community meetings, and celebrated with people who responded to direct or indirect questions alike. Their stories contextualize perceptions of and feelings about gentrification as reflected along the terrain of individual memory, status, experience, and group identity.

As another characteristic, *African Americans and Gentrification in Washington, D.C.* has an ethno-historical component signaled by the use of secondary historical sources and the participation of elder African Americans. The stories of men and women who are 60 to 90 years of age recreate life in Washington from the 1920s and 1940s through to the present. Their experiences during a period of expansion, immediately after World War II for example, starkly contrasts against what we see taking place among African Americans in Washington today. Their stories deepen the descriptions of place and experience but over the course of moving this project toward publication a handful of these elderly participants have passed away while others have developed dire physical infirmities or become impaired by the ravages of memory loss. Such tenuousness reinforces the importance of recording the reflections of elders while these treasured community members are still around to share them.

Elders shared what it meant to be young during their time and I determined what was important by taking my analytical cues from them as they talked about such topics as the marked contrasts between urban and suburban, exchanging "folk amalgamations of race and behavior"[4] through discursive constructions of the city, home, school, neighbors, store owners, mentors, family members and friends. The ideas and behaviors I note are the content of past and present-day cultural assemblages and these elements are the very focus of this book. All of the data do not make it onto these pages but essentially I am telling the stories and sharing the opinions of this diverse group by placing findings against the backdrop of contemporary urban transitioning.

Remembrances of the past, filtered through an understanding of the changing socioeconomic and political conditions over time, are also imbricated in the ideological and material construction of present-day interfaces. I have heard a range of viewpoints over these years of carrying out my research with African American D.C. residents; individuals who ranged from the native-born to those with no less than 5 years of residence. This is a diverse group, yet I found patterns among them concerning their personal assessments and individual experiences *vis-à-vis* changes in the communities from which they hailed or through which they regularly traversed. Age and world view were among the additional social variables that held sway over the formation of their personal standpoints and ideas.

The physical organization of communities has an impact on opportunities and the overall experiences of daily life and spaces continue to be racialized in and around Washington, D.C. The transformations this metropolitan area has undergone over the last few decades, moreover, foster further, almost perpetual shifts which differentiate local communities, making them stand out against each other. As a result group boundaries are fraught with meaning and the energy of cultural recreation. This city has been in a constant phase of change and, indeed, that is the nature of the human experience. Whether caused by outside intervention or occurring more organically, demographic modifications have been a historical

---

4   Page 5, John L. Jackson Jr., *Harlem World: Doing Race and Class in Contemporary Black America.* Chicago: The University of Chicago Press, 2001.

constant but with a consideration of these more recent population shifts, the current direction of change has charted very new territory.

In preparing to write this book, little of what I observed was safe from my notepad. Small remarks and momentary displays of attitude recorded as brief notes were on equal footing with what I gleaned reviewing the swaths of my field notes and transcribed conversations I acquired from extensive participant observation and lengthy oral history interviews. These are the sources I mined for information on African American family history, personal experiences, and discursive constructions of people, places, and ideas. Talking to people about their memories and insights revealed how African Americans have made sense of the past as well as contemporary everyday life to socially construct and, in essence, stake claim to this city. This is how I assembled documentation of the ways African American identity formation and race relations are fueled by fluid and complex processes (Bobo, 2011; Harris-Lacewell, 2004).

Rather than focus on one neighborhood, I duplicated the multi-sited fieldwork approach that has been discussed in both Clarke (2004) and Pardo and Prato (2012), and which was also utilized in *The Home* project. The residential areas I visited included, in NE, Brentwood, Ivy City, Lamond Riggs, Michigan Park, North Michigan Park, Trinidad and Woodridge and the NW neighborhoods of Bloomingdale, Columbia Heights, Eckington, Georgetown, Le Droit Park, Mt. Vernon Square, Petworth, Shaw and Shepherd Park. I also interviewed two former residents of the demolished Homestead Homes in SE[5] as well as six D.C. natives now living in Maryland, Philadelphia, Pennsylvania and New York City.

Following my work with *The Home*, another chance to gather data through an institutional affiliation arose in 2007 when I joined a local, grassroots organization located in the Shaw community of NW Washington. The group, called D.C. First (DCF), managed campaigns aimed at preventing the privatization of public property and focused on advocating for increased affordable housing and child care for working families and families with disabled children. I joined the public property campaign and was also asked to serve on the organization's steering committee. After more than a year of membership, I agreed to join the board and served on it for a year.

The executive directors of DCF granted me permission to become a participant–observer of the meetings and events I attended. During that time I offered my clerical and writing skills to DCF working groups and meeting coordinators. By joining this organization, I was able to practice a public anthropology as I engaged in community work while gathering ethnographic data. I also incorporated new residents into my project. This also advanced the gathering of ethnographic data on the Shaw community.

I also became acquainted with Ingrid Drake through my association with DCF and she played an important role in helping me to expand the volume of

---

5   The place name for this housing complex is also altered to protect the confidentiality of the former residents who participated in this study.

my data collection. Drake gave me access to oral history data on 20 current and former residents of one of the oldest African American enclaves in the city, the N.E. neighborhood of Ivy City These extensive life stories were collected by volunteers and supporters of a grassroots initiative funded by the Humanities Council of Washington of D.C. Portions thereof appear in *Ivy City Oral History Project*, a small publication that crams within its 31 pages, colorful photographs and in-depth personal reflections of community life from the 1930s to the contemporary period (2009). I was the only university-affiliated scholar to have access to all of these interview transcripts at that time and most of the personal data collected did not appear in the 2009-publication. Because this information already appears in the public record, I do not use pseudonyms when referring to these Ivy City residents.

Although this book is not a community study, I did conduct the bulk of my ethnographic explorations in a handful of specific neighborhoods. For extensive visits, I chose Michigan Park in the NE and Shaw in the NW. Having had a close association with these two neighborhoods, as I came of age in Michigan Park and my aunt having lived in Shaw for 10 years until her death in February 2011, conducting field research in these areas was at once both challenging and convenient. I had casual and more structured opportunities to gather field data and to combine this work with my obligation to visit elderly kin, but the real challenge came as a result of needing to look at a familiar setting with fresh eyes.

Ethnographic data facilitate the emergence of a sense of place. During the summers of 2008 and 2009, I recorded field observations on community life and periodic daily comings and goings from a variety of vantage points. Before or after interviews in Columbia Heights, Georgetown, and Lamond-Riggs, and Michigan Park I would sit in my vehicle and make jottings as I watched community life unfold around me. On other occasions, I would take up position in a bookstore or restaurant window to watch interactions within these establishments and activities occurring outside on the street. I also patronized an assortment of bars and performance venues in neighborhoods to observe the racial/ethnic and age make-up of persons in attendance.

The people of this study were all born between 1920 and 1970 and this foreshadows the constrained variation I was aiming for. Differences in neighborhoods were complicated by variations in participant's place of origin and type of residence. The women and men I spoke with also diverged by occupation and this resulted in differences of socioeconomic positioning and work-related status. Some of the people I engaged with were retired while others were either employed or in search of work. Performing and visual artists were represented, as well as former and current activists, administrators, radio personalities, educators, mail carriers, laborers, office support staff and one doctor, lawyer, police officer and midwife. There was also variation by sexuality, gender, ideological perspective and length of time in D.C. I incorporated these individuals into my project through a process of snowball sampling. Acquaintances knew people who knew other people and that gave me the contact information that I followed up on.

In gathering data for *African Americans and Gentrification in Washington, D.C.* I had long-term, face-to-face interactions with approximately 35 African Americans, the majority of whom are current residents of the city. I collected oral histories on most of these individuals and engaged in participant observation with them to varying degrees and in a range of settings. I also gained information on deceased kin which added depth to their stories. In the end, this book stitches together the narratives of approximately 100 Black Washingtonians to document their attachment to D.C. and ascertain their views of and responses to gentrification.

In addition, the hours I spent watching and jotting down observations were helpful as was the time spent consuming area resources in the form of food, live music, and other types of performance. These practices exposed the dynamic ways communities felt, sounded, and smelled. This strategy also presented entertaining options for observing the racial composition and interactions of restaurant and store patrons and audiences. Were patrons and crowds homogeneous or differentiated? Were there types of events, cuisines, or performances that attracted certain segments of the local populace, and what meaning could I glean from these observations? These are some of questions I considered through these particular explorations and data-gathering strategies.

I began the process of writing up my findings from this research in 2010 and would write during the spring, summer and winter breaks from my duties as an assistant professor. Ironically it was not getting tenure that enabled me to devote the time I really needed to edit my manuscript closely and finish the work at the end of 2012.

Exploring the Analytical Context

The volume of available research on gentrification (Butler, 2007; Cunningham, 2001; Curran, 2007; Freeman, 2006; Hartman, 2002; Lees, Slater, and Wiley, 2008; Niedt, 2006; Sternburgh, 2009; Zimmerman, 2008) has not diminished the call for additional contributions. The remaining need for studies on the subject is due, in part, to the continuing struggles communities are engaging in to lessen gentrification; whether they reel from its effects directly or watch from a distance but support those affected through activism. There is also a perspective which conceives of gentrification as an approach to urban redevelopment (Vigdor, 2002). There are subtleties in these different opinions as well as confusion about why gentrification occurs, who it benefits, the extent of its harm, and the complex ways class and race intersect and alter communities. Debates aside, what there is little equivocation about, among the long-term residents I engaged with for this project, is the look and feel of gentrification.

For many African Americans, gentrification means "not belonging" in areas of the city that were once commonly known or frequently traversed. It is visiting elderly kin in neighborhoods that have become unfamiliar, witnessing the declining use of informal but cherished place-names for parks and communities in public discourse and the mass media, doing a double take while walking by the tanning salon that has popped up in your neighborhood or the drawing of racial battle-lines at the local, listener-sponsored, progressive radio station. As this list suggests, gentrification affects community infrastructure, the availability of goods and services, and social relations. Micro and macrolevel outgrowths are central and figuring prominently among the topics and social processes examined in this book is the issue of social justice.

The family of the late dentist Brian Hundley felt a devastating impact of gentrification in the spring of 2002. After Dr. Hundley, a native-born resident of NW and graduate of Howard University School of Dentistry, was fatally shot by an off-duty police officer following a traffic incident (Leonnig, 2004), his widow and older brother took legal action against the Metropolitan Police Department (MPD). The family filed two lawsuits but the demographic changes brought about by gentrification played a role in court as both cases were heard by all-White juries (information derived from personal communication with Hundley's surviving kin). Each ended in mistrials because the incredulous jurors could not reach a consensus on the unarmed man's innocence.

I saw another face of gentrification in the heart of the historically Black Shaw neighborhood. I agreed to meet with another anthropologist at a new eatery and upon entering I noticed that practically every patron I observed in the place was White. After I crossed the threshold customers looked up from their drinks or conversations to glance in my direction. Although I read nothing sinister into their inadvertent but curious stares, I did pause and speculate about being out of place. I also wondered if this is what safety and comfort looked like in the new Washington. My friend forgot about our date so we rescheduled and met at the eatery a few weeks after that experience. The meal was tasty and I noted one additional African American diner in the restaurant.

Gentrification also generates mixed feelings. I spoke with middle-income, long term residents who vacillated between benefit and disadvantage; appreciation and resentment. While some individuals were torn in their opinions, added to expressions of angst and equivocation was the voice of Black residents like Simon Akers. This native-born Washingtonian of NE once said "gentrification is great!" because he could safely and comfortably sit on his front porch again in his Woodridge NE neighborhood. Akers saw his quality of life enhanced in the wake of these shifts and in this he is not alone. Interestingly, his comments indicate there was a time in his community, before gentrification took place, when conditions were not as viewed as so problematic or dire.

This book wades through personal expressions, like those of Akers' above, but *African Americans and Gentrification in Washington, D.C.* also places qualitative data gathered through face-to-face interactions within a larger context that takes policy making and socioeconomic trends into consideration. This tactic involves acknowledging, for example, that a part of living in Washington, D.C. today involves contending with the proclivities of neoliberalism—the theory and practice of a newly unleashed, or invigorated advanced capitalist economy.

Neoliberal projects thrive on unfettered avenues to markets, the privatization of public resources, and the commodification of history and culture (Harvey, 2005). These tenets make neoliberalism experimental at its core as the people and institutions orchestrating these enterprises flit about in search of lucrative income and wealth generating opportunities.

Literature on the impact of neoliberalism in U.S. cities draws attention to education and housing policy as well as programs purportedly designed to revive struggling communities and address urban poverty (Goode and Mavskovsky, 2001). Smith's (1996) work examining urban revanchism, or the reclaiming of cities by well-heeled, private interests, has been influential in critical urban studies. Discussing centrally-urban space during restructuring, Zukin (1991) writes that a place is both a locality and a "cultural artifact of social conflict and cohesion (p. 12)." She elaborates by focusing her discussion on the role of gentrification in reorganizing downtown urban spaces "at the expense of the inner city (p. 186)." Even the "small events and individual decisions that make up a specific spatial process of gentrification feed upon larger, social transformations (p. 186)." Zukin also reminds us that both the micro and macro must be kept in mind while making connections between these developments in urban settings.

Ethnographic evaluations of neoliberalism observe that these courses of action emphasize "consumption-based developments as mediums of progress and upward mobility" (Davila, 2004, p. 208). As deindustrialization has become entrenched in focusing our national economy more on "the selling of services and images than on making products," urban development models have become ever more dependent upon "trickle down strategies of privatization, marketization, and consumerism to promote urban economic revitalization" (Ruben, 2001, p. 435). This is a focus that takes precedence over attempts to increase the standard of living for poor and working class populations (Reuben, 1987).

Bullard takes this a step further and argues that disproportionate numbers of poor, African American residents face "urban removal" from successive waves of urban revitalization programming (2007). Powell warns that "local governmental entities may promote gentrification through policies that encourage home purchasing in the city. In areas with tight housing markets, the influx of higher income residents displaces people of color from their neighborhoods and forces them to seek housing in other, often economically struggling parts of the metropolitan region" (Powell, 2007, p. 53). Although the specific process needs more careful documentation in D.C., it is also very difficult to locate and follow displaced people. It is apparent that African Americans who are departing the city but remaining in the immediate region are choosing Prince Georges County in Maryland as a key destination for residency (Powell, 2007).

Racism and neoliberalism work in concert against populations of color in urban areas, and the interactions of these "isms" have been analyzed by researchers from a range of disciplines. Scholars working from a historical perspective make the case that U.S. neoliberal practices have their origins in the American south (MacLean, 2008), whereas others have taken a more global approach by examining racialized inequalities in Europe, Latin America, the Israeli-occupied territories, South Africa, and the United States (Goldberg, 2009). The linking of race and neoliberalism also offers a path toward framing African American susceptibility to the forces of urban dislocation and putting these within a historical context.

Moreover, because Washington, D.C. has also been a locus for heightened class stratification among African Americans (Gatewood, 1993), analyzing race and socioeconomic status together, while conceding the weight of contradictions, underscores questions of intersectionality and intra-racial conflicts. This analytical approach leads to the acknowledgement that some African Americans have benefitted from the unfairness of class disparities while others remain extremely vulnerable. Marable (2002) notes that inequality in the United States, has long been defined by "interlocking systems" that target the social variables of race, class, sexuality, and gender, and Cose (1993) and Feagin and Sikes (1994) draw our attention to the details of African American professionals' and managers' struggles with racism.

Critical Whiteness studies (CWS) offers a fresh frame for looking at issues of race. While some proponents of CWS note that White racial identity has frequently managed to remain strategically invisible and/or normative, others focus on how Whiteness is concurrently associated with racist subjugation (Delgado and Stefancic, 1997; Rasmussen, Klinenberg, Mexica, and Wray, 2001). This book draws on CWS to acquaint readers with patterns in the responses of many of the African Americans I spoke with who connected the presence of White newcomers to the social benefits accrued from being White. Although this assumption was arrived at by project participants largely through anecdotal information, there are data showing that White Americans are able to secure and afford mortgages and small business loans with assistance from personal networks (Oliver and Shapiro, 1999). Additionally, a study by the Institute on Assets and Social Policy (2010) revealed that the wealth gap between Blacks and Whites in the United States has more than quadrupled since the 1980s. This is a relevant development because gentrification occurs through the flow of capital and the influx of people who have access to this important resource. It is also the case that race influences who gains access to capital and how this access is differentially thought about and responded to both by those who receive it and by those who do not. These issues point to the second utility of CWS: its ability to put the current political and economic conditions into a broader, historical context.

The African American discursive constructions of Whiteness and White privilege that I observed form subaltern views of the dominant group. Thus documenting these views adds to race scholarship that deconstructs Whiteness from varied angles (Hartigan, 1999, 2005; Ignatiev, 1995; Roediger, 1995). The outlooks I present are external—constituting a "Black gaze" that examines Whiteness from the vantage points of non-members. This stands in contrast to the work of Conley (1994) or Brodkin's partially auto-ethnographic analysis of the role of White privilege and suburbanization in Jewish Americans becoming White Americans (1994). Instead, elements of *African Americans and Gentrification in Washington, D.C.* resemble the work of CWS scholars who examine the perceptions African Americans share with each other as they characterize White American motivations prerogatives, and privileges (Bay, 2000; Morrison, 1992; Yancy, 2004).

Some of the verbal depictions I recorded emanated from a place of an unabashed bigotry that a handful of respondents were all too eager to share with me. What others conveyed were critiques of historically-situated notions of White advantage that have been shared among African Americans across the intra-racial divides of class, region of origin, or generation. When distilled for racialized commentary on gentrification, these expressions and constructions become critical assessments of White supremacy. Because of the salience of White supremacy in African American history, these associations and assessments offer links to a past which many African Americans feel is threatened by gentrification. There are many aspects to Black American's relationship with the past, some of which are cyclical in nature. Thus the elders who remain in our midst, who have had the most direct experience with the perils of White supremacy, often feel it is their duty to inform subsequent generations of the pitfalls of racism.

At this point in U.S. racial and political history, making cogent arguments about the contemporary legacy of White supremacy to mainstream audiences remains a challenge. The backlash against the Obama presidency has spurred denial of the idea that racism is factor in the lives of Americans of color today. Indeed, a journal article on the psychology of race reported that a significant percentage of White Americans feel, to the contrary, that they are the most discriminated-against group in the nation (Norton and Sommers, 2011). While not as delusional, Frank Rich wrote that it is anti-White to espouse the idea that an African American would never be elected as president of the United States (2008). What is absent from these opinions, emanating from the much-vaunted editorial pages of the *New York Times* no less, is the nuanced deliberation that is refined by an intimate familiarity with the sting of racism. Then again, the rhetoric of right-wing pundits' surpasses, by a huge margin, any naivete, insincerity, hostility, and/or ill-advised analyses of liberals or inadequately-informed moderates.

The wave of anti-government sentiment directed toward the Obama administration has been plagued by racist overtones. The list of offenses has raised the hackles of African Americans who have read the reports in newspapers or learned of them through other media. Although the Internet has been the source for the most overtly bigoted attacks, right-wing public rallies have provided some interlocutors with more direct dealings with these hateful cadres. One former D.C. resident shared her dismay after unknowingly visiting D.C. during Glen Beck's much-publicized Tea Party protest in 2010. She told me she thought she had inadvertently stumbled upon a Klan rally on The National Mall.

Expressions of anti-Black racial hatred and insensitivity have become commonplace in the U.S. media.[6] This, in tandem with the uptick in right-wing violence (Potok, 2011), indicates we are in another period of White backlash. However unlike the post-Reconstruction and post-Civil Rights eras, the election of Barack Obama has not led to lessening of racialized social barriers, temporary or otherwise. The election of this country's first president of African descent has inflamed and frightened a vocal percentage of the White populace. Elected officials have not hesitated to add their voices to the race-baiting fray according to an article in the partisan political website Wonkette, which reported that Atwater, CA City Councilman Gary Frago sent a prank e-mail to a local paper announcing that nude photographs of first lady Michelle Obama were set to appear in National Geographic magazine (Layne, 2009).[7] African Americans I have spoken with have been unambiguous in their assessments of racism's resurgence.

Forthright White anti-racists also do not avoid making the obvious connections and one of the most prominent, Tim Wise (2010), says racism is at the center of this anti-Obama movement. In his critique of the association of socialism with the current U.S. president in the online magazine Znet, Paul Street asks:

> Does Obama's racial identity give a special edge and hook to the right's predictable red-baiting of the nation's first [*sic*] (black?) president? Do some, perhaps many, perhaps most, right wing whites connect the dots between (a) their reactionary fear/hatred of "socialism" and "redistribution" and (b) their related fear/hatred of black civil rights, affirmative action, and reparations for blacks (we might add their fear/hatred of predominantly Latina/o immigration and citizenship?

It is hard to contest this conclusion given the vitriol that was displayed in town hall meetings on health care reform and the ensuing campaigns to discredit and malign Obama. The Internet is littered with photographs of this President that have been digitally altered to make him look like an ape, a sock-monkey, an African in "native dress," or a member of the Taliban. One recent image I saw has President Obama appearing as if he has been lynched by hanging. These are acts rooted in fear, ignorance and hate. These deeds also constitute racist ploys that are designed to detract from the humanity of the individual and the legitimacy of the Black person in office.

---

6   There have been numerous examples of this, but I will cite two. One is the case of Fox news host Eric Bolling, who characterized the visit of an African head of state to the White House as "Hoodlums in the Hizzouse." The second is the May 15 article in the *Psychology Today* website entitled "Why Are Black Women Less Physically Attractive than Other Women? (2011).

7   http://wonkette.com/409928/yet-again-email-republican-elected-officials-repulsive-racism

Although I posit that race is central to these sometimes incoherent and frequently dishonest outbursts and right-wing mobilization strategies, there is also push back against the charge of racism from scholars and observers who ground their criticism of Obama on more empirical evidence (Pinkney, 2008). Some also remind us that corporatism and anti-left hostility may also play a role in constituting his opposition (Street, 2009). African American Muslim and famed hip hop artist Lupe Fiasco offered a different critical perspective, calling Barack Obama the greatest terrorist threat in the United States during an appearance on a televised web show (Ball, 2011). This perspective essentially takes the 44th president of the U.S. to task for not only maintaining, but even expanding, the surveillance and military operations of President George W. Bush against U.S. citizens and populations in developing countries.[8]

Discussion of this broader context illustrates how the economic and political are felt in personal ways and points to the conditions that can set populations apart on the basis of race, class, and subdivisions of these larger categories. The following chapter further examines sociocultural diversity by using elements of auto-ethnography to make researcher positionality more transparent and paint a detailed picture of portions of life in the District. I use these elements of my own personal story to highlight more so than to analyze.

White flight defined the urban racialized landscape of D.C. that was my home during the 1960s and 1970s. Whether my family was headed to see Pop Pop and Granny in what is now called Capitol Hill, cousin Shanice out in SE, or Grandpa and Dee Dee in NE, we travelled what had become an African American landscape.[9] Change has been a constant in this history, and though the tide has reversed, change continues unabated.

* * *

"Gentrification, Race, and Neoliberalism in Washington, D.C." is the first chapter of this book. Chapter 1 looks at the primary analytical frameworks I relied upon

---

8   Articles appearing in *The Washington Post* (22 May 2009) and *The New York Times* (24 August 2009 and 11 June 2010) as well as reports aired on the British Broadcasting Company (11 May 2010) and The Pacifica Network's Democracy Now (27 September 2010) discuss crackdowns on government whistle blowers, FBI raids on anti-war activists in Chicago and Minneapolis, Red Cross reports of detainee torture at a Black site at Bagram Airbase, and continued rendition of alleged terrorists under the Obama administration.

9   As I discuss these experiences, and acknowledge the impacts of racialization in the lives of the people I interacted with, I am reminded of the data which problematize any neat or uniform configurations. Through the participant observation I engaged in with community organizers, I met and worked alongside white residents who have deep and longstanding connections with African American residents and whose political actions reflect concern for ameliorating what they have concluded are the problems associated with gentrification and neoliberalism. These examples are instructive and useful for undermining rigid binaries of identity and action.

to generate meaning from the information I collected. Race and class emerge as key concepts in this book because of the way these hierarchies have shaped past patterns and contemporary conditions in this city. In exploring these issues, *African Americans and Gentrification in Washington, D.C.* engages the work of scholars who are concerned with race in the 21st-century United States.

This includes works from CWS to provide a framework for understanding how African Americans characterize gentrification and theorizing about the casting of a Black gaze upon the dominant group. In addition to critically engaging literature on race and class, this chapter also reviews theories of neoliberalism as a strategy for contextualizing current trends in urban development and governance.

This chapter also shares background information about my experiences growing up in D.C. to provide researcher transparency and a descriptive tool that paints a detailed picture of the social landscape. The former helps establish a context for readers to consider the links which may exist between standpoint, topical foci, and the methodological and analytical proclivities of a social science researcher.

Chapter 2, "Race and Class Hierarchies in D.C. History," examines a number of the key historical moments in the city with regard to racial formation and socioeconomic inequalities. It includes discussions of enslavement, emancipation, Jim Crow, and desegregation for further contextualization of contemporary social inequalities in D.C. and positing a connection between the present and the past. What emerges through the overall contribution of these data is the consistency of racism and class struggles in the overall history of African Americans in Washington, D.C.

The voices of the past and present continue to play off of each other in Chapter 3 "Arrival, Belonging, Difference: Exploring the Oral Histories of Elder African Americans." This chapter offers textured details on one cohort: African Americans between the ages of 65 and 92. This chapter recounts everyday life in relation to childhood, neighborhood associations, political views, socioeconomic strategies, and ideas around race and belonging. As Black residents talk about their personal lives and beliefs regarding work, families, leisure activities, and a changing D.C., particular attention is given to how these individuals became Washingtonians and how meaning around space and place is constructed and expressed. This chapter also introduces the oral history and participant observation data I collected, including stories I accessed through the Ivy City Oral History Project (funded by the Humanities Council of Washington, D.C.). This chapter gives readers a feeling for the past and a sense of what the passage of time—and more specifically, gentrification—can erase.

The focus on seniors is followed by "Race, Place, Representation, and Attachment." Chapter 4 examines mainstream depictions of the District and presents statistical data that paint an economic picture of D.C. residents' lives. This chapter also looks at the oral histories and participant observation data from African Americans in their 40s and 50s, revealing how these participants use their past relationship with the city and ideas about race and belonging to frame their views of gentrification.

Chapter 5, "Race, Class, and the Individual Dynamics of Gentrification" explores the connections between ideas, experiences, and macro-level political–economic shifts. This chapter delves more narrowly into an examination of African American residents' perceptions of and responses to gentrification. With such a focus this chapter also highlights how changes in D.C. are affecting cross-cultural relationships on the ground. It is followed by "Race, Class, and the Dynamics of Collective Responses to Gentrification." Chapter 6 continues examining how residents are affected by and reacting to gentrification and demographic change. By uniting a consideration of race, class, and resistance with the arts and expressive culture, this chapter looks at the work of activists who are banding together to prevent urban dislocation. By looking at collective responses to gentrification shared concerns emerge more clearly. This chapter also has implications for considering the formation of cross cultural relationships and the information presented here also connects with my central social justice concern that racism, classism, and neoliberal policies are the underlying culprits generating urban inequality.

"Furthering an Anthropology of Gentrification in D.C.," is the concluding chapter of this book. It suggests what additional research is needed to fill gaps in the literature on urban anthropology, and D.C. studies in particular. The key contribution of this final chapter is to summarize the overall implications of this study and inform readers of how this ethnographic examination of Washington, D.C. engenders insights for other parts of the U.S. and the world where populations are confronting gentrification and other forms of neoliberal urban reorganization.

Chapter 1
Gentrification, Race, and Neoliberalism in Washington, D.C.

D.C. residents have used oral histories to take discussions of gentrification into the public sphere. For people living in the swaths of subsidized housing faced with demolition, in particular, the collection of their stories has taken on a sense of urgency reminiscent of anthropologists embarking upon salvage ethnography. Individuals and groups have also used conferences and the Internet to disseminate these data.[1] Where African American remembrances of the past have looked askance at gentrification, these oral histories have been described in some quarters as "harkening back to a mythic, culturally perfect moment that was somehow destroyed by White middle class professionals" (Franke-Ruta, 2012). This is but one sign of the race and class oriented tensions that coalesce around this issue.

Handily simplifying and dispensing with the experiential memories of gentrification's critics has become normative in the mainstream. It is not coincidental that this practice appears correlated with the increasing pervasiveness and entrenchment of gentrification-related demographic shifts. The outcomes of gentrification are not tenuous. It is also apparent that the needs of the poor and low income earners of color which community-based organizations work to protect are conceptually subsumed under the desires of upwardly mobile people who often have entirely different requirements comparatively. Still, critical perspectives of gentrification face a backlash and all of this is taking place as inequalities in Washington, D.C. have sharpened in the face of what these indicators show are failed trickle-down economic policies (Nelson and Ojha, 2012). This previously cited online article is preceded by the subtitle: "The federal government has emerged as one of the most potent factors driving income inequality in the United States—especially in the nation's capital."

Rather than ignore the specter of uneven development, *African Americans and Gentrification in Washington, D.C.* acknowledges and historically contextualizes this as the inheritance of race and class-based inequality in the U.S. This book also connects the examination of long term hierarchies to the contemporary, gentrification-related outlooks of African Americans. What do the current ideas and experiences of Black Washingtonians indicate about the state of race relations today? How do the viewpoints and strategies of organizers who work with low income populations facing gentrification reflect upon race relations and social

---

1   Individuals affiliated with the D.C. Historical Society participate in conferences and exchange historical data about local communities through their listserv.

hierarchies in D.C.? These questions constitute the basis of this book and the legacy of racial inequality is central to the historical component of this study. As the past consideration of African Americans in Washington, D.C. reveals, the proprietary narrow-mindedness of some African Americans as well as the handful of exaggerated claims I collected do not lessen the crucial need to acknowledge the connections between inequality and gentrification in the nation's capital today.

As the introduction suggests, African American standpoint are a central aspect of this book along with the consideration of how myriad perspectives are formed. It begins by fleshing out brief details about my own background that speak to setting but this book is not an auto-ethnography. Essentially *African Americans and Gentrification in Washington, D.C.* makes its contribution to discussions of this topic through its ethnographic reiteration of what we already know about the link between gentrification and inequality. This connection largely exists because, in all of its capacity to whisk away the charred memories of uprisings and bring a form of restoration to urban environs in previous states of partial disrepair, gentrification is inextricably tied to the machinations of social hierarchies.

Poverty, alienation, and anger fed the firestorms of 1968 and what happened in their aftermath. As Schaffer writes, based on earlier oral histories with African American D.C., in addition to the desperate reactions to Martin Luther King's murder, "African Americans described a widespread resentment toward generations of political, civil, and especially economic injustice-the latter of which neither the civil rights movement not the federal government had yet to effectively address" (2003/2004, p. 6).

It is also the case that disinvestment occurs in spaces that have an association with otherwise neglected populations it should come as no surprise that these previously-discounted neighborhoods can become locations for intense human interaction when these trends in abandonment are reversed. Such factors tie gentrification to social inequality and this first chapter lays out the frameworks and concepts that have helped in the interpretation of contemporary events and understanding of the changes taking place for particular issues of race, class and social justice. Toward this end chapter one starts with a personal account and then moves on to discuss theories of racism and neoliberalism that help explain the data presented in this book.

Commuting to my Past

Openness about scholarly positionality helps place research within its wider social and historical milieu. For example, this book is about gentrification but at its core is a focus on the ways in which people make sense of themselves, this place and others against the backdrop of a rapidly changing city. *African Americans and Gentrification in Washington, D.C.* is also concerned with what project participants have to say about the relationships they form across the boundaries of race and class.

Gentrification is firmly rooted in class divisions that, in this instance, are expressed through the complex languages and experiences of race and class combined. As it relates to D.C., these are issues that I have had to come to grips with since my childhood. That is because I was born in Washington, D.C. in 1959 in a diverse setting that was also undergoing marked shifts rooted in the dynamics of race and class.

Portions of this book use auto-ethnographic elements. These are not included to declare exceptional insightfulness due to my native status. This decision was made to promote reflection on the ways researchers' experiences can shape the gathering, understanding and writing of ethnographic data. I also wanted to circumvent any pretense of neutrality. Researchers have pasts and the discussion of transparency and possible links between identity, methodologies and analytical frameworks reinforces this point. The circumstances of my upbringing provide texture and detail to descriptions of the local environment without any intent to monopolize authenticity.

I lived in D.C. uninterrupted from 1959 until I graduated from high school in 1977 which results in my view of change in this city being long and based on experience rather than the analysis of secondary sources solely. I grew up in a racially diverse community and became an outgoing, community-engaged person with a network of friends, kin and acquaintances that is varied and expansive. This chapter substantiates this description. It also provides a more detailed sense of context and how my perspective has developed over time.

My network is extensive for a number of reasons. I still maintain contact with people I came to know as a child attending elementary school, in addition to those I met in subsequent years. My D.C. work history is also far-reaching. My first paid position was as a nurse's aide at Freedman's Hospital during the 1970s. Since that time I have worked as an office clerk with the Department of Housing and Community Development and as a secretary at locations ranging from The World Bank to the K Street business district. During the late 1980s I was a staffer with the Washington Office on Africa under the leadership of Jean Sindab and, later, Damu Smith, with whom I also pushed back against environmental racism in the toxics division at Greenpeace. I have known, worked with, and befriended people from numerous walks of life.

Following post-college stints in Poughkeepsie and New York City, I returned to D.C. in 1984, only to depart again. In 1988, I moved to the Bronx to attend graduate school at the City University of New York in Manhattan. As this history indicates, this book is an ethnographic examination of a place from which I hail but have not been an inhabitant of since 1988. Today I reside in a planned community in Maryland that is located 30 miles northwest of the Nation's Capital. I came back to the area in 1996 and when I ride into the city to teach, conduct my research, visit family and friends, or patronize the arts, I negotiate geographic boundaries while maneuvering around old memories and dramatically altered facades. To reach my former home today, my commute also reverses the direction of pleasurable Sunday drives our family took during the 1960s and 1970s.

My childhood took place during a volatile period in U.S. history and this planted a number of seeds into my young impressionable mind. My brother and I were exposed the mundane, educational, exciting, and sometimes troubling when we were growing up. The list of experiences included attending political rallies with our parents, gawking at hippies as we rode through Georgetown, and being fascinated by sex workers around 14th and T Streets. In between taking music lessons, attending church, visiting family, attending school, and playing with friends, we witnessed the urban uprisings that followed the killing of Dr. Martin Luther King in 1968 and felt that something in the air had changed. One sign of these dimming memories was the National Guard presence in the many communities we were associated with.

With the help of the mass media I was mildly traumatized by the assassinations and riots of the mid-to-late 1960s but it was impossible to avoid exposure to information on the events that were sweeping the nation and my local community. Mom, an elementary school teacher and Dad, postal clerk, were habitual consumers of the news. David Brinkley, Chet Huntley, and Walter Cronkite were regular dinner guests at our house. We were one of those families that watched television while eating, and my mother also subscribed to *Ebony*, *Jet*, *Look*, and *Time* magazines. Plenty of reading material could be found around the house that covered the tumultuous happenings of the day. I became fixated on one particularly haunting cover of a July 1967 issue of *LIFE*. It depicted the, still living, body of a boy hit by gunfire in Newark, NJ. The figure of the injured child filled me with dread and fostered this unrealistic fear that I, too, would be struck by a stray bullet. For a while, this mild obsession replaced any trepidation I may have felt about the snaggle-toothed man I was certain lived in my closet.

This was the context in which our family's Sunday jaunts to the 'burbs captivated my young imagination and soothed my fleeting yearning for more bucolic surrounds. These short trips were also racialized excursions because the suburbs of D.C. were, to the members of my racially-sensitized household in particular, a different world. Entering spheres of Whiteness was, an act laden with intrigue and potential risk for African Americans. I didn't know what was on my parent's minds but the inscrutability my brother and I associated with the suburbs and its inhabitants was linked to our, largely, segregated daily lives.

Through my household's upward residential mobility, the complexion and class background of our friends and acquaintances became more diverse in 1966. We left the neighborhood of Lamond-Riggs to move into a larger, detached house purchased in the White-flight community of Michigan Park. In addition to having White friends and neighbors for the first time, there were such key, NE institutions nearby as Catholic University, The Model Secondary School for the Deaf, and Providence Hospital. This contributed to the community's heterogeneity and stoked our curiosity about the new neighborhood.

With this transition I gained an assortment of friends, including hearing-impaired teens of various backgrounds and the children of math, history, and anthropology professors at Catholic University. Their families were the noted group of Whites who did not flee integration. The hospital also did its part fostering community excitement by bringing into the midst of our urban, yet quiet, neighborhood that quintessential stimulant to the youthful imaginary: the stranger who came in the form of employees and hospital visitors who parked on our street. There were also the visits from rabbits, chipmunks, and, on one noteworthy occasion, an albino squirrel, which caused a mild commotion which the animal got stuck on the windowsill leading to my parent's bedroom.

Still, the suburbs were more spacious and unspoiled than anything we knew, even "nicer" than Shepherd Park, the Black middle class neighborhood along upper 16th Street NW that everyone we knew called The Gold Coast. Because my parents talked about race frequently in our presence, my brother and I tacitly understood that the White people who lived in our new neighborhoods formally, had moved to such areas outside of the city upon the arrival of African Americans. Understanding this city has been a process of learning about what in a sense has always been readily accessible knowledge. Not until the research for this book was complete did my parents inform me that they avoided taking us on drives through Virginia because this was a state many African Americans viewed as unfriendly to Blacks. I was also an adult before I discovered the extent of White enclaves that existed in D.C. outside of Georgetown.[2]

In actuality, all of these enclaves were foreign to me. We didn't know anyone who lived in Georgetown. Our only connection involved what my mother shared with me during an oral history interview about her father living there with extended kin after migrating to D.C. from South Carolina during the 1920s. As kids, my friends and I would take the bus there to buy raunchy comic books and cheap bangles. We were keen on getting sandwiches from Booey Mongers and shopping for jeans at Up Against the Wall. Yes, I was familiar with Georgetown but oblivious to the existence of American University Park, Chevy Chase, Spring Valley, The Palisades, or other White enclaves.

I continue to negotiate this urban—suburban and racialized continuum today. Leaving my home I commute to my past when I hit 95 South and head across the Beltway.[3] Driving through Prince Georges and Montgomery Counties in Maryland,

---

2   This is a personal history that I am not arguing is in any way tantamount to a D.C., African American experience. Upcoming chapters use ethnographic data to support the view that, among other variables, the familiarity with a range of neighborhoods in D.C. is determined by insertion into diverse networks of acquaintances and friends. During the 1960s and 1970s, as well as today, this would be heavily influenced by parental occupation and the school attended, as subsequent data will show.

3   In the discourse of political punditry, the Washington Beltway is a trite and overused symbol of the gulf between the "real world" and the workings of the federal government. This inside/outside dichotomy privileges politicians and those within their spheres of influence and interaction as the sole or legitimate resident of D.C., thereby ignoring the majority of local residents and overshadowing their place within this geographic context. This phenomena merits closer examination for researchers with an expertise in textual analysis and symbolic anthropology.

I head for Georgia Avenue, then 16th Street in D.C.'s northwest corner. Depending on my route, I may, consciously or subconsciously, relive old experiences in these spaces. Passing near the Kaywood movie theater elicits thoughts of the girls on my block keeping a sharp look out for cute boys with prerequisite large afros; catching a glimpse of Mudricks corner store off of Bladensburg Road, would always bring to mind us kids stopping on the way to and from Ruth K. Webb Elementary to buy button candy, edible necklaces, chewable wax lips, or Coke bottle—shaped candies filled with a colored liquid. When I take New Hampshire Avenue in I often cast a fleeting glance toward Nicholson Street immediately after crossing Eastern Avenue, because that was one of the last addresses for my dear Aunt Helen who died of a sudden stroke almost a decade ago. Before entering into the District a veritable buffet of immigration's stamp on the Washington suburbs lines the avenue in the form of restaurants and clothing stores established for the East and West African, Afro Caribbean and Latin American patrons who live in the area. In addition to being in close proximity to the city boundary, there are other connections to D.C. I was told by Mexican American and Los Angeles transplant and activist Sylvia Montenegro that many of the Latino youth she works with in Langley Park and Takoma Park Maryland are former residents of such gentrified communities in NW DC as Adams Morgan and Mt. Pleasant.

Conducting field work in one's home town forces the discerning ethnographer to sort out a hodgepodge of memories and spatial perceptions that both support and undermine that old adage that you can never go home again. As a native Washingtonian and a social scientist, I view this city through lenses that both illuminate and distort my vision. As such I have learned through experience why researcher positionality and its impact on praxis and analyses clearly come into play and should not be ignored. However, as I embraced the "union of possibilities"[4] of native anthropology, I also recognized the intersection of class, gender, age and the other differences that worked to separate me from my research participants (Slocum, 2001). This made me mindful about avoiding simplistic notions of field connectedness. Although my awareness was heightened around this issue I also learned that my origins proved advantageous given the wide networks I was and remain a part of in Washington, D.C. Mining the depths of my contacts resulted in access to a tapestry of African American people along with information that hasn't been previously discussed in ethnographies of D.C. The auto-ethnographic elements of this book help me emphasize the plurality of African American Washington and reinforce the acknowledgement of the self as a tacit guide. I do this while staying rooted to the understanding that ethnography

---

4   This concept comes from Kimberly Simmons' reflection on the role of race and gender confluence and divergence in her ethnographic study of women and identity in the Dominican Republic entitled "Passion For Sameness: Encountering a Black Feminist Self in Fieldwork In the Dominican Republic," in *Black Feminist Anthropology: Theory, Politics, Praxis and Poetics*, Irma McClaurin, editor, New Brunswick, NJ: Rutgers University Press, 2001, p. 95.

too heavily dependent on memory, nostalgia, intuition, and personal attachments is not good social science[5] because intimate knowledge of places and politics is no prudent substitute for participant observation and the other mainstays of qualitative inquiry in anthropology.

Auto-ethnographic reminiscences aside, I spoke at length with African Americans natives who hailed from different parts of the city and were of various ages and class backgrounds. Some, like me, came of age during the 1960s and 1970s, so I took my analytical cues from them in an attempt to grasp what it meant to be young at that time. They, too, talked about marked contrasts between urban and suburban and exchanged ideas about "folk amalgamations of race and behavior"[6] through discursive constructions of the city, home, school, and the people they know—local store owners, neighbors, mentors, family members, and friends. The ideas and behaviors I note are the content of past and present-day cultural assemblages and these elements are the very focus of this book.

The data from each generation provided patterns out of which a host of unifying ideas began to form. The women and men in their 70s and 80s shared stories that sometimes wedded contradictory themes such as scarcity and abundance. They told of grappling with Depression-era poverty and segregation while simultaneously leaning on the support of extensive social networks and being comforted by a profusion of music and leisurely enjoyment on the expressive culture scene. This is not to suggest this was a monolithic group. Some individuals had more personal hardships over the course of their lives than others, as well as differing ways of responding to life's difficulties.

The stories of my parents and grandparents are presented among the many others appearing on the pages of this book. As they face the ends of their lives it is a privilege to include accounts of them attending school or arriving to D.C. from the south or elsewhere, stories of the difficulties they attempted to overcome negotiating Jim Crow and so many other challenges.

The network I pulled from to find participants for this book includes people I have met through my community of origin but they only constitute a small portion of the individuals I spoke and interacted with. I have traveled around the world and lived in New York City for eight years of my life. My D.C.-network has been augmented by these travels and by working in the anti-apartheid and environmental racism movements. My job as an assistant professor at American University for 12 years also expanded the vigor and diversity of my personal network. Over the course of more than a decade of working in the academy, teaching two and three courses per semester with 20–40 students per class, I have taught over 1000 students and sat on panels with dozens of scholars and activists.

5   I am influenced here by the discussion of Rhoda Kanaaneh on p. 7 of *Birthing the Nation: Strategies of Palestinian Women in Israel*, Berkeley: University of California Press, 2002, p. 8.

6   Page 5, John L. Jackson Jr., *Harlem World: Doing Race and Class in Contemporary Black America*, Chicago: The University of Chicago Press, 2001.

The purview this leads to should expand any limited understanding of the potential for native anthropologists to make meaningful and important contributions to contemporary ethnography. Contrary to the concern of one outside reader of an earlier version of this manuscript, my status as a native Washingtonian enhances rather than compromises this work. It is because of the many experiences I have had in this city that the people I count among my friends and acquaintances are so tremendously varied based on their immigrant status, race and ethnicity, sexuality, U.S. origins, age, and socioeconomic position. It is from this network and complete strangers whom I have never met before that the data for this book emerge.

Finally, *African Americans, Race, and Gentrification in Washington, D.C.* endeavors to cut through some of the disharmony around discussions of gentrification by emphasizing the issue of social justice rather than essentializing notions of who does or does not belong in the city. Having witnessed both the cost of race and class-based contention and the potential for cross-cultural reconciliation first-hand, I have learned what it takes to facilitate better relations among people of different groups and to value the efforts involved in these processes. My contention is that disputation is not assuaged by ignoring the anger, fear and resentment that lurks on the many sides of debates about gentrification. It is more helpful to explicate and contextualize the strife and learn from the examples of people who are successfully mitigating some of the conflicts brewing around the confluence of contemporary urban change and difference.

Regardless of the specific theoretical analyses, contemporary urban studies must wrestle with the racialized and political economic timbre of these present times in order to be relevant and forward moving. We are living in an exceptional moment in the U.S. history with regard, but not limited, to the question of what progress the nation has made addressing the legacies of inequality. In terms of this study's findings, frameworks that grapple with racism and neoliberalism present unique opportunities to analyze what is happening on the ground when corporate and individualized wealth generating strategies and the ideologies that support these are challenged by forces issuing from working class and communities of color in D.C.

Race in the Analysis of Gentrification in Washington, D.C.

Our contemporary times have been dubbed the post-civil rights era and designated by others more controversially as the post-racial period (Mahon, 2004). To the merits of the first label, there are African American adults in positions of power who have come of age long after the passage of key civil rights legislation. The rights that were made into law more than 30 decades ago are the stuff of history books for some Americans and with the implementation of fair housing, affirmative action, voting rights, and other anti-discrimination policies, some Americans operate under the assumption that the forms of discrimination that have been so damaging in the lives of racialized minorities in the U.S. have been outlawed and swept away.[7] Contrary to this view, racial disparities and discrimination are still leading forces to be reckoned with in American life (Crenshaw, Gotanda, Peller, and Thomas, 1995; Fields and Fields, 2012; Massey, 2007).

Roediger takes on writers from the left and the right when he argues that this type of denial marks an analytical retreat from understanding both how race remains significant in American modern life and the ways it intersects with, rather than subordinates or yields to, class power (2007). The refusal to acknowledge racism today relates, in part, to ideas and practices set into motion by the White backlash against multiculturalism and racism's upbraiding during the 1980s (Bloom 1988). These precursors paved the way for the post-racial viewpoint to gain some traction and additionally, the election of Barack Obama to the presidency of the U.S. substantiates the assertions of Americans who are inclined to believe claims of racism are anachronistic today.

The proliferation of the post-racial idea was a practice of journalists before the Obama campaign savored their first victory. While not verified by the historical perspective of social scientists or the preponderant experience of people of color, the ideas of newspaper and television writers have far greater reach and more currency than they often merit. In a treatise on the White denial of racism, Wise (2009) quotes respected *New York Times* columnist Frank Rich who wrote "in defense of White America" and argued that people predicting racism would stymie Obama's road to The White House were being absurd and anti-White (2008). In another paper of record, *The Washington Post*, Richard Cohen suggested the post racial tenor of this period would catapult Obama into the presidency.

The gist of post-racialism, a less conservative counterpart to D'Souza's end of racism concept (1995), sees complaints about racism as anachronistic if Barack Obama can reach such a lofty political goal in a country with a checkered racial past. In order for post racialism to have legs, however, issues and experiences that complicate this rosy picture must be swept under the rug. These under-analyzed, ignored, or compartmentalized events would include the virulently bigoted responses Obama campaigners confronted as they carried out their work across the U.S. There are also a series of more subtle considerations that may be outside of the purview of mainstream journalists who lack the analytical tools to fruitfully venture into the complex issues of race in the U.S.

If, as noted by Wise, White Americans choose to vote for a candidate of color "only to the extent they are able to view that person as racially unthreatening, as

---

7   At the end of February 2013, Supreme Court Justice Antonin Scalia shocked many Americans when he shared the opinion, while hearing oral arguments in the case of *Shelby County vs. Attorney General Eric Holder*, that section five of the voting rights act is tantamount to a "racial entitlement." As reported in numerous television, radio and Internet news sources, these remarks sent shock waves through the civil rights community and prompted the determination by observers like myself that Justice Scalia is a racist because he shows no regard for the voters of color who have remained disenfranchised in elections across the country.

different from 'regular' Black people, as somehow less than truly Black, or as having 'transcended race' (a term used with regularity to describe Obama over the past few years), then White racism remains quite real, quite powerful and quite operative in the life of the nation."[8] The peeling away of these real, albeit psychosocial, issues that Wise describes requires a familiarity with racism that is more nuanced than what has been most commonly promoted in the mainstream media.

Tea Party protests against Obama's health care reform drastically undermined any idea of post racialism. The histrionics of these uninformed and racially homogeneous crowds were covered by the media and the Tea Party movement gained an unearned degree of political credibility over a short period of time. What has gone largely uninvestigated during the continuing hysteria is what impact these developments, and the equivocal response to them by the mainstream media, have had upon African Americans. Whether we consider the gun-toting Obama detractors who gathered a few miles from the National Mall as this president campaigned for a second term, lawmakers who refused to work with the President to foster economic recovery, state officials who erected barriers to minority-voter participation, or opposition figures who have expressed disdain about the national demographic changes that pushed Obama to victory in November of 2012, these issues not only mitigate the progression of post-racial ideology, they underscore the racialized context amid which African American demographic shifts in D.C. are unfolding. The lack of attention shown to the responses of Black people to the overt racism of the Tea Party movement for example, mirrors the attempts to silence dissatisfaction brewing as gentrification becomes increasingly rooted in the norm. There are race-related bodies of literature and frameworks which can advance the analyses of these developments.

One area of consideration is the writing of scholars whose work goes beyond the post-civil rights and post racial themes but still remains specific to the 21st century (Bullard, 2007; Hartigan, 2010; Logan, 2010; Markus and Moya, 2010; Winant, 2004). This includes summaries of how and why racial inequality remains a fact of U.S. life today by scholars who emphasize structural racism and educational disparities (Orfield, 2001) or the soaring impact of mass incarceration upon African American women and men (Alexander, 2012). There are also scholars who work directly with communities to apply their knowledge of inequality toward meeting the challenges people are facing in real time (Lopez, 2008).

These works have revealed that the extensive and longstanding institutionalization of racism has fostered a sense of normalcy that has obscured the contemporary impacts of these practices (Bonilla-Silva, 2010). Housing and job discrimination are two examples of racialized structural barriers that key segments of the U.S. population are completely unscathed by. Similarly, gentrification is a political economic process that has become status quo but the shifts it is associated with are enabled by inequality in household incomes, wealth accumulation, and urban housing markets. However, without exposure to the experiences of minorities

---

8   Page 23, *Between Barack and Hard Place*, Tim Wise, 2009.

and the working class it is unlikely that individuals who are benefitting from gentrification will develop a critical perspective about its implementation. The inadequate understanding of racial inequality has contributed to the phenomenon of *White-washing race* (Brown et al., 2005). As argued in Brown's pivotal volume, myths about racial inequality have proliferated and misled citizens about what remains a pervasive and entrenched force in daily American life.

In addition to studying the structural components of racism, analyses of its persistence has also turned toward understanding the links between racism and ideology in the U.S. today. Fields and Fields describe ideology as "the descriptive vocabulary of day to day existence through which people make rough sense of the social reality that they live and create from day to day" (p. 134, 2012). In deploying the terminology of sociolinguistics, this sociologist and historian also writes that ideology is "the language of consciousness that suits the particular way in which people deal with their fellows. It is the interpretation in thought of the social relations through which they constantly create and recreate their collective being" (p. 134, 2012). Racism has led to both material and ideological ramifications and critical Whiteness studies is a subfield that offers useful frameworks for looking at race and gentrification today.

One of the goals of CWS is to make the invisible visible (Rasmussen, Klinenberg, Nexica, and Wray, 2001). This involves moving into plain sight structures and expressions of inequality that are specific to the legacy of White domination such as racial apartheid and White supremacy (Kaufman, 2007). Another element entails looking at aspects of White racial formation that have been overlooked in the past (Brodkin, 1994; Hartigan, 1999, 2005; Painter, 2010; Roediger, 1991, 1994). In the U.S., racism "normalizes whiteness and problematizes color" (Segrest, 2001) and it is in part because of this practice that historically oppressed groups have been the focus of so much study, too often at the expense of widespread, directed analyses aimed at dissecting and categorizing the motivations, strategies and culture(s) of the more powerfully positioned *race*. CWS challenges this and while these studies are not uniform or without criticisms, research and writing occurring under the large umbrella of CWS examines racialized inequalities and race relations from angles many scholars previously sought to avoid.

The comments of the people I spoke with crystallized some of the concerns taken up in CWS and this reinforced the analytical utility of this frame for my study. I was pushed in this direction when participants would deploy the concept of White privilege when talking, for example, about the ability of young White residents to purchase costly condominiums or row houses in the city. This would also come up in what African Americans referenced as racially-biased or culturally-insensitive behavior of young White residents, most often associated with the use of public spaces. I look at these claims more closely further along in the book but other examples include reports of newly-arrived residents not greeting neighbors. Akua Templeton also described an incident where a dog held on a leash by a young White woman urinated on an African American church lawn. Newcomers' dogs also emerge as a recurring source of tension in communities with shifting demographics.

The comments that follow listserv content or community blogs on the topics of gentrification or the specter of African American displacement also reflected this trend of Black/White racial conflict. While perusing posts on topics ranging from street crime to the February 2009 incident where an African American detective brandished his gun at a group of White winter revelers who struck his vehicle with snowballs, the subject of White privilege emerges. Overtly or indirectly, persons virtually conversing either point to or contest the idea that White residents who are purchasing costly property or paying high rents in D.C. are benefitting from, unmarked, advantages. I investigated these attitudes more closely to see how African Americans arrived at these ideas and note the ways in which they were communicated.

CWS has another useful aspect which is also ethnographically under-explored. Whether explicitly stated or implied the White gaze has generated detrimental effects which have been documented in Black cultural studies and the historiography of African Americans. From the early periods of their experiences in the U.S., and frequently on a patterned whim, African American health and well-being could be sorely jeopardized if a White man or woman attached ill intent to the conduct or thoughts of African Americans—the murder of Emmitt Till is a startling example of this. More recently, knowledge of this possibility conditioned African Americans to anticipate the judgments and actions of Whites as a strategy that was protective of self, property, loved ones and economic opportunity.

This idea is an addendum to W.E.B. DuBois' concept of the double consciousness, wherein he describes the penchant for many African Americans to view themselves through both their own eyes and those of the members of the dominant society. DuBois brilliantly observed and wrote in *The Atlantic Monthly* (1897):

> It is a peculiar sensation this double consciousness. This sense of always looking at one's self through the eyes of others, of measuring one's soul by the tape of a world that looks on in amused contempt and pity. One feels his two-ness — an American, a Nero; two souls, two thoughts, two unreconciled strivings; two warring ideas in one dark body, whose dogged strength alone keeps it from being torn asunder.

Implicit in the double consciousness concept is the content of the Black filter. For centuries African Americans have modified their own behaviors by taking White American inclinations and sensibilities into close consideration. In contrast though, due to the racialized power dynamic in the U.S., has made it such that the Black gaze upon the bodies of White Americans has not been a critical factor shaping the behaviors or thinking of those being watched. However these observations still occur (Morrison, 1992; Roediger, 1998; Bay, 2000; Yancy, 2004) and the perceptions and constructions of Whiteness generate thought, modes of resistance, and elements of humor discursively shared, particularly when African Americans are among themselves. This book lifts the veil on some of that secrecy by exposing and attempting to make sense of African American reactions to the changing racial demographics of the District that reflect interpretations of White American identities.

The sentiments I captured reveal varying degrees of frustration, feelings of being left out or under assault and, in some interviews, a sense of loss. There were also people who were happy and excited about the changes. This latter view usually referenced the stores and restaurants in communities that gave a new energy to neighborhoods which interlocutors were very familiar with. Feelings on these establishments would breakdown among African Americans by age and income as the senior people among my project participants were less likely to patronize the more specialized of the new businesses opening in their communities.

I also uncovered pre-judgments associated with the Black gaze including the construction of all Whites as middle class or unfettered by economic burdens. Since few of the people I spoke with reported much personal experience with low income or working class White residents in D.C., this upper income association may be a specifically localized viewpoint. Putting this specific consideration aside, such observations as White equals rich, validate my conclusion that, with specific regard to Black/White relations at least, CWS can help ethnographers illuminate important and overlooked ideas and behaviors that pertain to race in the U.S.

Neoliberalism and Gentrification in Washington, D.C.

In addition to the post-civil rights and post-racial labels, these contemporary times have also been designated a neoliberal period. Feminist anthropologist Dana-Ain Davis writes that neoliberalism "represents an ideological coherence to the primacy of the private sector and is sustained by the creation of powerful non-state institutions that perpetuate the assurance of the market's self-regulating character" (2013, p. 27). Hackworth describes neoliberalism as a metaconcept rooted "in the trilogy of the individual, the market, and the noninterventionist state."[9] Its relationship to urban restructuring in general and gentrification in particular can be summarized by what Hackworth, citing Brenner and Theodore (2002), further posits as the dynamic, uneven and contested process of tearing down or barricading of preexisting artifacts, policies, institutions and agreements.

These targets include public housing and space, food stamps, and federal monetary assistance to cities and states and the stated goal is foster market freedom and all the good that will allegedly follow from that. Gentrification is the local reflection of these broad political and economic projects, beginning with the arrival of "small-scale owner operators" who "entered disinvested neighborhoods to rehabilitate individual homes for personal consumption." These shifts have been followed by an increased influx of investment capital and the people with

---

9   Page 10, *The Neoliberal City: Governance, Ideology and Development in American Urbanism*, Jason Hackworth, Ithaca, NY: Cornell University Press, 2007.

access to it, along with the altering of the landscape by tearing down the old to make room for the new (Hackworth, 2007).

People can naturalize these developments on all sides of debates about neoliberalism, gentrification and displacement and disagreements are often too complex to be described as merely two-sided. For some African Americans global economic restructuring was exclusively framed as an expression of White racial domination. A handful of the people I spoke with were familiar with the neoliberalism concept but also found some White cultural culpability in changing conditions. Some of these perspectives reflected a degree of essentialism but given how White Americans were benefiting from the changes taking place in communities, it was apparent that race was connected to urban restructuring.[10]

On another side of the debate a cadre of Whites[11] has a tendency to minimize the impact of structural inequality in shaping their place in a changing D.C. In this scenario urban "development" is viewed as an outgrowth of hard work and ingenuity.[12] Conversely, those African Americans who did not purchase or renovate their parents' homes or prevent crime from sucking the worth out of properties and the enjoyment out of city life, have failed to succeed in the game of modern, urban economic achievement. These attitudes are not the sole expressions of White Americans. I have written, elsewhere (Prince, 2006), about African American educators, writers and laypersons espousing, seemingly neo-conservative ideas of personal responsibility, a perspective that is not only perpetuated by middle class African Americans (Juan Williams, 2006; Cosby and Poussaint, 2009).

D.C. is a model neoliberal city. Given its penchant for capital accumulation (Harvey, 2005), the neoliberal project thrives upon unfettered avenues to markets, the privatization of public resources, and the commodification of history and culture. These mandates make neoliberalism experimental at its core; flitting about new strategies almost willy-nilly in search of lucrative income and wealth generating opportunities. Unfortunately and all too often things can go wrong when untested methods are applied to local governance and the social problems affecting people's lives. It also makes policymakers' support for unproven approaches to

---

10   These are concerns that link critiques of neoliberalism to CWS but responses to gentrification are also mitigated by age and other variables. African American youth have been more vociferously implicated in negative interactions with White residents of predominantly African American communities. More qualitative research on interactions with White newcomers to predominantly *minority* communities is needed to flesh out more of these concerns and questions.

11   I haven't conducted this research among White Americans so there is a degree of conjecture to this statement. I base this assumption on newspaper articles and blog responses from new identified or self-identified as White.

12   This is a perspective I gleaned reading discussions on a blog spot and community website called "The Prince of Petworth" after a posted short film on gentrification.

urban development and social service provision an imperative and this is why the neoliberal project is also a partnership between the state and commerce.

Commercial entities have been given free rein in Washington, D.C. With the help of friends on the D.C. City Council and ideological constructs that smooth their paths, developers have snatched up public housing properties, a bevy of schools, and waterfront locales previously held by the public trust. Housing activists have complained to me that corporations have an inordinate amount of influence over the policy decisions of elected representatives. For example, private corporations like the Corrections Corporation of America are now running prison systems and this has caused hardships for the families of the incarcerated and heightened the concerns of scholars and activists (Mattera and Khan, 2003).[13]

Its analytical utility notwithstanding, there have been noticeable degrees of continuity in the trajectory of African American history that suggest the "neo" in neoliberalism may deserve a closer look. Its hegemonic apparatus that appeals to the promotion of freedom, choice and personal responsibility are attractive to some. The conceptual power of these ideas fall flat when stacked against the life stories of Americans who have made the prerequisite sacrifices but remain in poverty. There is a certain illogic that must proliferate in order for neoliberal notions to gain currency but in content and communicative style these epistemologies replicate some of the most desperate but successful taxonomic ideologies of the past—including the pseudoscientific varieties that have launched attacks on the abilities of women and people of color (Gould, 1981; Baker 1998).

Blaming the vulnerable or turning a blind eye toward their predicaments is part and parcel to neoliberal ideology, as is victimizing the poor or persons at risk to racial disparities through deregulation and heightened exploitation. In a conversation about 19th-century Black life in D.C. with Carroll R. Gibbs, an activist and author of *Black Georgetown Remembered* and other publications, he shared that men who were commonly referred to as tramps were incarcerated in D.C. and the children of confined debtors were apprenticed out to prevent them from becoming dependents of the state (personal communication with author in 2009).[14] This piece of information indicates that the same oppressive vagrancy laws that re-enslaved African Americans in the deep-south from the end of the Civil

---

13   Residents have described D.C. as a city run as a social experiment. Vouchers and public charter schools, regarded by activists who fight against these programs as capitulations to private interest at the expense of the children, are examples of how neoliberal approaches have infiltrated the realm of education. The young and relatively inexperienced former head of D.C. schools, Chancellor Michelle Rhee, has become a national celebrity while achieving pariah status locally, at least from the perspective of the working class parents and other residents I spoke with.

14   Gibbs has guest-lectured in my Roots of Racism and Inequality in Washington, D.C. classes at American University and organizes a series of citywide lectures on African American life that are held on a yearly basis in local libraries. I attended a lecture and slide show on Jim Crow in D.C. at Frances A. Gregory Library on Alabama Avenue and 37th Street southeast which was attended by about 17 people on a Saturday afternoon. He is

War to the World War II-period, were also imposed upon Black Washingtonians (Blackmon, 2008).

MacLean maintains that the regional roots of neoliberalism in the U.S. can be traced to the American south (2008).[15] Writing as a historian, she labels 19th-century southern planters as America's first neoliberals and sees 1970s-antecedents of neoliberalism in the southern elite's responses to New Deal political machinations. MacLean says:

> The south's White elite both before and after the Civil War wanted low labor costs, a weak state as far as public welfare was concerned, and, above all, open markets in which to peddle its commodities. Southern leaders vehemently rejected the labor protections, quality public education, infra-structure investments, rehabilitative justice, and active federal government sought by northerners, moved by economic changes and social movements like those that led European national toward social democracy.[16]

Critical race theorist David Theo Golberg argues the neoliberal state can be exemplified as a more bounded, national configuration oriented toward a shift to protectionism, deindustrialization and liberalization of markets and associated with structural adjustment and tax rates that favor the upper end of income scale (2009). In developing a theory of race and neoliberalism, he also asserts neoliberal projects promote the flow of people, information, capital, goods and services as well as the functioning of the state as a traffic cop assigned to facilitate this stream and institute violence when this tide is disrupted or preemptive strikes when interference is anticipated. The neoliberal concept of race also has as much to do with invisibility and it does conformity. Goldberg further writes that goods and services are racialized as are notions of who should be protected in this process of accumulation.

Ideas about Whiteness greatly figure into who benefits from this shifting neoliberal project. Goldberg asserts racialized minorities can enter Whiteness by emulating sets of conditions such as upward mobility, home ownership, the displaying of certain values expressed in ways of acting and dressing, essentially through performance. At the same time, moreover, race is also muted in that the racial structures that we know to be real are ignored or taken for granted.

Finally, Goldberg says racial neoliberalism also frames capital, and goods and service flows with a rhetoric of mixture and social intercourse, as well as notions of engaging the global community. These ideas, along with emphases on global commercial interactions with an accent on racial hybridity, may sound

---

also a contributor to the film, *From Enslavement to Emancipation* which is a documentary published by the D.C. government to honor Emancipation Day celebrations in the city.

15   MacClean also emphasizes the role of the American west in proliferating the neoliberal project.

16   Ibid., page 23.

benign or even forward-thinking on the surface (2009). Pointing to the need for "more complete understanding of contemporary global processes," Clarke and Thomas advocate for "an integrated analysis of the historical precedents of current circulations of how imperialism and racial ordering have shaped global movements, and of the ways conceptualizations of belonging, membership and citizenship have been both imagined and institutionalized in racial terms."[17] A more critical view is fostered when racialized power is folded into the analyses as Clarke and Thomas suggest (2006).

Social Justice and Gentrification in Washington, D.C.

There are three ways in which researcher transparency, race, and neoliberalism make *African Americans and Gentrification in Washington, D.C.* a book about social justice. Although its benefits are not evenly distributed, gentrification is a policy-driven practice that has been sanctioned and subsidized by the marshaling of public entities and resources. Gentrification does not improve dislocation caused by the shrinking pool of affordable housing in Washington, D.C. and this is a central problem facing working class residents in the city today. Housing is this book's most pressing social justice-related issue and a topic that overlaps with my overall focus on the inequalities of race and class. This matter is at the center of an important body of literature that frames housing as a human right and poverty as exploitation (Desmond, 2012)[18] and this book connects gentrification to these key social justice concerns.

African Americans and Gentrification in Washington, D.C. also speaks to the rights of Black Washingtonians to embrace and defend their local histories without apology. It is problematic to minimize geographic belonging and autonomous self-expression about spatial attachment, particularly during a time of rapid demographic change. However it is also important to be mindful of how history creates contradictory battlegrounds and produces competing narratives. Where some African Americans imagine D.C. as a Chocolate City (CC) that has existed in perpetuity, there are also relative newcomers who push the rewind button on the history of the last decades to their own ends. Honoring the multicultural history of the city and unique contributions of African Americans are not mutually exclusive exercises and misrepresenting the past in order to diminish the presence of other groups does not advance the goals of social justice. An important requirement of social justice efforts is to attend to power analytically and orient research toward

---

17   Page 8, *Globalization and Race: Transformations in the Cultural Production of Blackness*, Kamari Maxine Clarke and Deborah A. Thomas, editors, Durham, N.C.: Duke University Press, 2006.

18   Edsall, Thomas. September 2012. Is Poverty a Kind of Robbery? http://campaignstops.blogs.nytimes.com/2012/09/16/is-poverty-a-kind-of-robbery/.

assisting vulnerable populations. This book works to sort out some of these complex issues of hierarchy.

Gentrification and integration are inferred in connection with the final way in which social justice relates to this book. Gentrification has been framed as a potential force for reducing segregation based on the idea that demographic shifts will contribute to the formation of multicultural spaces (Weinberger, 2011). Additionally, for proponents of gentrification, efforts to widen the tax base, bring in purported job creators, and privilege the needs of middle income earning residents are projected to foster an overall growth and prosperity that will trickle down to lower income residents. The promise of urban restructuring through gentrification has been promoted by capable advocates (Freeman, 2008; Vigdor, 2002) but the problems for the poor and working class still loom in the wake of marked transferals of resources and shifts in populations. The following chapter presents additional data on the fact that low income households in Washington, D.C. are facing severe economic pressures. In addition, there are households and communities that, due to their positioning in the social hierarchy, will not experience an improved quality of life as the result of gentrification.

Chapter 2

Race and Class Hierarchies in D.C. History

Washington, D.C. was created through the partitioning of Maryland and Virginia land parcels in the late 18th century. The city was born amid much judicial wrangling as congressional leaders worked to reach agreement on a location for the capital that would be "under the influence of wealthy plantation owners and out of the hands of eastern industrial capitalists" (The Smithsonian Anacostia Museum and Center for African American History and Culture, 2005, p. 3). From the past to the present, whether irregularly or explicitly acknowledged, Black–White relations and class divisions have been intrinsic to the city's origins and its subsequent history.

Race and Class in Washington's Past

For African Americans the past 100 years have seen old sociopolitical and economic barriers eluded, broken down, and succumbed to and more novel obstacles erected on their paths. The trajectory for African American inequality in D.C. begins with the legacy of enslavement, followed by the short-lived promises of Reconstruction and the disparities of Jim Crow segregation, leading to the dislocations of urban renewal, the devastation of riots, and the uneven impacts of contemporary urban restructuring.

D.C.'s distinctive modern-day characteristics are fashioned by the specificities of its founding. For example, the District was among the first American cities to achieve majority African American status although what some consider a positive development did not become a demographic reality through benign means. To the contrary, this status has its origins in the most difficult period of African American history: the appropriation of Black labor and inventiveness through chattel slavery.

Nowhere in the United States has slavery been so replete with contradiction than in Washington, D.C. Both enslaved and nominally free African American laborers helped build the White House, the Capitol, and other magnificent structures that stand, with all the allusions to freedom and liberty, as singular architectural symbols of the nation's capital. These edifices attract throngs of tourists who are most likely unaware of the oppressive circumstances under which these impressive buildings came to be.

There were also historical figures whose life courses symbolized the paradoxical existence of African Americans during the antebellum period in D.C. One of these was White House seamstress Elizabeth Keckley who, according to her autobiography *Behind the Scenes or Thirty Years a Slave and Four Years in the White House*, endured childhood beatings by her owners and rape, and then went on to become a successful entrepreneur and confidant of both Mary Todd and President Abraham Lincoln (Keckley, 1868; Lusane, 2010; Masur, 2010).[1]

Washington, D.C. was "a peculiar city" upon its founding, labeled as such because of its distinctive early 19th-century demographic features (Manning, 1998, p. 330). The census of 1800 reported that more than one quarter of Washington residents were slaves and a smaller percentage were free people of color. Manning (1998) says:

> This demographic feature distinguishes Washington from other Northern cities that attracted European immigrants to satisfy their rapacious labor demand. Unlike other Eastern Seaboard cities (New York, Philadelphia, Boston), it was neither a center of manufacturing nor of commerce. This profoundly influenced labor relations in the District by reinforcing the local economy's dependence on cheap black workers and thus its political-cultural ties to the southern caste system. (pp. 330–31)

These patterns appear to have shaped future migratory trajectories to the city by delimiting European immigration and encouraging the arrival of other African Americans. During the Civil War, the existing African American population was augmented by fugitive slaves or so called contraband and Black migrants traveling south in search of opportunity. The pace of these population movements would increase after emancipation in Washington (Masur, 2010).

A strategic location "on the Potomac, with easy access to the Chesapeake; … any kind of coastal trade" (Apidta, 1995, p. 14) would be lucrative for any city, but Washington's proximity to the largest slave-trading firm in the country, Franklin & Armfield, headquartered in Alexandria, Virginia, made the trade in Black captives exceptionally good business for D.C. (Apidta, 1995). There was a lot of money to be made in the selling and buying of Black people. Most of the captives were put on the market at local auction houses and taverns concentrated downtown. Addresses and intersections of those locations within the city limits included:

1. Robey's Slave Pen and Tavern, east side of 7th Street SW (between B Street and Maryland Avenue)
2. Williams Private Jail or The Yellow House, opposite Robey's Slave Pen between 7th and 8th Streets; also south of B Street SW and the Smithsonian
3. 3410 Volta Place, NW
4. The National Mall
5. Beal Street Tavern and Stables, Georgetown, NW
6. Miller's Tavern or F Street Tavern, 13th and F Streets, NW

---

1   Keckley became influential and prestigious through her skills with a needle and thread and her business sense. She also became a part of Washington's African American elite and helped organize the Contraband Relief Association during the summer of 1862.

7. Lloyd's Tavern, southeast corner of 7th Street and Pennsylvania Avenue, NW
8. John Beattle's Auction Block, 3200 O Street, NW
9. Montgomery Tavern, 1300 block of Wisconsin Avenue, NW
10. McCandless Tavern, Georgetown, NW
11. Lafayette Tavern, F Street between 13th and 14th Streets, NW
12. Carroll Row, Corner of First and A Street, NE
13. St. Charles Hotel, 3rd Street and Pennsylvania Avenue, NW
14. Decatur House, Jackson Place and H Street, NW
15. National Hotel, Pennsylvania Avenue and 6th Street, NW

There are no signs to mark the human dramas that must have come to pass in these locales but historians have described the commerce of trading human beings in and around these vicinities in vivid detail:

> Chained and handcuffed, Black men were driven in a double column followed by boys and girls. The women with little children were carried in vehicles, with the mounted white overseer, whip at the ready, bringing up the rear. Their route would sometimes take them right by the Capitol building itself to one of a number of slave markets throughout the city. (Apidta, 1996, pp. 16–17)

Abolitionists visiting from Europe were appalled by the conditions they saw enslaved African Americans living under in Washington, D.C. (Harrold, 2009). This city became a major depot in the trafficking of Black captives, but commerce in human chattel was not the only way 19th-century racism affected African Americans:

> There were also laws that oppressed both slaves and free blacks. It was illegal for African American to vote, hold office, testify against whites, serve on juries, or own firearms. An 1827 Washington ordinance subjected them to a 10:00 pm curfew. An 1836 ordinance attempted to restrict them to the most menial work. In Washington, Virginia and Maryland—as in most southern jurisdictions— the law presumed that all black people were slaves unless they could prove otherwise. This presumption supported the arrest of African Americans who would not document their free status. (p. 8)

With the institution of these Black codes, African Americans faced serious proscriptions against their liberties, accompanied by threats of physical danger and the potential for a host of nonlethal indignities Whites visited upon them. Despite the hostile environment, the tide of racism was poised to shift. Overall, African Americans worked to improve their life conditions, building institutions and developing benevolent associations and other organizations that were active but also restricted and closely scrutinized by Whites (Masur, 2010).

In 1840, D.C. became one of three cities in the U.S. in which the majority of the African American population consisted of free persons (Medler, 1997, cited in The Smithsonian Anacostia Museum and Center for African American History and Culture, 2005).[2] The proportion of unenslaved Blacks in this city helped instigate manumission efforts and the formation of institutions designed to aid former slaves (Masur, 2010). African American abolitionists like Frederick Douglass, Henry Highland Garnett, and leading African Methodist Episcopal minister John F. Cook Sr. were among the prominent Black Washingtonians who, along with Elizabeth Keckley, were working collectively against slavery (Harrold, 2003).

Their work was aided by antislavery legislators like Henry Wilson of Massachusetts, who opposed lawmakers who were advocating for slavery in the District and championed reparatory legislation to revoke the Black codes and post-emancipation barriers to African American achievement (Masur, 2010). The leadership of antiracist Washingtonians was augmented by the Black rights advocacy of regular visitors like Martin Delaney and Sojourner Truth, as well as non-natives who took up residence, including educator Anna Julia Cooper; religious leader and African nationalist Alexander Crummell; and feminist public speaker Maria Stewart, who established a school for African American children in D.C. (Lusane, 2010).

Despite the resolutions of the proslavery Washington city council and other legislators, President Abraham Lincoln signed the District of Columbia Emancipation Act into law on April 16th, 1862 (Masur, 2010). Gibbs (2002) notes that following this momentous occasion.

> The District's Black folks were ecstatic as well over Lincoln's signing of the Emancipation Proclamation. There were watch night church services, day-long prayer and thanksgiving sessions, and spontaneous eruptions of praise and prayer. (p. 19)

There was much to be grateful for at this transformative time and African Americans in the District made important initial gains at slavery's end, but racism would continue to toughen the road at each political and socioeconomic turn. The backlash against the real and perceived achievements that followed emancipation was swift, and Blacks were retaliated against through discriminatory practices in public accommodations and employment:

> As the number of black people in the city grew, hostility increased on the part of certain white Washingtonians. Congressmen, residents, and local officials who were opposed to black political power devised several plans in an unsuccessful effort to thwart black suffrage. (Smithsonian Anacostia Museum, 2005, p. 71)

---

2   The other two cities were Baltimore, Maryland and St. Louis, Missouri.

The establishment of African American residential areas like Anacostia and Barry Farms in SE, in addition to communities that existed where the Library of Congress, Federal Triangle, and other D.C. landmark buildings now stand, took place during the post-Emancipation stream of Black migration to the city (Fitzpatrick and Goodwin, 1990). There were rapidly erected alley dwellings and other sites in the city where impoverished residents struggled to make ends meet and became vulnerable to illnesses associated with exposure to swamps and open sewage (Smithsonian Anacostia Museum, 2005). Borchert reports that an 1880 survey of 3,000 male alley dwellers showed that many of these men were employed as carpenters, barbers, shoemakers, blacksmiths, plasterers, and brick masons, with close to 20 percent "described as rag picker, rag gatherer, rag man, rag dealer or junk dealer and one third employed as peddler, jobber, huckster and horse trader" (1980, pp. 167–8). Employment patterns for women in similar forms of housing showed an overwhelming involvement in domestic service (Jones, 1929; Swinney, 1936).

Racism made the search for gainful employment and adequate housing intertwined difficulties for African American residents of D.C. at the end of the 19th century. Lesko, Babb and Gibbs cite an 1879 housing survey which showed large numbers of Blacks in Georgetown living without indoor plumbing or in wood framed rather than brick homes and write, "Blacks and whites originally lived side by side in the Grace Street-Cherry Hill-Cissell Alley neighborhood west of Wisconsin Avenue and south of M Street, an area with many dilapidated houses and poor city services. By 1910, however, most of that neighborhood had become predominantly black as whites abandoned its narrow, crowded streets for better housing and employment elsewhere in the city" (1991, p. 41).

Leaving an area to obtain improved housing and job opportunities is one form of demographic change. The turn of the 19th century would see African American out migration from Georgetown taking place under circumstances very different from what White residents experienced. Black dislocation from Georgetown also points to an ignored problematic of gentrification. Over a period of decades and through the efforts of civic organizations African Americans were pushed out of what is now an affluent area under the auspices of *slum removal*. In discussing concerns about the area's African American residents, Georgetown Citizens Association documentation strips away all pretense and reveals a candid bigotry in referencing a *colored area* "in close proximity to a number of fine new homes belonging to white persons" (p. 91). Concern and emphasis was on property values and not the well-being of the communities of African Americans which dated back to the Civil War.

Another factor in this social justice conundrum was that while the housing of Black alley dwellers was by all accounts unsanitary, inadequate and in need of improvement (Borchet, 1980; Lesko, Babb, and Gibbs 1999; Moore, 1999), these areas were also important sites for community building and cultural exchange. Moreover, as contemporary examples with the HOPE VI federal housing program implementation also show, by and large the vulnerable populations do not uniformly benefit from the infrastructural improvements which follow the destruction of their communities. Instead the poor, of both the past and present, become displaced through the renovation process and after the improvements are completed, there are no reliable policies for reinserting the dislocated. There is also insufficient action taken by policy makers and elected officials to ascertain where the poor have gone and how they fare after such disruptive transitions. As I show in subsequent chapters, this scenario has been played out in numerous instances over time.

Another outgrowth of the Washington housing crunch was seen in the Shaw area during the 1880s. Known today as U Street because of the centrality of the 14th and U intersection, the neighborhood had its alley dwelling predominated by Blacks but it was also known for residential intermixtures of race and class born out of dearth rather than harmonious relations across these boundaries (Ruble, 2010). This portion of NW achieved historical significance in part because of the performers and professionals who lived or worked in the area. Shaw was also in close proximity to Howard University and the adjacent Le Droit Park, an all-White enclave of stately mansions that was gated in order to remain off limits to the African American students and faculty of the nearby historically Black University (Fitzpatrick and Goodwin, 1990). African Americans who would repeatedly tear down fences that were erected to keep them out thwarted the ability of White residents to remain segregated and Le Droit became Black by the turn of the century. This change represented another form of demographic change. This was an instance of Whites fleeing an area that had a close proximity to African Americans but maintained a good reputation and was not characterized as an area in sharp decline.

Georgetown, U Street/Shaw and, after White out-migration, Le Droit Park also had an elite African American stratum which consisted, early on, of those who found work in the domestic sphere by serving in the homes of well-to-do Whites. Propelled by the new opportunities brought about by Reconstruction, this would become a cohesive grouping by the 1880s. Moore (1999) notes that:

> After the Civil War, the establishment of black universities such as Howard and more liberal admissions policies at white universities made it possible for some members of the next generation of elite to prepare to enter professions. During Reconstruction, the legal profession took on great importance for blacks, who saw it as a stepping-stone to politics. At this time a great many black men also trained for the ministry—a field that would remain open to blacks as long as there were black churches. The professional most in demand in the 19th century, however, was teaching. (p. 25)

African American elites were entering areas beyond service to Whites and although Black business owners, professionals and government workers were not as rigidly affected by a racial division of labor as were manual laborers and the poor, they had their own degree of challenges to contend with. The ascendance of Jim Crow segregation in Washington, D.C. eliminated some of the White competition for African American owned business owners but Blacks of various socioeconomic backgrounds who received unequal pay for comparable work had to hold multiple jobs to compensate for lost wages (Moore, 1999). Black patrons were reeled into African American owned businesses with the ideology of racial solidarity while some African American elites buoyed by uplift ideology cooperated with White charities and worked independently to advocate for low rent housing for the poor (Moore, 1999). The turn of the 19th century would see continuous population movements, growing housing and employment needs, and the professionalization of Black elites.

D.C. had "the largest urban concentration of African Americans in the U.S. up until World War I — more than New York City during the same period" (Manning, 1998, p. 332). African American communities experienced progress and setbacks after Reconstruction, but the inauguration of President Woodrow Wilson ushered in a much-feared period of racist retrenchment. The racial illogic of Jim Crow was soon realized after Wilson's arrival in Washington:

> Black employees in federal offices were screen off from their compatriots and restricted to newly designated Jim Crow restrooms and lunchrooms. Civil service applicants were required to submit photographs, and the few federal appointments that blacks had been allowed to receive in the past were now reserved for whites. The combined impact of reintroducing stringent segregation in public facilities, withholding federal employment opportunities, and the lack of citywide elections and the leadership opportunities lost therein all chipped away at the political and economic infrastructure of black communities in Washington, DC. (Smithsonian Anacostia Museum, 2005, p. 75)

The effects of Jim Crow resulted in stratified political—economic circumstances for African Americans, but this was not unusual or D.C. specific. However, Washington, D.C. was a company town; in time most residents would be employed by the federal government. For those African Americans who did not obtain government employment in D.C., there were possibilities for entrepreneurial opportunities in segregated neighborhoods. The old elite's ability to gain status and income from working in the domestic sphere was a paradoxical feature of this urban scenario. Black servants of the White wealthy had a degree of clout but after the turn of the 20th century, a nascent Black middle class emerged that consisted of a combination of the old Black elites; professionals; and business owners who serviced, educated and informed members of the African American community (Landry, 1987).

Colorism—an outgrowth of racism whereby lighter skinned Blacks gain increased social status and privilege—was a common aspect of African American communities across the U.S. However, the light-skinned elite of D.C. have been singled out for their distinctive income-generating opportunities and lifestyles that, over the years, have differentiated life in D.C. from that of nearby cities (Gatewood, 1993). Intermarriage and separate social interaction among African Americans of high status and lighter skin represented attempts at social detachment from darker and/or poorer Blacks who were limited by the realities of racial segregation. Whereas the social status of elite Blacks was based on patron—client relations with prominent Whites as well as skin color, proper comportment, and family ties, this had changed by 1920. It was during this decade when well-off African Americans began looking to Black communities for approval after discovering "that whites did not make the same social distinctions that they [the Black elite] so carefully cultivated" (Moore, 1999, p. 3) Gatewood (1993) writes that this was a key transition in Black elite life after the turn of the 20th century; however, the rebuffing of Black elites by former White patrons certainly did not eliminate skin color prejudice continues to plague African Americans in terms of intraracial stratification, gender, and shifting aesthetic values within Black communities.[3]

Among the many ironies of colorism are those instances wherein its beneficiaries emerge as ardent and effective warriors for social justice and anti-racism. In D.C. this description was fitting for a long list of politicians, educators and otherwise accomplished African Americans such as Robert and Mary Church Terrell, Angelina Grimke, W.E.B. DuBois, Roscoe Conklin Bruce and others. These leaders had lynching, dislocation, and the maltreatment of Black GIs as issues to rally around. In her autobiography, Terrell (1863–1954) writes about the numerous encounters she had with law enforcement and White business owners as she went about the work of subverting segregation and other forms of racial mistreatment in D.C. (1940). She was an anti-racist and womanist warrior up to her death and Terrell was also embroiled, along with her husband and other African Americans in Washington, D.C., in the increasingly acrimonious jostling for influence between Booker T. Washington and adherents to his Tuskegee Machine philosophy and those who opposed his immense power (Giddings, 1984).

There were also social justice advocates who were not members of Black society such as Perry Carson and Nannie Helen Burroughs. Burroughs was the founder of a school for *colored* girls and a member of the National Association of Colored Women (Giddings, 1984), She was nationally-known for her charitable work but her dark skin color and modest background contributed to Burroughs being a fiercely loyal race woman who was largely unaccepted by and most disinterested in the D.C.'s Black elite social scene (Moore, 1999). Whether concerning the working class or upwardly mobile; followers of Washington's accommodationist approach or DuBois' more confrontational stance, D.C. was a locale of heightened social justice advocacy at the end of the 19th century. These seeds of activism set the stage for the battles and victories that would be

---

3 A nine-minute trailer for a film titled "Dark Girl," by actor/director Bill Duke, shows the pain and difficulty experienced by dark-skinned African American at the hands of other Blacks and has been making the rounds over the Internet. I was e-mailed the trailer from three people in my network and also forwarded it widely.

fought for and won by Black Washingtonians during subsequent decades and the legacy of within-group class differentiation would also continue to divide African Americans on the ideological front. Upcoming chapters will show how the intra-racial socioeconomic differences and competing schools of Black political thought also shaped African American experiences with gentrification.

Ideology and the political and economic conditions of the postwar years had a symbiotic effect and created the conditions that would give rise to gentrification in subsequent decades. Nationally, Black residential exclusion was fueled by notions of White superiority and enforced through violence, legal maneuvering and governmental housing policies. In discussing the logic of federal intervention in the United States housing market and the role of private capital in these processes, Freund (2007) writes that the Federal Housing Authority (FHA) "structured the housing market along racial lines. Guiding agency operations was a theory about race and property values first articulated in planning and real estate circles before the Depression" (p. 129). Cities Destroyed for Cash (Boyer, 1973) also documents the negative racialized impact of housing policy. The passage of the Home Owners' Loan Act in 1933, led to redlining and the denial of insured loans to African Americans and residents of racially-mixed urban neighborhoods. Not only was suburban development strategically subsidized, these policies also deprived minority communities of much needed resources (Johnson, 2009). This racism and neglect through public policy created the conditions that preceded gentrification.

In postwar Washington, D.C. there were additional events unfolding that would also shape demographic change and hence, gentrification. For example, schools in the District were desegregated with the Bolling *vs*. Sharpe decision in 1954 (Balkin, 2001). The case was initiated by the Consolidated Parents Group, residents of Anacostia who wanted the new John Philip Souza Junior High School to open as an integrated facility. The 1954 decision prefigured the loosening of additional Jim Crow era restrictions and marked a decisive period in the local history of D.C. In the ensuing decades, housing opportunities opened up for African Americans and the number of White Washingtonians began to decline. The city's overall population dropped from its height of 803,000 in 1950 to a little more than 606,000 by the 1990s. However, the African American population increased between1950 and 1970 until it, too, began to decline during the 1970s. These are demographic shifts which were initiated for different reasons but, as with previous patterns, they were rooted in racialized and class-related processes. Oral history data I collected from seniors are discussed in the following chapter and show how interpersonal relations unfolded on the micro-level as White neighbors began fleeing transitioning neighborhoods like Trinidad in NE during the 1940s and 1950s.

Most of the women and men I talked with to complete this book were also present during the riots of 1968. The violence and property destruction which took place after the assassination of Dr. Martin Luther King had a huge impact on political-economic developments moving forward. It affected subsequent demographic shifts and shaped the housing and urban development policies of the following years. The riots also had an influence on individuals who became involved in local politics after these events transpired. As this young generation of leaders emerged after the establishment of home rule in 1973, the City Council and, later, Mayor's office was characterized by supporters and detractors alike as run by The Student Nonviolent Coordinating Committee or SNCC. This was a reference to leaders like the Reverend Douglas Moore and former mayor Marion Barry who served as a local SNCC director during the late 1960s (Ruble, 2010).

Nineteen sixty-eight is also important because African American outmigration emerged as an issue in Washington, D.C. during that year and this demographic shift was related to the riots. Gentrification is contingent upon disinvestment and dearth in urban environments and Smith and LeFaivre posit that gentrification is the end result of a deliberate cycle that begins with neighborhood devalorization (1984). The destruction of 1968 presented the need for action and the intensification of investment in the people of these communities. However, the urban unrest also stoked pre-existing racist ideologies about Blacks and their urban domains. As a result abandonment ensued.

This was the socio-historical context in which future urban development strategies were formulated and because these scenarios were repeated in cities across the U.S., these developments also fit into broader national debates through varied bodies of literature that has connected Black outmigration, particularly of middle class households, with deterioration in the tax base, a decrease in the allocation of city resources, and the alleged decline of role models for the children of struggling African American households.

Between 1950 and 1970 the White population of Washington, D.C. decreased from 518,000 to 210,000 while the African American population increased by 257,000 during that same period (U.S. Census Bureau, 2008). Following this significant White exodus Washington became one of the earliest among the major cities to gain an African American mayor in the Civil Rights period (Pohlmann, 2009). Walter Washington was selected by Lyndon Johnson to be mayor of Washington, D.C. in 1967, the same year that saw the election of Carl B. Stokes and Richard G. Hatcher as the first, respective, Black mayors, of Cleveland, Ohio and Gary, Indiana (Pohlmann, 2009). By voting for Washington in 1975, Washingtonians preceded proximal east coast cities in their efforts to elect their first African American mayors. Baltimore, New York, and Philadelphia elected Kurt Schmoke, David Dinkins, and Wilson Goode, respectively, during the 1980s.

It is also the case that Walter Washington did not enjoy powers comparable to those of other mayors. Home Rule was enacted in 1973, the same year that the legislative branch of the local government—the D.C. City Council—was established by Congress' Columbia Home Rule Act (Congressional Digest, 2007). In spite of this victory and the symbolism attached to the office, D.C.'s mayoral decision-making powers are subject to the authority of the federal government. No other mayors have to seek the approval of Congress to pass their budgets or enact legislation. This power dynamic comes to bear on many aspects of the local residents' lives and is a critical distinction between conditions in D.C. and those of other U.S. cities.

The absence of a voting representative in Congress for District residents has been framed as a civil rights issue by many Washingtonians. Taking it a step further observers like the late Senator Edward Kennedy attributed this unique form of disenfranchisement to the racial make-up of the city (Meyers, 1996; Modan, 2007). Jaffe and Sherwood (1994) went as far back as the 19th century to trace how the role of racial hostility toward Black Washingtonians influenced future voting rights legislation. The authors also quoted John Mitchell, the disgraced Attorney General under President Richard Nixon, referring to D.C. governmental officials as "the Amos and Andy Cab Company" during a period of predominantly African American calls for greater political self-determination and statehood (p. 100–101).

This Black people's history of Washington, D.C. highlights the extent to which African American residents have had their work fighting for socially just conditions cut out for them. After the tremendous staying power and lasting sacrifices of so many, the African American population showed a decrease between 1970 and 1980 for the first time (U.S. Census Bureau, 2008). Given the extent of social upheavals and population losses the city had endured, urban planners, activists, and the newly-elected officials who made history in 1973 had tremendous postwar-years challenges. In time it would be African American leaders who would work in concert with the real estate industry to set gentrification in motion by building market rate housing and subsidizing private investment.

In the face of these shifts there has also been significant grassroots push-back against neoliberal urban development. In 2002, for example, Washington Inner City Self Help, Latino Workers Rights Organization and the National Coalition for the Homeless mobilized residents to march against gentrification and occupy abandoned buildings in response to what they saw as an emphasis on the demands of private investors at the expense of the needs of working families (Wilson, 2007). This coalition of activists from the NW community of Columbia Heights issued demands "in a highly symbolic act...to the City Council and Mayor's Office" that all affordable housing units lost to residents through deals made with developers be replaced, that the warehousing of vacant public property cease, and that living wages be paid to working families (p. 142, 2007). Activists also called on public officials to "commit to providing a full range of services including supporting housing for the disabled, treatment on demand for those with drug and alcohol problems, and assistance in locating and securing both housing and employment" (Wilson, 2007, p. 143). These concerns align very closely with those of the activists I would work and collect ethnographic data decades later.

Washington, D.C. Today

Washington, D.C. is officially composed of approximately 100 neighborhoods, the names of which range from being familiar to residents to completely obscure. Sometimes designations change stemming from developer's or newcomers' efforts to rebrand gentrifying neighborhoods. The case of Truxton Circle poses a unique example of this. For decades, long-term residents commonly viewed the area as a part of Shaw. However, a *Washington Post* article noted the stoking of tensions between these residents and White newcomers who began calling the area by the original, yet largely unheard of, name of Truxton Circle. The practice provoked the ire of long-term African American residents who sensed appropriation in the making.

The article, "An Identity Reclaimed—Gentrification, With a Few Discontents, Transforms a Corner of Shaw," appeared in the "Where We Live" section of *The Washington Post* (Abrams, 2011). The title begs questions of how something so new to a population can be framed as reclaimed but privileging the proprietary sentiments of newcomers is not an uncommon practice within mainstream discussions of gentrification. Like many of its type in *The Post*, this piece ineffectively grapples with the power dynamics at play when members of a dominant racialized group wield their influence to synchronize the status quo with the pace of their desires.

The city's Office of Planning structures D.C. communities down to the most local level within Advisory Neighborhood Commissions (ANCs),[4] and then into larger wards and clusters. Residents often speak in terms of wards and even ANCs, but few talk about neighborhood clusters.[5] Before beginning this research I was completely unfamiliar with Burleith, Woodland-Normanstone Terrace, Hawthorne, Barnaby Woods or Wesley Heights, among a lot of other neighborhood designations. Some of the people I spoke with had no idea what their community was called while some gave two names when asked the same question on other occasions. There were also instances where communities blended into each other so seamlessly that their boundaries were indistinguishable. In NE, for example Lamond Riggs becomes North Michigan Park somewhere around South Dakota Avenue which, then, flows into the Michigan Park neighborhood that borders Brookland. Traveling southeast on 12th Street eventually leads to Rhode Island Avenue, which is a main artery for heading to Woodridge, toward the left, or downtown, to the right. Staying on 12th Street then leads to the neighborhoods of Brentwood, Ivy City, and Trinidad.

All of these communities, with the exception of Lamond Riggs (Ward 4) and downtown (Ward 2), are in Ward 5, and based on 2008 U.S. Census data

---

4   There are 37 ANCs. According to the language on a D.C. government website, ANCs "consider a wide range of policies and programs affecting their neighborhoods, including traffic, parking, recreation and street improvements, liquor licenses, zoning, economic development, police protection, sanitation and trash collection, and the Districts annual budget http://anc.dc.gov/anc/site/default.asp.

5   Neighborhood names with associated wards and clusters can be found at the following website courtesy of NeighborhoodInfo DC. http://www.neighborhoodinfodc.org/pdfs/ward_cluster.pdf. It was made available on 14 August 2008 and was last accessed on 14 March 2013.

percentages, the communities of Wards 5, 7, and 8 have the highest numbers of multigenerational African American[6] residents and the lowest of number of Whites. In contrast, Ward 3 has the largest amount of White residents and the fewest African Americans (Social Compact, 2008). The majority of people I obtained data on for this study hail from Wards 1, 2, and 5, with only a small number living in Ward 2, in Cluster 4.

Each quadrant has its neighborhoods, resources, statistical indicators, and physical attributes, but the city can also be discussed as differentiating from north to south or east to west. For example, the western region of D.C. experienced an increase in job growth between 1985 and 1995, whereas the eastern portion saw a decrease during that same period (Brookings Institution, 1999). Jobs almost doubled per capita in those areas of D.C. farthest west and southwest (Orfield, 1999). This is good news, but only for distinct segments of the local population.

The overall number of employed D.C. residents has increased from 292,000 in 2000 to 307,000 in 2007, but unemployment has also increased and this disadvantage is experienced disproportionately across the city. Contrasting indicators also show that Wards 5, 7, and 8 have the lowest average household incomes, while Ward 3 has the highest at $128,000 (U.S. Census Bureau, 2008). Conrad (2010) cites statistics showing residents living in the western part of the District, in Wards 1, 2, 3, and 4, have rates of unemployment that are below the city's average, and those from the eastern part of the city, living in Wards 5, 7, and 8, have the highest levels of unemployment.[7] None of these figures "reflect the most serious effects of the recent economic downturn because the disparities in median household income and unemployment rates in the Washington region predate the national economic recession" (p. 8, Conrad, 2010). D.C. Fiscal Policy Institute data make the racial component to these disparities quantitatively apparent and these can also be found in Conrad's 2010 paper.[8]

---

6   This is a variant on a concept used by Arvenita Washington in her dissertation "Reading, Writing and Racialization: The Social Construction of Blackness for Middle School Students and Educators in Prince George's County Public Schools." This ethnography looked at the social construction of Blackness in a Prince Georges County, Maryland middle school. Her version of the term multigenerational Blacks distinguished African American youth with lengthy ancestry in the United States from those whose parents spoke English as a second language as immigrants from West Africa, Central America, and the Caribbean.

7   This paper was last accessed at http://aladinrc.wrlc.org/bitstream/handle/1961/9255/Conrad%2c%20Emily%20-%20Spring%20%2710%20%28P%29.pdf?sequence=1 on 14 March 2010. In it Conrad includes the following graph: Unemployment Rates (%) by Ward, May 2008, Washington, D.C.

Courtesy of D.C. Dept. of Employment Services, Office of Labor Market Research and Information.

8   Ibid. In it Conrad includes the following graph: D.C. Median Household Income, By Race/Ethnicity per the D.C. Fiscal Policy Institute Analysis of the 2008 American Community Survey.

SW is the smallest quadrant with the least number of residents. In addition to being the site for massive urban dislocation through restructuring, SW is home to the wharfs of Maine Street, where seafood restaurants are patronized and watermen and women provide fresh seafood. What happened to the SW quadrant was the subject of a documentary made by Delores Smith in 1991 through funding from the D.C. Humanities Council.[9] The stated goal of her film was to provide teachers with a visual tool to educate D.C. Public School students about what occurred beginning in the 1940s. During that time SW D.C. lost approximately 23,000 people in connection with the razing of homes and other buildings to make way for a highway. A D.C. Humanities Council website describes the film topic as being about "former Southwest residents as they remember the streetcars, markets, seafood, and neighborhood camaraderie before their community was torn apart."[10] Williams (2009) maintains that these development schemes "created Bantustan-like public and private complexes in wards 7 and 8 east of the Anacostia River."

D.C. is also unique in its special challenge of combining city, county, and state-level responsibilities. Meyers (1996) points out that:

> No other city in America has the District's state functions of welfare and Medicaid responsibility, maintenance of a state court, prison, and parole system, a state-level university, a state-level employment service and job training administration, disability compensation, state occupational safety and health enforcement, state licensing and utility and banking regulation, motor vehicle registration, and the like, in addition to such county functions as a county hospital, nursing homes, community mental health facilities, alcohol and drug abuse services, and public libraries, along with the usual city services such as police, fire, public works, traffic control, and recreation. (p. 47)[11]

Because D.C. is not a state, the city lacks the flow of revenue offered by a state structure to support the needs of its citizens. As Meyers further states:

> [N]one of the 50 states lacks the authority to tax non-residents who earn income within the state's borders and 45 currently require withholding on income earned within the state's borders (p. 47).

Predatory lending is another systematic and structural form of inequality that has affected life in the District. One outgrowth has been high rates of foreclosure in Washington, D.C. (Williams, 2004). The city also has elevated rates of poverty. According to a report by the D.C. Fiscal Policy Institute (DCFPI) the income gap grew over the last two decades in correlation with increasing wage inequality and stagnating incomes (Lazare, 2006). A second DCFPI report indicates that support

---

9   http://www.wdchumanities.org/dcdm/items/show/995.
10   Ibid.
11   Page 47.

provided by the Temporary Assistance for Needy Families (TANF) is insufficient, stating, "while the District has taken a number of steps under its TANF program to help parents move from welfare to work, D.C.'s TANF cash assistance benefit levels leave families with children well below poverty and are lower than in a majority of states, including Maryland and Virginia."[12]

The availability of affordable housing is central to discussions of gentrification, economic vulnerability, and African American mobility. In addition, expiring Section 8 housing contracts are connected to this issue. There are 7,800 project-based Section 8 units set to expire by 2013, and of those, 5,400 units—55 properties in total—are owned by for-profit landlords. Many for-profit owners decline contract renewal because of opportunities to charge higher rents and generate more rental income on the open market (Leaks, L., personal communication).

With each blow against Section 8 contract renewals the number of affordable housing units in DC is substantially reduced. The representatives of two grassroots groups that work with low-income populations maintain that these shortages increase obstacles to economic sustainability for low-income residents in Washington, D.C. The poor in Washington, D.C. are predominantly Latino and African American, and community-based organizations serving these populations report that their members face dislocation as gentrification and accompanying developments drive up property taxes, increase rental rates, and diminish the available stock of affordable housing. With meager financial resources, low-income minority populations face the risk of enduring substandard living conditions, exemplified by overcrowding, displacement, and homelessness. This discussion continues in subsequent chapters but two, large-scale quantitative studies discussed below clearly demonstrate how individual challenges can build into cumulative effects.

A macrolevel picture shows stark findings on racial disparities in the United States. The Institute on Assets and Social Policy published a report that showed wealth inequalities between White and African Americans have quadrupled over the last generation (May, 2010). This study was based on a longitudinal study that gathered economic information on the same set of families from 1984 to 2007. It concluded that the wealth gap between Black and White households increased from $20,000 to $95,000 during this 23-year period. Shapiro, Meschede, and Sullivan (2010) explained the causes for this discrepancy as resulting from:

> Historical and contemporary factors but the disturbing four-fold increase in such a short time reflects public policies, such as tax cuts on investment income and inheritances which benefit the wealthiest, and redistribute wealth and

---

12   This report also found that in D.C. the monthly benefit for a family of three that lack any other income is $379; an amount that is only 38% of the federal poverty level. Moreover, TANF benefits have fallen approximately 40% since 1990, when D.C. eliminated annual cost of living adjustments. Lazare and Tallent advocate raising TANF benefits to almost $600 monthly for a family of three.

opportunities. Tax deductions for home mortgages, retirement accounts, and college savings all disproportionately benefit higher income families. At the same time evidence from multiple sources demonstrates the powerful role of persistent discrimination in housing, credit and labor markets. (p. 2)

The previously-discussed study followed upon the heels of *State of the Dream 2009* (Rivera, Jueza, Kasica, and Muhammad, 2009), the Institute for Policy Studies' report that raised alarms about continuing problems of income inequality, job access and low-level job attainment for African Americans. This 2009 report also supported the rectification of an "asset [housing, stocks, bonds and savings] gap caused by historic and contemporary structural racism" as a strategic goal for the future (p. 9).[13] The authors of both reports remind us that the statistics from these studies are the numerical reflection of punishing consequences in people's lives.

The history of discrimination and unfolding hierarchies in D.C. shows that, from enslavement to the present, the tentacles of inequality and vulnerability have wrapped African American Washingtonians in a corrosive embrace. Although the chronology and specificities may differ in the contemporary period, discrepancies rooted in class and race shift but remain intact and demographic change is not separate from this process. Population movements associated with gentrification, in particular, occur and are being perceived in relation to past events and conditions, although not necessarily linear ones, African American responses to these changes are added linkages to this history.

Whether or not the minutia of community or genealogical history is known all people walk with the past. For African Americans that means stepping in footprints that have been molded, in some form or fashion, by racism (Prince, 2004). This process may be mitigated in certain corners but race leaves an impression on perspective (Hochschild and Herk, 1990) that far too often results in the kind of discord rooted in experience, status, and identity that surfaces on community listserv exchanges about gentrification in D.C. Discourses of positionality are more than theoretical and their impact, whether real or imagined, shapes what people know and experience in life.

Hence, consigning these events to the past, alone, moves to erase associations between history and the present. It also implies that groups that have wielded power over time and benefit from current societal structures bear no responsibility for addressing the contemporary legacies of these oppressions. The triumph of hegemony notwithstanding, many of the elders who participated in this project both lived and discussed days gone by. These women and men had to confront Jim Crow, secure family members during community upheavals and contend with

---

13   Additionally useful is a study conducted by the National Community Reinvestment Coalition that used data on Washington, D.C. to document the role of race in the subprime mortgage problems. This study concluded that, regardless of income, African Americans were 80% more likely to receive a less-than-optimal loan arrangement and 20% more likely to go into foreclosure.

strikes and unemployment. These are also the people who shared their memories and feelings about their grandparents who had been enslaved. As a part of America's shameful and unevenly acknowledged history slavery, then, emerged as a viable ethnographic frame through which African American thought, action, and culture could be analyzed. This centuries-long political economic and ideological system of labor exploitation also presents a history that is, at once, national and intimate, and though the locations for former auction blocks in D.C. are largely unmarked and unacknowledged, they, nevertheless, are physical spaces that have presence and meaning when their history is revealed and made accessible to people.

The D.C. auction block data I include here, for example, were obtained from a, somewhat underground publication entitled *The Hidden History of Washington, D.C* (Apidta, 1995). The book is subtitled, *A Guide for Black Folks*. This combination implies at the outset that this information has been overlooked or, even worse, secreted away in a deliberate attempt to keep this from the people the author feels have the greatest need to get their hands on it—African Americans. This history, while not widely disseminated, is available for those who are motivated enough to go looking for it.

The celebration of Emancipation Day is a second example of conscious efforts at reclaiming the past and has been occurring each spring by various community-based organizations working to commemorate the end of enslavement in the District. African American residents have become increasingly aware of their bonds to D.C. history and the contemporary ramifications of this past. Community-based organizations also have uncovered the history of D.C. by putting people to work researching their own neighborhoods.

The following chapter elaborates on how my findings are connected to this past: the outmigration of blacks from Georgetown, the elders who attended Dunbar High School or my mother's friend who would visit the elder Anna Julia Cooper in their Le Droit Park neighborhood when this informant was a young teenager. History resonates in an assortment of ways throughout this book but the larger point is that, whether it resides in structural barriers or is hidden in the untold stories behind the presence of shiny, downtown facades, inequality has left its mark on the lives, landscapes, and memories of African American Washingtonians. This history affects demographic and ideological outcomes and includes views of White Americans (Bay, 2000). From the earliest presence of African Americans, enslaved and free, CC was set in motion as a key component to the making of contemporary Washington, D.C.

Chapter 3
Arrival, Belonging, Difference: Exploring the Oral Histories of Elder African Americans

I arrived early and found a seat about half the distance between the podium and the last row. I immediately began rifling through my pocketbook until I recognized the reassuring feel of my note pad. I was in SE for another of the occasions when my field research took me to a D.C. public library. On this fall day, I came to hear local historian C.R. Gibbs talk about the history of Jim Crow in the District. I am on his listserv and regularly receive announcements of his various media appearances and presentations across the city. Gibbs is a published author with an impeccable grasp of local history. His series of library talks have explored Black inventors, peoples of African descent in the Diaspora, and Blacks during the Civil War, among other topics, and as such are a particular draw for African American audiences with an Afrocentric or Pan African orientation.[1]

Pan Africanism was embraced by a number of the people involved in this research project, as demonstrated by adoption of traditional West African religious practices, clothing and hair styles, and names.[2] Socioeconomic class can affect these practices and beliefs. Although this is not uniformly the case, it is possible that college educated and professional managerial workers may predominate among Pan Africanists, compared with the Black poor and working class, because this population has higher incomes and access to both the social capital and strategic information that allow them to nurture their awareness with travel to Africa and develop their tastes to afford and acquire Afrocentric accents to beautify their homes. On more than one occasion, I discovered instances where my middle-aged

---

1   Algernon Austin posits there are two ways the term *Afrocentrism* can be understood in his study of 20th-century Black nationalism, *Achieving Blackness: Race, Black Nationalism, and Afrocentrism in the Twentieth Century* (2006). It may be used as a general referent to Black people who express pride in their African heritage or the cultural centrality of Africa in the African American experience.

2   There has not been a lot of research on this. Michelle Chatman is a Ph.D. candidate in the department of anthropology at American University who is currently completing a dissertation based on an ethnography of an Afrocentric charter school in NE D.C. She is specifically looking at how ideologies of race and pedagogy intertwine and uniquely shape the policies and practices at this school.

project participants were exposed to Pan Africanism through their octogenarian, college-educated, parents and other elder kin.

The crowd gathered to hear Gibbs that evening was small—I counted 17 people in attendance. Everyone was African American and no one in the room appeared to be younger than 30. His talk included discussions of job and housing discrimination. Gibbs also presented slides of existing and defunct African American businesses, along with shots of well-known and anonymous African Americans who confronted Jim Crow in the city. Just like the people Gibbs mentioned in his presentation, the elders who participated in my research project are the forbearers of native Washingtonians living in the city today. They are eyewitnesses to this continuing history and their stories add up to a forceful testament about the contradiction of the American promise. Another layer of power relations is added to this history in the ways gentrification has altered the landscape and dismantled many representations of elders' past existences.

Below is a listing of elder participants by pseudonym, neighborhood of residence, and year of birth. Where available, I also indicate their occupation at retirement as an additional point of reference. An asterisk is placed by the names of those whose children I also interviewed or interacted with for this book:

1.	Egbert Hallowell*	Woodridge	1921	police officer
2.	Jacqueline Hallowell*	Woodridge	1925	school teacher
3.	Verina Potter	Shaw	1933	government
4.	Nathaniel Potter*	Michigan Park	1926	postal clerk
5.	Francis Potter*	Michigan Park	1929	school teacher
6.	Marie Studdard	Trinidad	1992	homemaker
7.	Olivia Mebane	LeDroit Park	1930	government
8.	Martha Key	Columbia Hts	1920s	nurse
9.	Bernice Cofield*	N. Michigan Pk	1924	school teacher
10.	Vivian Brightwood*	Georgetown	1929	homemaker
11.	Harold Dunn	Georgetown	1924	veteran
12.	Horace Campbell	SE	1920	store owner

People over the age of 65 make up 11 percent of the D.C. population (U.S. Census Bureau, 2011), and more than 10 percent of the people whose life experiences are detailed on these pages were born within the first two decades of the 20th century.[3] The majority of these elder informants have already surpassed outlooks for life expectancy among African Americans in the Washington, D.C. based on

---

3   As this study is primarily based on ethnographic data, this book focuses on the contemporary period. It reflects field research I have carried out between 2005 and 2011. Some of the information I present here also comes from oral history interviews, archival research and the reading of secondary sources. Given these methods and because some of my project participants were born in the 1920s, it is safe to say that this book, while contemporary, also covers the period between 1920–2011.

a Congressional Research Service report on this issue (Shrestha, 2006).[4] This is presumably linked to their socioeconomic status. Although not all were college educated, most were professional managerial workers prior to retirement.

Only four of the 12 in this group were male, and two of these men were the eldest members of the group. All of these participants were born in the 1920s, with the exception of Olivia Mebane, who was born in Harlem in 1930; she moved to D.C. with her mother and brother at the age of eight. Despite their differences, all of these individuals were in a position to corroborate what Gibbs presented with first-hand observations from their own lives.

Conversations with these folks focused primarily on themes of segregation, community and family life, migration, housing, and recreation. We talked about racism and conflict within Black communities during the 1940s and 1950s, as well as what their work, educational, and social lives were like. There were numerous connections between Gibbs' talk, my secondary historical research, and what I discovered through oral history data. In addition to providing first-hand accounts of social justice issues, the qualitative data I collected from interacting with elders also showed what D.C. was like before gentrification became so entrenched.

The Content of Elder Profiles

Cofield was the only octogenarian I spoke with for this project who also had a parent who was born in D.C. She told me hers is the oldest African American family in the U.S. and went on to discuss how extensively this fact is verified in documentary film and other archival data. During one conversation we had at her North Michigan Park home, Cofield told me about the far-reaching investigations one member of her kin network had completed. Her family member discovered that, along with other connections to Africa, her surname is derived from a Ghanian language. After other key discoveries about her family's links to Africa were made, Cofield and her daughter, journalist Femilayo Saunders, made a momentous trip to West Africa, where they were grandly received by their kin. For the Cofields, the bond to Africa is tangible and familiar rather than vague and romanticized.[5]

There was a mutuality of experience among some of the elders with whom I engaged. Women and men had similar race-related ideologies, whereas others had social status elements in common. Outside the margins of race, these informants

---

4　This report can be found at http://aging.senate.gov/crs/aging1.pdf.

5　As Cofield's daughter, Femilayo Saunders was among the five other participants in this project who were in their 50s and 60s whose parents I interviewed for this book. She is a person who has traveled to Africa many times and also embraces a West African belief system as her religion of choice. Saunders is one of two project participants who practice this traditional African religion but she is a part of a larger number of people I spoke with who are consciously aware of their African roots.

shared other linkages with project participants from their age group. For example, Jacqueline Hallowell and Francis Potter were the only women on this list who lived with their husbands.[6] Both couples had to be diligent with the budgeting to manage household expenses, for neither was wealthy and both lived on fixed incomes.

Francis Potter's sister-in-law, Verina Potter, never married, and Olivia Mebane was divorced. All these women and men lived alone, with the exception, again, of, Hallowell and Potter, as well as Marie Studdard who shared her house with an adult grandson. Other similarities connected Cofield to Jacqueline Hallowell and Francis Potter. All three women were retired school teachers. Francis' husband Nathaniel Potter, like his deceased brother John, Bernice Cofield's husband, Mason Cofield also worked with the U.S. Postal Service. At some point I conversed with each of the three widows about their husband's occupations and their earlier lives in the city.

Bernice Cofield, Vivian Brightwood, Martha Key, and Marie Studdard were widows. All of these women spoke affectionately of their husbands. I was shown photographs and other objects and pieces of information about or belonging to the deceased men during visits to their homes. Studdard showed me a book on the Pullman Porters in which her husband's name was mentioned (Tye, 2004), and Brightwood's husband is pictured and discussed in *Black Georgetown Remembered* (Lesko, Babb, and Gibbs, 1991). Martha Key explained how, upon marrying her husband at the age of 32, she moved him into the house she owned in Columbia Heights. She worked as a nurse at Walter Reed Hospital, and among her many patients were wealthy, high-ranking military officials who appreciated the care she gave them so much she was given gifts. The family of one of her patients bought Key a car. Her income allowed Key to purchase her NW home as a single woman.

Cofield talked with me about meeting her husband during one exchange and also elaborated on his work history:

> BC: My husband lived at 24th Street Northeast. I didn't know him then, but we met at Howard University. He had come back from... he went into the service and when he came out of the service he came to Howard University I think on the GI bill.

> SP: Good for him.

> BC: And this is when we met. He was working at the government printing office at night and attending Howard in the day. But we fell in love and we got married. And he graduated, he went to work in the post office and that was considered a top job at that time back in the '40s, in the '40s and '50s. And he was a letter carrier to the special people that lived in Georgetown. He delivered mail to Justice Frankfurter, and to Senator Ted Kennedy, to Mrs. Auchincloss who was Jackie Kennedy's mother. Well around 31st and M and Dumbarton Avenue and

---

6   Jacqueline Hallowell passed away in July of 2011, leaving her husband to be the only widower among the male elders who participated in this study.

all around there, they received their mail special and my husband was the one who delivered their mail.

SP: Oh wow, that's interesting. I never knew such a thing existed; it makes sense.

BC: And through that experience he was given tickets to operas and etcetera, etcetera and he loved music and so this is how we got hooked on going to operas and all the concerts at the Kennedy Center and the Washington Opera.

SP: Well that sounds like a beautiful life together.

Cofield beamed with pride as she waxed nostalgic about her deceased spouse. Her reference to her husband's employment with the Post Office points to a position that was highly coveted by African American job seekers in the years after World War II. The household heads that obtained this work were not professional managerial workers at the outset, but employment with the U.S. Postal Service presented opportunities for career advancement and provided such benefits as pensions and life insurance that helped move postal workers into the burgeoning African American middle class of the 1960s. These Washingtonians did not constitute members of the new Black middle class defined by Laundry (1987) as college educated professionals who achieved their positions during the post-civil rights era but this and similar forms of governmental employment were vital for D.C. households. Moreover, these men and women were spared the work of their parents who labored in fields, stockyards, and homes of White households. This cross-generational mobility improved the opportunities and quality of life for these workers and members of their households. This is corroborated by the stories of arrival that discuss the employment histories of these elders' parents.

I also noted the pleasure both Cofield and her husband took in his status as a mail carrier to elite Washington families. There was prestige associated with this role as well as the assorted perks Mason Cofield derived from this work such as sums of cash during the holidays and, as indicated on the previous page, tickets to the opera and other performances. Out of all the White enclaves in D.C., Georgetown is one of the most exclusive. Ironically, as will be discussed in Chapter 5, this historical community was also an early site for African American dislocation in D.C.

During this interview, Cofield also mentioned that her husband delivered mail to African American households in Georgetown, including that of the Brightwood family. I visited the home of Vivian Brightwood twice and, as was the case with Cofield, had a chance to do a videotaped interview with her and her son Jonathan Brightwood. Although some of the relationships between project participants were either known about ahead a time and/or anticipated, this connection between the Cofields and Brightwoods was purely coincidental.

For the four native-born elders, as with the majority of African Americans, race and class formed the basis for a complex of ideas and experiences that were essential indicators of both intra and interracial interaction. That consequently influenced how other people responded to them as well as the opportunities they were afforded in life. From such open-ended questions as, "What was school like?" emerged specific answers about identity, security, and general feelings of self-worth and well-being. Other factors such as education, status, and skin color figured into these processes. Elders brought these issues up both in response to my questions and in unsolicited comments.

For example, Cofield informed me, in a mildly defensive tone, that she graduated from Cardoza High before I had broached the topic of school ranking. She took this stance because, of the three primary high schools attended by the majority of African Americans students during the 40s and 50s, the highest regard was reserved for Dunbar, established in 1870 as the Preparatory High School for Colored Youth and later known as the M Street High School. Graduates included poet Sterling Brown, educator Nannie Helen Burroughs, anthropologist Allison Davis, physician Charles Drew, and jazz pianist Billy Taylor, and faculty included W. E. B. Dubois, Mary Church Terrell, and the father of Black history month, Carter G. Woodson. Feminist writer, activist, and former Le Droit Park resident Anna Julia Cooper was the school's principal before leaving to attend graduate school at the Sorbonne in Paris, where at age 67 she would become the first African American woman to obtain a Ph.D. (Giddings, 1984).

Dr. Cooper died in 1964 at the age of 105, and interlocutor Olivia Mebane (Dunbar class of 1947) spoke with me about growing up in Le Droit Park and visiting with Dr. Cooper when they both lived in this same neighborhood. Mebane described entering the large home and being greeted each time by an African American woman assistant who directed the young visitor to her host's bedroom. Dr. Cooper would be in the bed during their informal talks and Mebane took great pleasure in the esteemed educator's interest in her college education.

The two other high schools known for educating African Americans were Cardoza and Armstrong. The cornerstone of Cardoza's reputation was its role in training clerical workers, with Armstrong bringing up the proverbial rear as a vocational school. These categorizations and the educational experiences afforded by each school carried an assortment of sociocultural implications. As a Cardoza graduate, Cofield moved to set the historical record straight when she stated:

> It's so funny you hear about attending Dunbar High School, but at Cardoza High School you could take college entrance courses, you could take business courses. So when I graduated from Cardoza High School I went directly to Howard University, I didn't have to take any elementary—well—undergraduate courses or…I had all of my calculus, algebra, language, English requirements, everything that was needed and yet there are many, many people who are graduated from Cardoza that you do not hear about and I feel that Cardoza High School produced many, many leaders in the Washington area as well as Dunbar High School.

Francis Potter talked about growing up poor in D.C. and attending Dunbar High School. She felt she received a stellar education at this institution but also recalled the specter of elitism she faced as member of the Dunbar class of 1944. Class and colorism colluded, she remembered without fondness, to marginalize this smart but poor, brown-skinned girl who lacked the social capital to respond affirmatively to the loaded questions a particular African American teacher would ask only certain students. For example, such queries as, "How have your parents been since the last time I saw them?" were never asked of Potter because her parents were not acquainted with schoolteachers. Potter's parents' were laborers and in the social atmosphere at Dunbar this fact of her background contributed to a self-described sense of alienation and fostered a lack of confidence that may have played a role in her decision not to pursue her dream to become a doctor. Even though she grew up poor, looking around, she also realized that plenty of her cohorts at church and school were in much worse shape than she was. In one conversation Potter described a brief and lone visit she made during childhood to visit a young friend who lived in D.C. alley community:

> I went down there by myself—I guess things were not as dangerous then. When I got down there to see her it was like being down in the deep south with some plantation shacks and stuff. Everybody was all squeezed in together. I guess it was warm weather and everyone was out. I never went back because I was scared to death. I think I was a bit hoity-toity. I was poor but I didn't think I was poor.

This was not the first time I heard this refrain. Most of these elders grew up in poverty but did not have a sense of this until they matured and gained greater insight into their parents' economic challenges. As younger people, these elders negotiated their way around the intra- and interracial borders that socially constructed and separated people by class and race.

I had the following conversation in the home of Vivian Brightwood, with Georgetown native and Navy-veteran Harold Dunn, in response to my questions about relationships with Whites during his youth:

> HD: I'm speaking for myself. What I think as a whole, it was good.
>
> SP: Yeah?
>
> HD: It was good because I had buddies. I was smart not to interfere with the White boys, because I had some good buddies, some White buddies. And I go right along with them. And they would—
>
> VB: Just like that man that owns the liquor store down there corner. He's leasing it now, but he lives on top of the liquor store. He and ------, I'm going to start calling you ----- he and -----, they went and played golf what three weeks ago?

HD: Oh yeah. He and I always didn't bother because when we were here in the Kew Gardens [apartments], see, right next to it, on 27th Street. We always had a good playing relationship. Bobby and his sister. They were Whites. In fact, they were—

VB: They were Jews.

HD: Yeah Jews.

VB: They were Whites, they were Jews.

HD: But then I had some buddies and they were just across the bridge. Right at 22nd and P. The boys/ father owned two restaurants on 22nd and P. And I had, I had been on Wisconsin Avenue. Actually this is me personally. My brother and I we used to hang out with them. But as the whole, we had no problems with the ones here. We had our problems with the soldiers. When they were in Fort, over at Fort Meyer. When they come in to M Street, you know, we lived here, they were in our territory.

SP: And you all didn't want them over there?

HD: No they would come over and start it. They would come over and say oh you Blacks and so and so and so. When they did that, we really did them in.

SP: Wow. That's interesting

HD: Yeah. That was the military. Because we didn't have—the ordinary, the ordinary Whites in the area, it was the soldiers that would come over from Fort Meyer. But we didn't have any problems when we would just knock them out, bust them in the head and do all that stuff. Yeah.

SP: You wouldn't have any problems with the police having those different confrontations with Whites?

HD: Oh yeah! They come get us the next day up to the precinct and we would be on the bench. Because they knew us, the police did, just like we knew them. We knew their name and they knew us by names.

VB: And back then the police walked the beat. And every so many corners they had a call-in box. And they had to call and I guess they had call to report that they were doing this or whatever. But they had calling box.

HD: But the ordinary Whites that lived on Wisconsin in that area. We didn't have any problems. We would play football down there in Rock Creek park. Standing in the park, the Blacks and the Whites [when we were kids] we didn't have any problems. Our only problem was with the soldiers from Fort Meyers when they would come across the Rosslyn Bridge, over there on liberty and if they see us on Wisconsin Avenue. That was our territory. That was Georgetown. But other than that the White and the Black relationship was good over here.

Proprietary language predominated throughout this conversation with Dunn. When he talked about *his* community and what was *ours*, he used discursive constructions of race that moved beyond the White/Black dichotomy into distinctions between neighboring and outsider Whites. Brightwood and Dunn also emphasized their authenticity as Georgetown residents when they talked about nearby communities that are often mistakenly considered part of Georgetown. On a few occasions, Dunn emphatically stated that this or that area was actually Foggy Bottom or Dupont Circle and that "if you didn't cross a bridge, you weren't in Georgetown."

On the day I had this particular conversation with Vivian Brightwood and Harold Dunn, my plan had been to interview her 54-year-old son Jonathan Brightwood Jr. who grew up in this household. Jonathan no longer lives in Georgetown, and many of the African American residents he knew as a boy have died. His father, Jonathan Sr., passed away in 1995 in the same room in which he was born in 1927. Jonathan Sr. was the second generation of this family to occupy this house, which was purchased by his parents in 1923.

I climbed the metal stairs in front of the Brightwood house after successfully navigating the cobblestone sidewalks out front and discovered Jonathan would be unable to keep our appointment. His mother and Mr. Dunn had just arrived from the funeral of an African American neighbor and kindly agreed to chat with me, although they were eager to loosen their clothing and unwind on what ended up being a typically sticky and humid D.C. summer afternoon. Weeks later I interviewed Jonathan at his mother's house, and while he echoed some of Dunn's views about good relationships with neighboring Whites, he also talked about being racially profiled by White police officers as a youngster, particularly when running home through the streets of Georgetown to beat his parent's curfew. As a graduate of Sidwell Friends High School, however, the majority of his classmates were White.

Some of the most gripping stories relayed by elders related to their arrival in Washington, D.C. Only four of the 12 project participants I personally interacted with—Bernice Cofield, Harold Dunn, Jacqueline Hallowell, and Francis Potter—were born in D.C. All but two had roots in the American south, the exception being Hallowell's husband of more than 55 years, Egbert, who was born in Barbados, West Indies in 1921.[7] The remaining seven migrated from Virginia, South Carolina,

7   There were other native Washingtonian elders whose lives are documented in this book; however; their information comes from the Ivy City Oral History Project.

New York, and Colorado at varied points as adults and children. When we talked about these early years the descriptions of the population movements that brought these individuals to D.C. had similarities. The commonality of poverty and other forms of vulnerability stuck out in the stories of almost each individual's lives.

Vivian Brightwood was born in Virginia and migrated to Washington, D.C. as a young girl. She married a Georgetown native and took up residence with her husband's family in 1952. In migrating out of the south, Brightwood and her family joined the scores of African Americans who left this region for a city that figured uniquely and prominently in the history of this northward migration (Wilkerson, 2010). In her sweeping monograph on the African American great migration, native Washingtonian Isabel Wilkerson says of D.C. that:

> Up and down the east coast, the border crossing for Jim Crow was Washington, D.C, which was technically still south of the Mason Dixon Line but was effectively the honorary north, as it was the capital of the union during the Civil War. Later, it was the first stop on the migration route up the east coast, the place where colored southerners could escape the field or kitchen and work in doors for the government and sit where they liked on the buses or streetcars. But to blacks in the deep south, Washington had a significance beyond perhaps any other city in the north (p. 200).

Verina Potter's family was also a part of this Great Migration. She was 86 when I spoke with her in her U Street condominium in N.W. It was 2009 at the time, and I recorded her oral history while she sat propped up by a series of pillows. I was seated at the foot of her bed in a padded, wooden chair. Having moved to D.C. from North Carolina during the 1940s, Potter had lived in a handful of different neighborhoods since her arrival. She had had her share of ups and downs, the most jarring of which, in addition to her own health challenges, was the loss of her younger brother, John Jr., to pancreatic cancer almost a decade ago. Neither Verina nor John had ever married, and they lived together for most of their lives.

Junior's passing was the impetus for Potter to leave the four-bedroom house she had shared with her parents and three brothers for more than 30 years. As retired government worker with health insurance and an adequate pension, Potter invested in a two-bedroom, two-bath condominium in the rapidly gentrifying Shaw neighborhood.

Uncertainty was a cornerstone of her arrival to D.C. story. In talking about this Potter said:

> We arrived here on a Saturday night. My father got us in a place on Third Street southeast and it was kind of brick-like; I think they called it cobblestone or something. I was saying to the cab driver, where are we? Are we in the country? He wanted to know where we were from. Then my father got us a place around the corner off Virginia Avenue and it had outdoor plumbing.

During those days, things were not bad. I didn't realize that we were poor; we always had a place to live, food and a change of clothes, you know. My father broke his foot two summers in a row at an ice house where he worked and mymother had to work. That was the only time my mother worked. She went to clean at Miss Anne's house.

Racism, poverty, and the derisory prospects of a segmented labor force were what faced these African American migrants to D.C. In listening to the stories of octogenarians, women and men who were also in the same generation as my parents, I was reminded of our proximity to African American enslavement and the continuities of the rigid racial and sexual divisions of labor that their parents were subjected to. Like so many of the enslaved, the male kin of these elder retirees were, just a generation before them, doing the physically demanding work that often left their bodies broken and scarred. For the women, as Potter described of her mother, the most common employment options for them were working at "Miss Anne's," a term originating in slavery that identified White women of means. As other people Verina Potter's age would report about being poor at that time, poverty for her meant little to no access to even the most minor of luxuries but never being hungry or without shelter.

Potter's father, John Henry Sr., was born in Belton, South Carolina in 1899, just 36 years after slavery's end. The Potters decided to leave the south after witnessing their kin experience near-deadly altercations with Whites in South Carolina. They eventually settled in an area gentrification has now renamed the Atlas District, parallel to the H Street corridor in NE. Potter's father held a number of jobs over the course of his lifetime as a Washington resident, working as a truck driver, janitor and Pullman porter. John Henry Potter, Sr. passed from lung cancer in July of 1966.

John and Cecelia Potter had four children, all of whom went to work for the D.C. government, the males upon the conclusion of World War II. The youngest son died due to complications from alcoholism at the age of 55, but the remaining two sons worked with the U.S. Postal Service while their sister, Verina, went from the Internal Revenue Service to the Department of Housing and Urban Development. They stayed with these agencies for decades, until each retired in his or her 60s. These siblings were not particularly mobile, although the third generation of Potters in D.C. would go on to relocate, leaving the area in the pursuit of education, employment, and more desirable housing.

Only the two youngest sons of the Potter household married, and the in-laws of the middle son, Nathaniel, were the Johnston family. Claude Johnston, Nathaniel's father in law, migrated to D.C. from Greenwood, South Carolina at the age of 17. Like the Potters and others I spoke with who moved to D.C. decades ago, young Claude Johnston bounced around from place to place in search of housing he deemed adequate for his specific situation. As a young, single man, Johnston moved in with cousins in SE and began finding work where he could. Other family members would join this kin network, some residing on Capitol Hill while others rented in Georgetown.

Francis Johnston Potter was the last surviving daughter of Claude Johnston and his wife Josephina. I conducted extensive participant observation with her and interviewed her several times in 2009 and 2010. Born in the District in 1929, as she shared portions of her parent's and siblings' experiences in D.C. Potter conveyed stories of migration, personal tragedy, economic success, racial discrimination, and the love and loyalty of kin. Her oral history also highlighted the role of southern culture and life in the lives of these new transplants, a theme examined in an earlier ethnographic study of Washington (Williams, 1988).[8]

Claude Johnston momentarily left D.C. after turning 18, returning shortly thereafter with his young bride, Josephina. According to Francis Potter, her mother did not work right away, and Claude, a member of a family of former sharecroppers, was in the habit of pooling his earnings with his cousins, aunt, and uncle. By the late 1940s, urban renewal had hit those pockets of African American renters in Georgetown. More of Johnston's kin crowded into the SE residence and these living arrangements did not mesh with Josephina's vision of her married life together with Claude based on Potter's recollections of her mother's views. In response to this lack of financial independence and density of extended kin, "mother," in the bluntly stated words of Potter, "wasn't going for that shit." She further recalled:

> All those strong personalities weren't working but they stayed and mother wanted to leave. Uncle Joe, my mother's oldest brother, told Daddy to get a place of his own or he was going to bring her up to Philly. Daddy went out the next day and got a spot for them. It was a roach-infested room but mother said it was their own.

From there the Johnstons went to a rented row house on 5th and M Streets, NW, not far from New York Avenue. I rode by the neighborhood with Francis Potter one day and she showed me where their home once stood. The three Johnston sisters were born at this M Street location and when this property was sold by the owners, the family of five then moved into the Homestead Homes projects. I pause in telling the remaining portions of the Johnston family story to note

---

8   The impact of the south on life and culture in D.C. is a contested issue. As noted in a winter of 2011 *Washington Post* article written by Steve Hendrix entitled Dixie and D.C. Region Drift Farther and Farther Apart, there is imprecision in determining if D.C. is located in the south or not despite the work of 19th-century surveyors Charles Mason and Jeremiah Dixon. Perspectives on answers to this question have much to do with the regional origins of the persons being questioned. Hendrix acknowledges that people from the north see this area as southern while southern migrants view D.C. as more of a northern city. Moreover, as the reporter indicates, while scholars use such measures as pronunciation styles or the locations of McDonalds restaurants that offer sweet tea to assess the southernness quotient, Greg Carr, chairman of the African American Studies Department at Howard University, maintains such markers as an entrenched Black elite and a "paucity of white ethnic neighborhoods" indicate D.C. is very connected to its southern roots.

some key connections to gentrification in Washington today. Potter's home, in the neighborhood known as Mt. Vernon Square, was demolished to make way for new development. The area has housing stock that is rich in architectural detail and currently deemed an *up and coming* community.

The usual, visual signs of gentrification are apparent in Mt. Vernon Square—refurbished facades, condominiums, and the requisite service providers and gathering places that help newcomers attach. These perfunctory outgrowths were augmented by the observations of resident Claudette Bynum. This judge-turned-midwife shared her formula for ascertaining the point at which White newcomers felt at home in their new surrounds. With her biting sense of humor, Bynum assessed that White contentment levels were marked by the size of their dogs: Yorkshire Terriers replacing Rottweilers signaled a transition into a new level of comfort in the community.

Like those of Bernice Cofield and the Potter family, the experiences of the Johnstons had associations that overlapped with topics and incidences that have been conveyed in other portions of this book. As an example of these links, the public housing complex the Johnstons moved into in the 1940s is the same facility written about by playwright Zahira Kahlo in her one-woman performance *The Home*. Potter shared poignant stories of her years living at the Home and Kahlo's play was ethnographically oriented because she based the script on the time she spent working with children in the Homestead Home's recreational center when the building became threatened with demolition.[9]

Francis Potter was the youngest of the three Johnston sisters - her brother Paul died from a congenital heart ailment at two before she was born. Her oldest sister, Lucinda, found work in the housing office at Homestead Homes but the additional income made the family ineligible to remain in the subsidized complex. In 1943 the family relocated to Queen Street in the NE neighborhood of Trinidad as first-time homebuyers.

Before the move Potter's Dad didn't think they had the down payment for the home, but Josephina Johnston surprised her husband when she produced the savings she had secretly accumulated to finalize the purchase. On how her mother pulled this off, Potter shared:

> When my mother would go out and do day-work, she told us, "if your Dad [calls], tell him I am out at the store." He wasn't working at an office so he didn't have access to a phone really. He would only call if there was an emergency. Meanwhile she was leaving my eldest sister in charge, saying no one can come

---

9 Implementation of the federal housing program HOPE VI razed the Homestead Homes in 2002 in what some observers consider the dubious quest for mixed income housing. Housing activist Barbara Best maintained the community already was mixed income, a point made not to diminish problems that are exacerbated by concentrated poverty but rather to push back against the reluctance to see these communities in all of their nuance and complexity.

into the house. She would clean at White people's homes; suburbs, Capitol Hill, or upper northwest. She would take the street car and it wasn't an 8-hour day.

Then, in public housing she worked cleaning rooms in the (Longworth) senate office buildings at night. That was her last job but my mother was a good money manager. Daddy was surprised she was able to come up with all of this cash for a down payment. She had saved.

The interpersonal contact and private nature of domestic work made African American women vulnerable to the sexual advances of White men, the cruelty of White women, and the burden of caring for their children (Clark Lewis, 1996). Black women avoided domestic work when possible, but this type of employment also provided opportunities for women to earn incomes and support their families economically (Jones, 1985). This was exactly what Josephina Johnston—a woman described by her daughter as little, stubborn, and good with money—accomplished.[10]

It was in 1950, seven years after the Johnstons were forced out of public housing and moved to Queen Street, when a newly married Joseph and Marie Studdard arrived on this NE street in Trinidad. Francis (Johnston) Potter was around 21 at that time, and although her parents and other African Americans residents welcomed the young couple to the neighborhood, the Studdard's portion of the block was not integrated. The young bride would quickly find out that her White neighbors were not happy to have the Studdards in the community.

When I met Marie Studdard in 2005, she was 85 years old and still a resident of the street where Potter's nuclear family spent key, formative years. I arrived with my four-year-old daughter in tow and was welcomed by a lunch of tuna fish sandwiches and crackers. I can still hear the sound of Studdard's voice in my mind as she giggled like a school girl while recalling her arrival to the neighborhood and the reception she received from her White neighbors. With one toddler and a second daughter on the way, Studdard had been living in apartments since her arrival to D.C. and was eager to have a porch to call her own:

As soon as we got in the house I had told Joe…I said I am so happy to have a porch I am going to buy a glider. We didn't have too much furniture but I was pregnant; I had one daughter. She was 15 months old and I was pregnant again. So I sat on my glider on my porch and the two White neighbors on either side

---

10   Attention to the intense and complex emotions associated with African American women domestic worker in White households were publically reignited due to the release of the film, *The Help*. That highly charged discussions over the omissions and depictions of Black women servants during Mississippi during the 1960s still occur serves to highlight the subject's importance. The feature-length film was released by Dreamworks Productions in August 2011. It was directed by Tate Taylor and adapted from Kathryn Stockett's best-selling novel of the same name. http://www.imdb.com/title/tt1454029/.

would come out and if they saw me on the porch they would go back [inside] like a tiger was out there.

In that time we didn't have a dryer so we would hang out clothes in the back yard and if I would go outside and they were outside talking, they would go in as if something horrible had come outside. So I was real mean; sometimes I wouldn't do my work because I would go outside to see them run they behind back in the house.

Yes I did, I would go out there and I heard one of them say, "It's not that I dislike colored people but I just don't want to live next door to them." So we moved in on Tues- day and on Thursday the "For Sale" signs went up on oneside and then on the others, cause they were busy trying to get out too.

Elders such as Studdard observed White flight occur in different phases. Francis Potter saw it take place in Trinidad during the 1950s and again during the mid to late 1960s, after she married and moved to the vicinity of Brookland and Michigan Park. It is in these stories of population shifts that elements of race, class, and prejudice are clearly played out.

Close to 50 percent of D.C. residents born in the U.S. came here from other parts of the country (U.S. Census Bureau, 2008). In terms of African American long-term residents, the most common states that have given rise to the Black Washingtonian are North and South Carolina, southern Maryland, and Virginia. Most of my native-born project participants trace their family's origins to these states. At another end of the spectrum, Studdard was born in Denver, Colorado. She grew up having very little contact with masses of African American people. To the contrary, she and her four siblings were the sole African American children in each of their classes.

As a keen demonstration of how the racial realities of Colorado impacted her identity, Studdard's life took a tragic turn when she was only seven. Her beloved father suddenly passed away. "He just dropped dead and left five little children orphaned," she told me and quietly shared that she went on to "die the death of a rattlesnake" in the wake of this intimate heartbreak and misfortune. This was not a phrase I had heard before but one I interpreted as a metaphor for the precipitous decline in her quality of life. From her perspective when her father died her life became worthless.

Studdard's mother had passed away when she was three, and after her father's death, her siblings were split up and dispersed to family members across the country. Studdard was the youngest and went to live with an aunt in St. Joseph's, Missouri which was a place she described in most unpleasant terms:

St. Joseph is akin to the lowest place in Mississippi. It was horrible, horrible. I had to go to a segregated school. I had never been and I was frightened half to

death of all these black children. I had never seen that many black people in all
the days of my life.

Studdard chuckled about the racial irony of her childhood predicament, displaying
an attitude that became routine in our talks. She shared a number of sad stories
while never showing any signs of melancholy as she recalled her difficult past.
After talking about the serious challenges of the early period of her long life, she
described the years between her young adulthood and middle age in a more joyful
tone. One particular topic we discussed was how she found her niche and became
active in community organizing very soon after moving to Trinidad.

Studdard described the people in the community as frustrated and herself as
motivated by a desire to change the segregated conditions they contended with. For
example, she and her husband could not send their eldest daughter to Ruth K. Webb
school which, although the closest elementary school to their home, only admitted
White children. Instead, Studdard and her daughter walked 14 blocks to and from
school to the segregated and under-resourced Alexander Crummell Elementary
School which was named after the 19th-century evangelical–abolitionist and
Pan Africanist who was a contemporary of Henry Highland Garnett and Martin
Delaney. Crummell's views about African American unity and identity went on to
influence W.E.B. DuBois and Marcus Garvey (Rigsby, 1987; Wilson, 1989).

Ivy City Oral History Project

Marie Studdard's oral history showed that relationships were formed between
residents of Trinidad and Ivy City due to the close proximity of these adjacent
communities. The Ivy City school she walked to, Crummell, closed in the 1960s,
but the boarded-up building, still standing in this historic community, is at the
center of grassroots efforts to oppose the D.C. government's approach to the
dispensation of public property.

The small wedge of Ivy City was incorporated into D.C. in 1872, and thanks
to Ingrid Drake and the community members she worked with, it is also the
neighborhood for which I have the largest amount of oral histories on. Authors of the
Ivy City oral history begin their profile by describing the neighborhood as one of the
smallest and least known in D.C. The community is located in Ward 5, sandwiched
between New York and West Virginia Avenues NE. It was established by Frederick
W. Jones, who sold the 205 lots to African Americans for $100 each (Ivy City Oral
History Project [ICOHP], 2009). One of the neighborhood's most notable residents
was community leader Perry Carson (1842–1909) who served as a delegate to the
Republican national convention and a Marshall for D.C. Emancipation Day parades
after he settled in the District during Reconstruction (Kraft, 2004).

Carson was described as a "leader of colored people" and a "silver-haired
giant" in an obituary that appeared in *The Washington Post* (November 1, 1909).
The Ivy City Civic Association wanted their crumbling, wooden Ivy City School

to be named after Carson, but the District Commissioners refused, and the building was dedicated as Alexander Crummell School in 1911 (Kraft, 2004).

The listing below shows that the majority of the people who participated in the oral history project were born in Ivy City:

Ivy City Oral History Project Participants

Name	Place of Birth	Date of Birth
Aaron Aylor	Ivy City	1964
Charles Brown	Ivy City	1952
Alfred Coates	Ivy City	?
Theodore Coates	Ivy City	1928
Clifford Coulson	Pennsylvania	?
Jackie Council	Trinidad, D.C.	1946
Erika Crews*	Ivy City	1992
Remetter Freeman	North Carolina	1930
Eleanor Dade Grant	Ivy City	1930
Sarah P. Hunter	D.C.	1917
Marjorie Jones	D.C.	1928
Joel McPherson*[2]	Ivy City	1973
Audrey Ray	D.C.	1953
Dorothy Scott (Nicey)	Ivy City	?
Elaine Smith	Trinidad, D.C.	1946
Kenneth Tapscott	Ivy City	1932
Romaine Thomas	?	1930s
Charlotte Tyner	North Carolina	1919
Daisy Wroten	Ivy City	1930

Two individuals, Charlotte Tyner and Remetter Freeman, were from North Carolina, and Clifford Coulson moved to Ivy City from Pennsylvania. The most elder participant in the oral history project was Sarah P. Hunter, a native Washingtonian who was born in 1917. Closely trailing Hunter in age were Tyner, who was born in 1919, and Marjorie Jones, another native, who was born in 1928.

Migration emerged as one of the key themes in these histories as current and former Ivy City residents situated their presence within the history of family members' movement into and around the city. Points of origin for the parents and grandparents include St. Mary's County and other parts of southern Maryland, as well as Georgia, Virginia, and the Carolinas. Other parts of D.C., such as Georgetown, Foggy Bottom, and Trinidad, were also home to kin before they settled in this NE community. In addition, a handful of these residents no longer reside in Ivy City but have moved on to other communities in D.C. or Maryland. Margaret Rice, for example, left Ivy City at the age of 18 but still attends church in the area. Other former residents said they return to the neighborhood regularly to visit kin and friends or attend services at Bethesda Baptist. The excerpts below speak to these population shifts. Eleanor Dade Grant said:

> My family came to Ivy City, my mother and father came to Ivy City from N.E. D.C. My grandmother lived off Benning Road N.E. Well, my mother and father were both born in D.C. My grandmother, my mother's mother was born in Virginia. And my mother's father was born in Annapolis. They bought the house when it was new. That's all I know.

Clifford Coulson reported:

> I was born in Pennsylvania but my mother came to live here in D.C. when I was a young boy, a young baby. We moved to Ivy City in 1942 during the war, and we've been here ever since.

Charles Brown's family moved to Ivy City 50 years before his birth. Migrating from Fredericksburg, Virginia, his kin wanted relief from what he said were slave-like conditions. Remetter Freeman's family also arrived from the south. She said:

> My husband's father was born in Georgia, but he left there—oh, golly—when he was a child. My husband was born here. But his grandmother, all of them were from Georgia. But they'd been there for years. I think they were among the first established in Ivy City. They were some of the founders of Bethesda [Baptist Church].

Today, the area has also been zoned for commercial development. There are factories, warehouses, and a nationally known nightclub that has irked local residents who say that the parking needs and disruption at closing time are problematic. Elders' descriptions of Ivy City in the 1930s and 40s speak to a more rural, almost bucolic, existence. Residents talked about fruit trees in the area and their families and neighbors raising chickens, pigs, and other livestock. There were descriptions of outhouses, piles of coal in the backyard that were used to heat homes, and the nightly lighting of the street lamps by workers who would return after sunrise to extinguish them.

Margaret Rice described the predevelopment landscape of Ivy City:

> All of that was woods, where that little mall thing is, all of that was woods. And we made a path through there too. It was nothing but woods. Oh, you know it had trees, sycamore, pear trees, and blackberries and stuff like that…poke salad, watercress.

The words beautiful, peaceful, and quaint were frequent references to the Ivy City of old and the community still has an old-fashioned charm about it. The remaining symbols of this past provinciality are the small, wooden houses that hearken back to another time. Segregation was also a harbinger of this past. But, while racial exclusivity established separate and unequal conditions at schools and workplaces, these residents who were born prior to World War II attested to a community that had an assortment of mom-and-pop stores, a laundry, playgrounds and community centers where the youth played ping pong and basketball (ICOHP, 2009). These diverse community resources provided support and respite for residents.

Marjorie Jones was born in D.C. in 1928 and grew up on Corcoran Street in Ivy City. She was raised in a three-bedroom brick house and described her childhood as very "pleasant," saying:

> The child life up there was good. There were those frame houses on the hill;
> they had pear trees and apple trees. People had peach trees and there were woods
> and paths all around. Up where Gallaudet College is...all that back there was
> nothing but woods.

Jones said that she and her siblings and friends picked acorns, blackberries, and strawberries back then and also bought sugar, flour, candy, and cigarettes for pennies. Some of their neighbors taught at Crummell which was the school she and her siblings attended. Her older siblings were delivered by midwives who cared for many of the pregnant women in the area when she was growing up. Jones also said her brothers and sisters never went to a doctor. She said her father would place poultices on their chests when they got a cold, elaborating:

> We had mineral oil and my father would cut up oranges and give you a teaspoon of
> mineral oil and then give you a slice of orange to take the bitter taste out. I remember
> my mother used to have a little jar like this and she used to call it juniper tar.

Dorothy Scott was another resident who was raised on home remedies. Her parents depended on a concoction of castor oil and soda to soothe ailments in their household. Scott also discussed the prospects for urban development in Ivy City. When asked about plans to rebuild Ivy City, Scott said it would be good, "as long as everybody can have their own. But then, I don't know. For the poorer people what going to happen cause when they start putting those big house in there, I don't know."

The topic of race was not prominent in these oral histories. Of course it was implied in discussions of segregated housing, schools, night clubs, and recreational facilities such as beaches and swimming pools, but based on my reading of the transcripts interviewers did not query subjects on this issue very frequently. Marjorie Jones said her parents, who hailed from South Carolina, did not talk about race very much at all:

> My father and mother never talked about it really. The only thing they talked
> about is their school days. They both went to school down there, they both
> graduated at 16. My father played football—my mother told me about how my
> father played football—they went to games. But I never heard them talk about

race issues in the south. They never did. All they talked about was school and
how they had to walk to school. They put cardboard in their shoes…they'd talk
about how they walked 5 miles to school, 5 miles back and they would talk about
the holes [in their shoes].

When Drake asked if Jones' parents talked about race at school or at church, she
responded:

> Well, during that time back then, the blacks went to black schools and the Whites
> went to White schools so how could there be an issue? You were with your own
> race. Okay and when they came here it was the same thing. We went to an all-
> black school so we didn't get entangled with the White.

Where it was raised there were interesting responses to questions of race. It
was certainly a factor in their lives - all project participants had to contend
with a racial division of labor and this contributed to the hardship associated
with poverty that existed in the economic, if not social, arena. It appeared
that living in these segregated environs insulated African American residents
from the most overt forms of racial discrimination. All of the interviews I read
emphasized the supportive and familial atmosphere they enjoyed growing up in
this community.

In spite of these positive reports, Ivy City has faced numerous challenges over
the course of its existence. In another exchange with Ingrid Drake, Margaret Rice
pointed to nearby buildings to register her complaints about the present and to wax
nostalgic about the past:

> Rice: This is what messed Ivy city up right here. All those apartment buildings
> with all these different type people moving in that wasn't like the people in Ivy
> City. They just…I don't know…now all the people weren't bad. There were
> some people that were nice but they didn't stay here that long I guess. Now stuff
> like this, you know I mean we never had nothing like this.

> Drake: What, trashcans outside?

> Rice: No, we didn't have that kind of stuff. No indeed. You knew when the trash
> man was coming, that when you put your trash out back. You didn't set no trash
> out no front and stuff like that.

> Rice: Oh, there's the Dream Club. The Dream Club, you've heard of the Dream
> Club…now that used to be what they called Okie Lounge.

> Drake: and what's Okie Lounge?

Rice: It was a night club. It was segregated of course, you know but that's what it was before they took it.

Drake: Oh, who got to go there?

Rice: It was White people. It was segregated you know.

Rice: You could go in the front part and order something if you wanted it, like a sandwich or something like that. But you couldn't sit down in there. And they had a telephone booth in there that they allowed us to use, because most of us at that time didn't have telephones. No this was a long time ago, back in the 30s, Because the Dram Club just came. I don't know what they did after they closed the lounge or if they closed it up I don't know but the Dram Club hadn't been there that long.

Drake: Did the White people live in the neighborhood around here?

Rice: They lived on West Virginia Avenue, Trinidad and all those little side streets going down there like Holbert and...I don't know the name of those streets....Queen and all of that, they lived over there. And Montello Avenue, black people lived on Montello Avenue which separated West Virginia Avenue from Trinidad Avenue. And then when they built the New Capitol Avenue, White people lived there.

Change also came in the form of nearby, large-scale development schemes. One of the earliest was the proposed expansion of freeway construction that would have totally obliterated Ivy City and neighboring communities. The oral history authors write that, "the fight against the freeway is one of D.C.'s most important civic battles which brought together Black and White residents in the creation of the Emergency Committee on the Transportation Crisis and included over a decade of organized community protest" (ICOHP, 2009, p. 12).

Ivy City residents faced the specter of dislocation again when the local government's Office of Planning proposed to zone the area for commercial development and relocate all residents (ICOHP, 2009). This plan was thwarted, and the neighborhood's responses made it clear that organizing into advocacy groups created community leverage against plans that residents deemed of more benefit to developers than themselves.

Today, residents have to deal with the typical, modern-day threats to urban quality of life such as drug distribution and other forms of crime in their immediate midst. This neighborhood lost a third of its household members during the 1990s so the impact of abandonment has been closely felt. It is for these and other reasons that mainstream media accounts associate Ivy City with the word blight[11]

---

11   An example of this is "Renewal Takes Root in D.C.'s Blighted Ivy City: Real Estate Investors Betting on Neighborhood," a Washingtonpost.com article by Paul Schwartzman

but, whether it involves encroaching development or internal challenges residents have not been passive when confronting challenges.

Community organizers funded by The Institute for Cultural Affairs helped Ivy City residents with a four-year plan for human development (1976–1980). These efforts resulted in the creation of the Ivy City Preschool and the Ivy City Corporation, and, according to the oral history report, the latter "promoted commerce in the community…and established block clubs, organized health fairs, participated in voter registration, organized a youth group called the Jets, and participated in a host of other activities" (ICOHP, 2009, p. 12) This work was done to attend to the spirits, health, and overall well-being of residents but still didn't address the concern that "revitalization" would displace long-term residents. The concern for dislocation motivated residents to form The Historic Ivy City/Crummell School Revitalization Coalition.

There was also community involvement throughout the entire process of seeing the Ivy City Oral History Project to fruition. Prior to publication of the Ivy City oral history (2009), the same Humanities Council of Washington, D.C. grant that made that book possible also funded completion of the Ivy City Guide to Historical Resources (2004). This guide was generated by the enterprising activities of Ciara Levenberry who was a senior at the Hine Charter School at the time. With the help of local archivist Marya McQuirter, Levenberry scoured the city to compile a list of locations where materials on Ivy City could be found. In its introduction, the goals of the guide are expressed as intending to:

> spotlight the history of Ivy City and to encourage residents, researchers, students, and social change activists to research, write, document, and film the Ivy City neighborhood. We hope that this guide will help provide a fuller understanding of Ivy City and will empower individuals and groups to continue to work together to transform it into a place of vision, fulfillment, and action for current residents.[12]

History can be used to brand communities in accordance with the proclivities of gentrification in an approach that counters the historical orientation of the Ivy City project. In her analysis of historic preservation along the U Street corridor, Frank (2005) argues that the work of cultural heritage tourism agents is narrow in scope because their efforts are revanchist in nature. Walking tours and other mechanisms

---

(2005). This piece describes Ivy City, as well as Columbia Heights and Trinidad, as "long-forgotten" neighborhoods. It also includes quotes from middle class professionals who have moved into the community and also describes the intention of investors to flip or quickly resell properties for profit.

12   At this writing, Ph.D. anthropology student Sean Furmage of American University is in the process of making a film about Crummell School and its role in the Ivy City community. It is my intention to show some of this film, along with footage of my interviews with African American Washingtonian widows, when I go on book tour in the city.

for sharing the neighborhood's past with the public are thematically centered on Black middle-class histories and Frank also draws our attention to, not only an emphasis on the Black elites of Shaw, but also a bemoaning of poverty and the 1968 riots as sullying factors of bygone era of a greatness.

Frank (2005) uses treatments of the newly restored Whitelaw Hotel to support her position. Described as "created by and for African Americans," the hotel opened its doors in 1919 and immediately catered to middle-income Blacks amid a throng of establishments that prohibited African American patronage. The hotel now provides housing for low- to moderate-income residents and is constructed in cultural tourism literature as a phoenix, rising from the ashes of urban blight, and posited as a metaphor for the neighborhood. However, as the neighborhood takes on increasing numbers of well-off residents, Whitelaw tenants do not comply with the mainstream representations of Shaw which historical preservationists would like to promote.

Another problem with the narrow interpretation of the Whitelaw is that it focuses only on those who created it, lived there, and visited. Frank asks what about the people who worked there and made it the high-class establishment that it was? Perhaps their working class status would mar the upper class image. This is just one of the ways that demonstrates that the "phoenix" narrative is not the only way to frame the story of the Whitelaw Hotel.

In contrast to the attitudes Frank decries (2005), the Ivy City project was enacted in association with a progressive, grassroots organization as a pushback against gentrification. The women leading this project wanted to document the history of those elders who are key holdovers in transitioning neighborhoods. The attachment of older African Americans and their younger kin to their homes and communities is sometimes mocked by residents who want to see more of an ethnic mixture[13] in these areas but as these histories indicate, African American communities already possessed a rich cultural diversity.

Moreover, elderly, long-term African American residents carry the memories of communities and the essentials of belonging as determined by relationships established with neighbors, community work in local churches and schools, and other forms of contact and involvement. In addition to being cared for, these populations should be seen and treated as invaluable resources in these communities. The next chapter looks at the generation immediately following informants who were born in the 1920s and 1930s. African Americans who came of age during the 1960s and 1970s confronted a transformed racialized landscape that created differentiated experiences with race, class, and belonging in the District when compared with those of their parents and grandparents.

---

13   In the documentary *There Goes The Neighborhood* that aired on Al Jazeera English (Rebecca Kaufman, producer) irony ensues when a new White resident of Anacostia decries homogeneity and uses a formulation of diversity that implies fewer African Americans.

Chapter 4
Race, Place, Representation, and Attachment

The post-World War II period brought about a rapid pace of change in race relations in Washington, D.C.; however, the promises of the civil rights movement and the opening up of employment and housing opportunities did not douse the angst and conflict associated with the divisions of race and class in the District. The features of these tensions have varied from community to community based on each area's particular history and the specific ways racial interactions have affected the status and experiences of the people involved. Describing his observation of the out-migration of Whites from his racially divided community in SE, 56-year-old David Robinson told me:

> We had White folks living on the other side of the fence that separated two apartment complexes. They used to throw rocks at us and yell nigger. Of course we threw back and yelled whitey. That was short-lived because those White folks moved out of Dodge.

Sharon Barnes, 52, grew up in the predominantly African American Lamond Riggs neighborhood in NE. She attended Bunker Hill, a local public elementary school, for only a few years before her mother enrolled her into a private school in the District. As a result of this, she reported:

> One of my best friends—her name was Susie—lived in Adams Morgan and she was a White girl. She came home with me from school to play and one of the girls in the neighborhood said, "Why would you bring this White girl over here?" This guy said we ain't supposed to be friends with White people.

Whether people were living in diverse or racially homogeneous environments there was no abeyance in the marking of communities and the peoples within them in racial terms. This is a process which occurred both within groups and externally.

In keeping with the themes represented by the racialized discord Barnes and Robinson experienced during their youth, this chapter looks at memory, competing views of D.C., and the influence of socioeconomic and racial hierarchies upon the ideas and encounters of African American Washingtonians who came of age after World War II. In doing so it exposes the dynamic and sometimes inconsistent impacts that have affected Blacks' views of the city and the identities of African Americans in relation to D.C. over time—all culminating in this marked period of demographic change, neoliberal development, and gentrification.

In the stories of the 40- to 63-year-old women and men who live across the city, it is evident how meaning and attachment are infused into place through memory. Advanced age does not produce a hierarchy which values the memories of elders over those of the young. The fact that older people have lived longer and gathered more memories to sort does distinguish their experiences in this regard. It is also the case that due to the passage of time the content of memories that relate to social hierarchies uniquely shift across the years along with the changing political, economic, and historical contexts. These developments give rise to multilayered standpoints that shape thought and action (Collins, 1990). Social forces of integration and upward mobility, more specifically, have made cross-generational comparisons more stark because of the lessening of racial and class barriers experienced by many African Americans of the post-World War II generation.

In acknowledging these social processes it is also important to note that this city does not have one authentic past or experience despite its "CC" status. There are residents who trace their ancestry to El Salvador and other Central American countries, who initially settled in the Adams Morgan and Mt. Pleasant neighborhoods upon arrival during the 1980s (Modan, 2007). Ethiopians and Ethiopian Americans have an important and obvious presence, as do immigrants from Asia and the Caribbean and their descendants. Chinese immigrants have been in D.C. since the 19th century when this population was initially concentrated on Pennsylvania Avenue NW between 3rd and 6th Streets (Chow, 1996). This community was displaced in 1929 during the start of The Federal Triangle construction project and, despite White resistance, Chinese residents were relocated to its current, albeit dwindling, location along the H Street corridor NW (Hathaway and Ho, 2003).

All these populations add demographic depth to what had previously been a more dualistic racial–ethnic configuration in D.C. This added diversity has been an invaluable catalyst for cross-cultural exchange and social justice activism although, in far too many instances, conflict has also ensued. Of additional importance, this ethnic diversity attests to the idea that African Americans do not have a monopoly on belonging in this urban space nor are they the sole population with close and lengthy ties to the city. Numerous groups belong and attach meaning to being a resident of the District including immigrants and their native-born descendants, as well as residents of different class and racial/ethnic backgrounds.

Mainstream Representations of Washington, D.C.

Unlike other major cities within a 300-mile radius, Washington, D.C. is small: only 68.25 square miles in size, with a population of less than 600,000 (U.S. Census Bureau, 2008). Neither large, nor of great population density, Washington's mainstream claim to fame is its place as the seat of the federal government. The city also welcomes hundreds of thousands of visitors annually who, in addition to being drawn by the political aura and memorial vistas, also come to tour the Smithsonian

Institution's extensive exhibits and enjoy festivals and spectacles like the cherry blossom parade in the spring. Many are also lured here because of additional attractions like four-star restaurants and hotels, as well as performing arts venues. These are among the more ubiquitous representations of this nation's capital.

Along with its size, Washington has a host of characteristics that set it apart from other major urban centers. All cities have socioeconomic diversity, but the smallness of D.C. amplifies the impact of class bifurcation. Divisions are stark—although not solely dualistic—and an unadulterated view of the scope can be had along the "Rodeo Drive of the east coast," where Wisconsin and Connecticut Avenues meet and residents intimately familiar with Jimmy Choo, Louis Vuitton, and Gucci shop and dine. The resources that high-income segments of the population access extend far beyond what average, local residents gain obtain. For those who consume information from conventional sources, views of D.C. are limited and defined by the Chambers of Commerce and realtors' selling points: as a tourist mecca and stomping grounds of the rich, powerful and connected. This is the picture of D.C. perpetuated by a bevy of new reality shows set in Washington, including Top Chef D.C. (Bravo), The Real World D.C. (MTV), as well as offerings on HGTV and The Food Channel.

One of the most problematic of these was the short-lived Real Housewives of D.C. This television show featured five area women who were described as local residents, although three lived in the D.C. suburbs. One of the women was African American and, in keeping with its established "real housewives" brand, the show mandated that these women attend parties, engage in petty conflicts, and showcase their upscale lifestyles. I highlighted what this series overlooked in its profile of D.C. during an interview with National Public Radio reporter Neda Ulaby, sharing alternative views with her, but most of my insights were not included in the broadcast.[1]

The corporate media have been particularly adept at presenting widely disseminated views of Washington, D.C. The delineations and meanings of D.C. these outfits concoct are at odds with what I heard and observed in my interactions with residents but mainstream depictions can have a huge effect on the way people who live outside D.C. conceptualize and interrelate with natives. During the 1980s, for example, nightly news portrayals hammered the idea of D.C. as the "murder capital of the U.S." into viewers' imaginations. Eventually a plethora of crime novels emerged that were set in D.C., and James Patterson,[2] George Pelecanos,[3]

---

[1] http://www.npr.org/templates/story/story.php?storyId=128935825.

[2] Patterson has written numerous novels including his suspenseful and dark series set in D.C. featuring protagonist Dr. Alex Cross, an African American psychologist and detective who lives with his family in D.C. and solves murders. The first of the series was Along Came A Spider (1993).

[3] Pelecanos' D.C. quartet series began with The Big Blowdown (1996) and was followed by King Suckerman (1997), The Big Forever (1998), and Shame the Devil (2000).

and other authors added to the popular imagination of this city as an inimitable place of danger.

Films have influenced views of D.C. as well, and shaped the national reputation of the city without much of a focus on residents of color or the working class. Some of the major releases that have made Washington, D.C. the primary setting include *Absolute Power* (Clint Eastwood), *Clear and Present Danger* (Harrison Ford), *Enemy of the State* (Will Smith), and *Minority Report* (Tom Cruise). Thematically, these cinematic offerings are more geopolitical than Georgia Avenue. The storylines involve international intrigue and other matters connected to governance rather than the concerns or representations of the "every-person," that is, long-term, local residents.[4] Will Smith notwithstanding, these processes either render African American residents of D.C. invisible or reduce them to mere glimpses of backdrops. In most of these instances the imagery is centered on that which is White, upper-income, and conventional.

Vying for the attention that mainstream media representations practically monopolize is a contrasting focus on D.C.'s perceived urban dysfunctions.[5] This is where long-term, African American residents move to center stage - in discussions of failing schools, crime, disease, "broken" families, and African American children misbehaving in various public settings. Flanked by these divergent narratives are peoples, experiences, and histories that, while not hidden, are also not as readily visible as they should be.

The use of the word other is one way to distinguish between federal Washington and its related upper echelons and residents with much less political/economic power and access. The word can be heard in informal conversation or can be the subject of articles such as "The Other Washington," *World Magazine,* Vol. 25, No. 7, 10 April 2010. Stories of "the other Washington," are ironic since the title refers to the largest single demographic group in the District—African American working people. Such designations are frequently but not always top-down. American University students in the School of Communication make use of this terminology to label people and experiences that have been ignored or overshadowed. This usage was designed to convey marginalization but this paradigm could be just as reasonable shifted to designate those who are not of color or among the lower income and working class.

---

4   Slam, starring spoken word artist Saul Williams and The Wire's Sonia Sohng was a huge exception to these cinematic treatments of D.C., but it was an independent film.

5   The August-2009 premier of the HBO documentary on former Mayor and current council member, Marion Barry, keenly illustrates where D.C. fits in the American mindset. Certainly other politicians whose personal struggles and frailties have come and gone from our national memory and/or been re-elected to the chagrin of outsiders, but the D.C./Barry story is the gift that keeps on giving to journalists, documentarians, comediennes, and hosts of others. It also cements a pathological view of a city that is so dramatically divided and misunderstood.

A nuanced, multicultural chronicling of life in this city, one that considers the interconnectedness of the individual, neighborhood, and community, broadly considered, promotes a wider view with alternatives to the dichotomy of the disadvantaged versus the privileged; marginalized habitats contrasted against the stately. These oppositional pairings, what Modan observes as the building-blocks of the Washington/D.C. or Washington *vs.* D.C. divide,[6] do not negate the existence of areas where Washington overlaps or rubs elbows with D.C.

There are further indications that the Washington/D.C. divide may not be uniform. Cultural and existential nuances in D.C. have a tendency to become smoothed out amid discussions of poverty and social problems, obscured amid a mainstream preoccupation with the goings-on in White and middle-class enclaves. But counter-narratives are widely evident; shared straightforwardly over office cubicle walls, in hair salons and barbershops, in places of worship, through the ties of kinship, in gatherings of community organizations, and through independent media networks (Harris-Lacewell, 2006). These avenues of African American everyday expression are rarely featured in *Washingtonian Magazine* and never covered by the more patented guide to luxury living in D.C., Maryland, and Virginia, *Washington Spaces*. However, it is through the mundane comings and goings of residents that personal experiences are expressed and culture, history, and the meaning and significance of place are defined, shared, and questioned.[7]

Of course, there is not one African American Washington, D.C. Sexuality, age, class, and location, as well as discordant notes of ideology and political allegiance, divide African Americans and chip away at crude notions of a monolithic Black community in this city. Belonging is an uneven process constructed through shifting conditions, occurrences, and beliefs (Prince, 2004). Its potency waxes and wanes, but feelings of attachment can intensify in the face of shared threats. The people I have interacted with over the years verify the view that specific neighborhoods cause important. When people spend many years in one community, these areas can loom in experiential narratives as places where people discuss belonging or feeling most at home.

At the same time, characteristics or processes that take people outside the confines of their immediate neighborhoods, such as transience, upward mobility, aging, or geographical curiosity can expand notions of residential belonging. Gentrification is another force that pushes at the boundaries of neighborhoods. In

---

6   In her ethnography Turf Wars, Gabrielle Modan writes as a sociolinguist who interprets the difference between residents who say they live in Washington and those who live in D.C. "Washington," she argues, represents the White, more middle to upper class, tourist-accessible portions of the city, whereas while D.C. represents the neighborhoods that are frequently go unmentioned or may be less known.

7   Weekly newspapers attempt to redress this kind of neglect by covering stories of "ordinary" Washingtonians. A list of these includes The Informer, The Afro American, and The City Paper; however, these outlets do not exist without racial and classed-based conflicts being played out within their pages.

addition to changing community demographics and new neighborhood monikers, gentrification connects various groups of African Americans who share a sense of unease over dislocation. My data showed such disquietude centered on concern about the physical displacement of people as well as the disarticulation of cultural elements that symbolize the African American presence. People feel threatened with loss and use places and things to create competing constructs of Black belonging in Washington, D.C.

Auto-Ethnographic Representations of Washington, D.C.

Whether I was overtly cognizant of it or not, my experience growing up in D.C. intersected with the formation of social hierarchies and battles for social justice. My people, places, and things had other layers as well and included half smokes and the Beatles; tennis at Turkey Thicket; family nights out at Ruby's Restaurant in Chinatown; and TV dinners while watching what Johnny Quest, Haji, and Bandit were up to. In my adolescence were added bus rides across town in a forced march to charm school, or to people watch voluntarily after buying risqué comic books in Georgetown. In the years that followed I was attending African Liberation day celebrations in Malcolm X Park with a veritable cornucopia of Pan Africanists. Occasionally, stalwarts of the All African People's Revolutionary Party, dressed in white, would innocuously jostle each other during rallies in their attempts to walk alongside event and organization founder Kwame Toure (Stokley Carmichael).

I was also inserted into a network of politically conscious, Black gay and lesbian performing artists. This eclectic grouping consisted of friends of my brother Chris Prince: actors, poets, and musicians who either performed at the Coffee House[8] or were holdovers from his much earlier summers with the late Mike Malone and Peggy Cooper (Cafritz) in the Workshop for Careers in the Arts. These drama and dance classes, taught by Owen Dodson, dancer-choreographer and director Debbie Allen, Mike Malone, and other instructors were held on the campus of George Washington University. This vibrant program ultimately gave birth to The Duke Ellington High School for the Performing Arts. Participation funneled more than a handful of African American students into Julliard and also fed the career success of singer, and native Washingtonian, Ami Stewart, who recorded a hugely successful dance cover of the soul tune *Knock on Wood*.

My brother's friends and artistic collaborators included poets Essex Hemphill and Larry Duckett and filmmaker Marlon Riggs. Essex, Marlon, and countless other gay African American men who constituted Chris' family, were lost to

---

8   The Coffee House was the name for a performance space made out of a 19th-century carriage house located in an alley along the H Street Corridor, now called The Atlas District. The neighborhood became infamously associated with the brutal murder of an African American woman by teens who were her nearby neighbors. Poet and Coffee House participant the late Essex Hemphill, wrote a poem about this attack.

AIDS but their work and my relationships with them helped bolster awareness of heterosexism and, in the process, expanded my understanding of what fighting for social justice looked like.[9]

I asked Chris how being in D.C. specifically informed the work of his community of artists. His response reflected D.C. as a muse of sorts. I return to the subject of how art can be associated with politics in this city in Chapter 6, but in a more general reference, Chris asserted that D.C. was important to his creative processes and relationships he built with other gay artists he collaborated with:

> Everybody's work did not talk specifically about Washington. Our work was informed by the nature of the city, informed by the fact that Washington had a thriving Black middle class, an educated Black middle class, and I think it was also because it was the nation's capital, and politics is something that is preeminent in people minds. That is a part of what was going on and at the time it was a majority-Black city. That did it as well; it wasn't like Baltimore where it was all working class. D.C. has a large number of middle class Black people, which is unusual, isn't it?

> There was already a group of gay Black people that was established as well. D.C. had social clubs and the oldest Black gay bar on the East coast, Black-owned. That was Nob Hill. We had the D.C. Coalition for Black Gays and Lesbian, and I think there was only one other and that was on the west coast. All of that was rare. There was a unique combination of things going, and that informed our art and gave me an audience. One thing fed upon the other.

Over the years I have observed that the majority of Chris' buddies have purchased homes in D.C. and remained in the city. It is also true that only a smattering of his gay friends are parents. Whatever their specific lifestyle, the stories of these women and men, whether they be native Washingtonian or not, single or involved long-term partners, with or without children, helps us acknowledge the layers of the African American experience in Washington, D.C. Sexuality, like age,

---

9   Stories of gay Black men and women in Washington, D.C. have been recorded through the Rainbow Oral History Project. This project also documents the experiences of gay and lesbian artists in D.C. and includes contributions from my brother, Christopher Prince, and members of his cohort. Further contributing to D.C.'s association go the African American gay experience, Chris was pictured alongside his friends Larry Duckett, Essex Hemphill, Wayson Jones, and Ron Simmons in the Style section of The Washington Post in 1991. The article appeared in conjunction with the airing of Tongues Untied, the Marlon Riggs documentary that examined aspects of the Black gay male experience in the U.S. on Public Broadcasting System (PBS). The D.C. residents pictured in the Post article all did voice over work for the film, the airing of which on was hugely controversial because conservatives objected to the subject matter.

gender, and class, intersects with race to give place meaning and texture and frame experience (Lutz, Vivar, and Supik, 2011).

Landmarks shoring up my sense of place, coming of age, were the Shrine of the Immaculate Conception on Michigan Avenue in NE, a building that can be seen from long distances in the city, and Providence Hospital, also in NE. My neighborhood friends and I treated the hospital gift shop like a corner store and had our first puffs of cigarettes in the first-floor bathroom. For other Washingtonians, their signposts were the Shrimp Boat on East Capital Street SE, or the Scottish Rites Temple on 16th Street NW, where Bill Sykes and his middle brother Chuck would sit and smoke marijuana under the ruse of going out to walk the dog.

I found belonging within another D.C. when I fell in with a group of dreadlocked, orthodox Muslims, only to face my mother's cold stares and dismay over my unconventional appearance. It was 1981, and I was 22 and smitten with long tunics, handmade skirts, and earth shoes. I also met Black people from Africa and the Caribbean, like Trinidadian Isa ibn Musa whose hair was shaped into two clumps of matted locks that resembled palm trees planted above each ear which prompted his fellow Muslims to say he had Mickey Mouse dreads. It was around this time that I too stopped combing my hair in egregious violation of "the politics of respectability" (Higginbotham, 1993, p. 185) to which my mother adhered. Unfortunately for me this was decades before the second natural hair revolution would take place during the 21st century. The thunderstorm this unleashed within my household reinforced what I already learned from first-hand experience, that competing narratives can be rooted in intra-racial differences such as class, religion, or nationality just as easily as any other form of human variation.

As previously shown, race and class had deep impacts on our youthful views. I cannot pinpoint when or how I began to call people living in my older cousin's SE neighborhood by the popular insults of the time, *bamas* and *tackheads*. She, my brother, and I all grew up on a relatively quiet and tree-lined streets in our two communities, but differences seemed to abound in perceptions of our neighborhoods. Perhaps it was because the distance we had to travel seemed lengthy or that my brother and I thought people talked and dressed funny "over there." Perhaps it had much to do with the fact that she lived in an apartment. Youthful parochialism and ultimately ignorance emboldened us to view SE through this same disparaging lens, even though SE, then and now, was diverse in terms of class and housing stock.[10]

It was the northwestern quadrant that generated the most fascination for the girls on my NE block as we were coming of age. Whether it was the racial/ethnic diversity of Chinatown and Adams Morgan or the solid architecture and bustling streets of Embassy Row and downtown, NW captured our imaginations, looming as a world

---

10   Some of this is simply rooted in class prejudice. These areas did have lower income residents and despite the impoverished roots of both of my parents, anti-poor bigotry was still learned from, what I would argue, were messages communicated from sources outside of my immediate household.

far removed from our more staid neighborhood. The upper-class portions were where our grandparents labored as domestics and our parents "put on their White voices" when talking to store clerks in order to be completely seen and understood.

Each generation had its emotional and identity oriented struggles that accompanied institutional and structural racism. In the mid-1960s we emulated whiteness with the draping of towels along our hairlines and the pretense of being a June Taylor Dancer with long flowing manes that skimmed our imaginative, gorgeous and equally flowing gowns. This ritualized imitation of dominant aesthetic standards of gendered beauty was practiced before James Brown demanded we say we were Black and proud out loud and we took him up on the offer. It was also prior to *Julia*, the Jackson 5, or the Bill Cosby half of *I Spy* making any visible impression on our self-esteem. Before "Black is Beautiful" became our mantra, everything White was pretty, graceful, wealthy, and desirable, and these positive evaluations also influenced spatial perceptions of class and community.

Interlocutors on Race, Class and Place

How did project participants use race and class to portray place in the conversations I had with them? One of the quotes opening this chapter is that of David Robinson, who was born in D.C. in 1955. Experience with racial strife in his SE community was brief from his standpoint, cut short by White outmigration. Robinson's family moved to Suitland, Maryland when he was in the 9th grade and took him, he says, on a journey from a Black to a White world. He shared a pre-move memory in reference to his community in SE:

> Growing up in a Black neighborhood we heard it all…"Say it loud…I'm Black and I'm proud" and the other part "Say it low…I'm Black Negro" Thanks JB…

After moving, the racial tide shifted:

> We were the minority and not the majority like in D.C. and had to deal with the awkwardness of being the Black kid in a White classroom. Teachers were White, the students were White and the principal was White. A whole different mind-set came in to play. I felt obligated to break the old stereotype of being Black and dumb. I had to show them I was just as smart as they were.

Robinson also added that he did not have any close, personal relationships with White people, "not until I moved out to Maryland, and they were more like acquaintances not friend friends," like he had while living in D.C. Not surprisingly, neighborhood of origin was a main factor in determining the background of one's friends.

Marcus Jackson also grew up in a predominantly African American community, but at the top of Washington, D.C., in NE. Unlike members of the

Robinson household, his parents never left D.C. His view of place was packed with references to gender, race, and color and took the following form:

> Growing up in D.C. Black in the 1960s and 70s provided a highly treasured experience. I had little contact with wealthy people and mostly knew working poor people like my immediate (and extended) family. Mostly these people were Black. This empowers my world view and racial identity.
>
> I was in the 6th grade when I heard Dick Gregory on a live WHUR broadcast from Crampton talking about how Black children were taught to dream for Whiteness as a measure of success. At age 11 or 12 the talk made me, for the first time, see my dark brown mother as a very beautiful woman. This funny man opened my eyes to the lovely world I discovered, home, in NE D.C.

There are multiple meanings communicated in Jackson's quote. As he reflects on his childhood, he is connecting to the moment when he recognized the impact of White supremacy on his thinking. His increasing insights into race occurred as he matured and this underscored the links between the political and the interpersonal. In terms of D.C., Jackson gained a greater appreciation of his immediate NE surrounds via Dick Gregory's bid to foster awareness. Jackson grew up in Brookland, which, like Michigan Park, was in proximity to Catholic University. These areas were unique for NE neighborhoods, and although most of the young people he knew in D.C. were African American, he had a handful of White friends whose parents were associated with the university. A few were also the children of his federal office worker parents' colleagues. Jackson attended St. Anthony's, a Catholic high school located at 12th and Lawrence NE for a couple of years and graduated from Wilson Senior High School. He took the time to list the White families with whom he had interactions growing up:

> We had houses of Fox, Flannery, LaFranchise, Daly, and Mullens, all White Catholic families with kids my age. Mike Fox did not play tennis or go to the playground, but he had pet rabbits and turtles around their house. His older brother had a motorcycle and pickup truck he would clean in the alley behind their house.
>
> My closest friends were Black. But any gathering of a dozen of us from Brookland would have someone from these families. James Flannery graduated Saint Anthony's eighth grade with me and we played baseball. St. A's introduced me to the Heffernans, Corboys, and Wards. Before St. A's, I knew the Mullens for our piano lessons; the LaFranchise gave an early invitation to their home after we moved here. Their large household gave us a babysitter a couple of times.
>
> I first knew Kathy Daly and her sisters at the playground while I played tennis. The Fox household two doors from ours had two boys, the youngest a year older

than I. Our three homes were bound/separated from other homes on our block by an encircling alley that began and ended on our street.

Jackson's story overlaps with mine, as I also attended St. Anthony's. Our communities are close to each other, and we, too, had a smattering of White households in our midst. I lived in Michigan Park and graduated from St. Anthony's in 1977 after attending D.C. public schools up to the 9th grade. My only White friend growing up was Anna Kenny, the daughter of an academic who lived across the street from me. Her dad was a Latin Americanist who also headed Catholic University's anthropology department for many years. For decades, the parents of people like Anna, many of whom are now deceased, lived without incident as minorities in the predominantly African American neighborhoods surrounding Catholic University. Not surprisingly, the children who grew up in these White households had close relationships with African Americans that continued as they matured, and more than a handful of their female children married African Americans. The experiences of these household members as children and adults are untapped resources that can engender new meaning in the workings of race and class in Washington, D.C. These stories need to be told in order to refresh our conversations about life, history, and culture in the District.[11]

Some of the discursive constructs I noted for exemplifying D.C. life and culture for the people I spoke with invoked the metaphor of Chocolate City (CC). What I did not anticipate was the practice of inflating the ratio of African Americans in the city. This characterization was popularized long before I raised it with my interlocutors. Native Washingtonian, Nkechi Omolade, 52, had lived in each quadrant of the city except SW. From her standpoint:

> D.C. used to be 99.5 percent Black so I always referred to DC as Chocolate City and I loved living in an all-Black community and an all-Black city. I was proud to be Black and living amongst Black folk; it did the soul good.

What Omolade is describing is a chocolate overdose. She didn't quite have her math right, but overstating the percentage of African Americans residing in the city during earlier decades was not an uncommon practice. Record producer/ computer technician Skyler Bishop has lived in France and New York City and traveled to Brazil, Germany, Morocco, Romania, Vietnam, and a host of other

---

11 I encourage ethnographers interested in the study of race in D.C. to research Whiteness and/or the layered experience of White Americans in D.C. Any number of theoretical frames would be useful for understanding particular neighborhoods in D.C. or broader themes of race and class in U.S. society. An example of the compelling type of stories that are yet to be told is that belonging to the daughter of a famous D.C. ethnographer. She once shared her experiences on the day Martin Luther King was assassinated. Fearing for her safety, a teacher walked the young woman home before the violent reactions were to be felt across the city.

countries. Also a native Washingtonian, he too engaged in this type of hyperbole when he told me his hometown was 96 percent African-American when he was a child. Inexplicably, I have also been guilty of this, as I can recall telling a college classmate that D.C. was 85 percent African American.[12] It appears some people exaggerate in this manner for effect, while others were simply unaware of the actual statistics. Whatever the motivation behind this demographic construct, the resulting representation was one of genuine predominance and racial exclusivity. It spoke to the essence of place which, in this instance, was steeped in the legacy of population movements and struggle within racialized and classed hierarchies. Over time, these people and their stories become the soul of the place.

The original CC label is not solely about having a Black majority among the residential population. CC pertains to Black political power or perceptions thereof. Marcus Jackson answered my questions of what the concept of a chocolate city or CC meant to him with, "advancement in government service and higher education, exploded middle-class Black populations in D.C. with steady work, advancement, and decent pay." David Robinson, like others, prefaced his comments by giving credit to Parliament-Funkadelic for originating the brand and then said, "At the time the album came out, the city was predominately Black...all the key positions were held by Black folks."

Asha Machel was born in Ohio in 1957 but has been a D.C. resident for 38 years. For her, CC is "a label for Washington, D.C. when it was overwhelming Black in population and when Black people held positions of authority." Responsibility, control, and predominance emerged as unifying themes. The reference to CC as something of the past expressed skepticism about the label's current veracity. Machel says that since her teen years, she has seen:

> More Black people leave Washington, D.C., less emphasis placed on Blacks in the arts, increase in Latinos in the city; many Blacks moved to the suburbs and the migration of Whites back into the city.

> It's more expensive to live in the city. I slowly saw the people on the 42 Mt. Pleasant bus change from predominantly Black, to Black mixed with Latino and a few Whites, to almost all Whites and Latinos and a few Blacks.

Skyler Bishop noted other disappearances taking place. He argued that gentrification had destroyed "traditional black neighborhoods and festivities and businesses which cater to them." Black-related festivals and other cultural events were being curtailed, while venues for the indigenous go-go music were becoming more customarily

---

12 In a personal communication with friend and former colleague, Dr. Rachel Watkins, she informed me that her family members told her, during visits to the D.C. home of her aunt and uncle in the 1970s, that African Americans were 85 percent of the District's population.

found in Prince George's County (Based on personal communication Ikram Ally during the time he was conducting research on this subject in 2010).[13]

"This just feels like a takeover," Samuel Hallowell told his friend Kevin Deshales as they settled in on their discussion of gentrification in D.C. Deshales, a middle-aged White male from the Pacific Northwest and former high school teacher who came to D.C. in 1968, agreed. The majority of people with whom I engaged for this project were, like Hallowell, either native born Washingtonians or African Americans who had lived here for more than 20 years. Almost 40 percent of Washingtonians are born in the city according to the U.S. Census Bureau, but this statistic is not broken down by race (U.S. Census Bureau, 2008).

Among the native Washingtonians whose views and life stories I sought was a network of friends in their fifties who grew up in adjacent neighborhoods in NE. With the exception of one who still resides in Washington, D.C. the remainder of the group now lives up and down the east coast ranging from Maryland to New England. They have also gotten together with more frequency over the last 15 months due to such milestones as 50th birthdays, children's high school and college graduations, and the deaths of parents.

Samuel Hallowell, Nkechi Omolade, siblings Sandra and Darius Olivette, and Sharon Barnes are included in the same friendship network of native-born Washingtonians. Darius moved to Philadelphia in 1987, and his sister Sandra's close friend, Nkechi Omolade, married early and left the city during the early 1980s. Sandra and Nkechi were among the first classes to finish at the new Duke Ellington High School for the Performing Arts. Sandra Olivette left D.C. for New York City before her brother departed. She has pursued a career in entertainment while Omolade and her husband, recent empty-nesters, have put their house in New England on the market and relocated to another rapidly gentrifying urban area, Harlem, New York.

Barnes finished law school at Catholic University in 2000 and began working as an assistant district attorney in lower Manhattan during that same year. She lived in the borough of Brooklyn but left New York City in 2004. Today Barnes resides in Upper Marlboro, Maryland in Prince George's County but she is in the process of moving to Silver Spring, Maryland at this writing into the home of her female partner who she plans to marry.

---

13 Discussion has taken place on the radio and through other local media outlets and venues about the curtailing of the annual Caribbean Parade. The parade has taken place along Georgia Avenue each year in D.C. for over 20 years, but the summer of 2010 marked the shortening of the parade route by 1.5 miles. The proposed reduction led to a vociferous outcry from supporters of the event. Subsequent reports emerged about members of the Metropolitan Police Department (MPD) hurrying revelers along during the parade and when it concluded. Most unfortunately, several people were hurt and one innocent bystander, Mr. Robert Foster, was killed when gun shots and fisticuffs broke out after the event ended. http://www.washingtoncitypaper.com/blogs/citydesk/2011/06/27/a-tense-saturday-for-the-caribbean-parade/.

The individual acts of outmigration represented by the movements among the people in this network are a part of a larger pattern of Blacks leaving D.C. during the 1980s and 1990s. African Americans who are now elders mulled over options to leave the District during the 1960s and 1970s. Other cohorts, members of the generation that followed that of current elders, discussed leaving Washington after graduating from high school during the late 1970s and early 1980s. This was around the same time I, like so many others, went off to attend college. Middle aged interlocutors talked to me about leaving to get graduate degrees or find a job, commence married life in a new state, pursue a career in the performing arts, or find more affordable rents. As this group aged, investing in housing stock in Maryland and Virginia became ideal attractions due to affordability and perceptions of safety.

James Hall, 51, was the sole member of this group of companions who still lived in D.C. This native of Brentwood in NE graduated from Coolidge High School in 1978 and, after attending Howard University, traveled and then lived in Cambridge, Massachusetts and New York City for a few years. As of this writing, Hall currently lives alone in his childhood home that he previously shared with his father Simon, a native Washingtonian whom I was supposed to interview. Simon Hall passed at the age of 85.[14] James Hall was unemployed and this was a situation that made his life economically tenuous. Joblessness also gave him a degree of freedom he had not enjoyed while working. It fostered a lot of creativity on his part.

Until a gunman robbed him of his laptop and the few dollars that were in his pocket, Hall would scour the Internet for jobs, ideas for cheap dates, and other activities to keep him busy. If I could not attend, Hall would still let me know about the anti-racism awareness meeting he attended at the Potter's House, assorted film festivals in the metropolitan area, or what the latest was with the City Council. During the recent elections, he also kept up with developments in various mayoral campaigns and was active on the listener-sponsored board of a local radio station.

Our relationship was an ethnographic match made in heaven. Due to his unfortunate job situation, his schedule was very compatible with mine. I hoped that he would secure employment, but I marveled at how he managed to keep a positive attitude. A recipient of two master's degrees from Harvard, it was not unusual for Hall to make it to the shortlist and land periodic job interviews. He was discovering, over the course of his years-long job search, that seeking employment from the position of joblessness was hindering his efforts to secure work.

Samuel Hallowell, a close friend of Hall's, has lived in Montgomery County for 12 years. Hallowell is the son of a D.C. native Jacqueline Hallowell and her husband Egbert. He left the city to attend business school in 1983 after graduating from Howard University and went on to reside in New York City and Philadelphia.

---

14 Declining health prevented me from interviewing Simon Hall. James also confided that his Dad has become crotchety in his senior years, giving me the sense he was trying to protect me from any potential unpleasantness that may spew forth during our discussion. I decided not to pressure Hall for the interview but I am certain the conversation would have yielded interesting data.

He expressed an intense desire to leave Maryland and move back to D.C. but also identified the current cost of housing as a prohibiting factor blocking his return. He echoed Hall's thought in a separate interaction with a spatial characterization of D.C. that also symbolizes the way race and class intertwine to constitute core meanings around how and why people "belong" in specific neighborhoods.

For as long as many can remember, the phrase "west of the park [Rock Creek]" has been a coded reference to the "White part" of D.C. In another allusion to race and place, I did not receive permission to reprint a map which accompanied a tea party posting related to an upcoming rally that was slated to take place on The National Mall. A leader out of Memphis, Tennessee used the Internet to warn attendees to stay off certain subway lines, most notably the yellow and green lines. *You* know what kind of people ride *those* lines was the message of the posting in which the people who ride the green and yellow lines of the D.C. subway system are marked as non-White or African American, depending on how specific we want to get with our educated guesses.[15]

Space and life in the District are characterized by a Black/White dichotomy along with additional oppositional models such as inside/outside the Beltway or the Washington/D.C divide already noted. Modan described how people living in NW DC assigned meaning to spatial belonging and wrote about the way groups deployed other ideological dualities as they created and asserted their sense of a *moral geography* upon Mt. Pleasant, a gentrifying and contested neighborhood (2007). Her use of the moral geography concept described interpretations of how, "through the use of alignments and oppositions among people and places," residents reinforced that you fit in and how you fit in—that you and the landscape are well matched" (p. 90). Such characterizations also symbolize difference or discord engendered by the influence of power on material and ideological position but however they were formulated, adherence to rigid dualities can obscure overlapping nuances and other complexities. That being said, a Black/White discursive binary was shared with me, unsolicited, by women and men I spoke with.

Although this was the case, there are still parts of the city that are neither White, upper-income enclaves or fodder for race-baiting fear-mongerers. Communities such as Brookland and Michigan Park have remained integrated throughout the heightened period of White flight during the 1960s and 1970s. This is the part of D.C. from which I hail, and although Whites were a definite minority in these neighborhoods, their presence was not viewed as odd or anomalous. There are also those vicinities that began gentrifying many decades ago and these, including portions of Capitol Hill, as well as Adams Morgan and Mt. Pleasant, remain diverse, albeit not untouched by tensions around race and class, as well conflicts over ethnicity and immigrant status.

Added to this typological list are the more recently gentrifying neighborhoods of D.C. While some, such as Petworth, LeDroit Park, and Shaw, are deemed historic or culturally significant for African Americans (Fitzpatrick and Goodwin,

15   http://dcist.com/2010/08/view_the_tea_party_guide.php.

1990), it was White Americans who predominated in many of these areas up until the 1950s. These are among the neighborhoods that have seen fluctuating rates of population shifts, with much less stability than in the upper-income, predominantly White parts of the city. Conditions are in rapid flux, and the information shared with me about these predominantly Black neighborhoods and how things used to be constitutes the makings of a "Chocolate City." The place-making components are also influenced by history.

A conversation with Samuel Hallowell as he waxed nostalgic about the summers of early adulthood reinforces this point. He longingly described how he and his buddies would ride bikes throughout the city, sometimes late into night. Hallowell made frequent use of an us/them dichotomy, saying:

> I thought of it as our city; it belonged to us, even though they belonged in the real ritzy part. White people were just Georgetown and Connecticut Avenue. Certainly, as a teenager and driving, actual contact with Whites accentuated the idea that this was our city because they clearly had their part and when we went to their part we were suspect. We knew that we were somewhat out of place. I had a sense they had their little section, but it was our city.

Travelling through enclaves and being the targets of law enforcement scrutiny reinforced the sense of not belonging in those areas of D.C. that Hallowell called "their little section[s]." Today, gentrification is undercutting old assumptions about who lives where and why and reformulating the meaning of chocolate city and its conceptual nemesis, chocolate chip.

Bernadette Thompson's reference to chocolate city was unsolicited. The reasoning behind this Cleveland native's move to D.C. came across in a conversation we had at her duplex in Eckington, NW. During our talk Thompson said she was drawn to this city because of its differences from Detroit, her previous home. She also distinguished between these two chocolate cities by emphasizing that:

> And you know the uh, Detroit was a steel town, you know was a car town, a factory town, so a lot of people in the population had factories and stuff they were making good money they'd buy their homes they were attached to their homes you know so it was heavily residential and all that kind of thing.

The following exchange is long but revealing and begins with a discussion of D.C.:

> BT: So it's chocolate city, there was always something to do. It was the mecca of entertainment. You know there was always somewhere to go. You know the atmosphere seemed to me to be more cohesive in terms of Black people and everything and it was like a, an integration of all these people from all over the planet. Kilimanjaro. You know all these different places where people would hang out from different ethnicities from the Diasporas.

SP: And Detroit is also a Black city too.

BT: Right, but Detroit to me wasn't as progressive as DC was. And it wasn't as diversified as DC was. You had the influence of Coleman Young back then, who was…like a little gangster, but I wouldn't call it gangster, but baby boy was running the city, [a] fuck you, kiss-my-ass kind of guy, you know.

SP He passed away didn't he?

BT: Yup. My uncle at the time, he wanted to find the museum of African American history, they had a big rivalry going on and stuff; they hated each other. It was crazy. But anyway so it was a different type of thing. You had Jheri curls there, you had our hair wearing our Jheri curls; they said what's wrong with your head? You know that kind of stuff. So [D.C.] was far more progressive than [Detroit] was in terms of fashion, things of that nature.

SP: Did it live up to expectations in terms of after you came here?

BT: Yeah, but I had been here before because I used to come here all the time to visit [her cousin] everybody.

SP: Right.

BT: So that's what I knew why I wanted to come here. And I wanted to go to an HBCU.

Thompson arrived from Detroit in 1986, coiffed in a shiny Jheri curl. She received a Ph.D. in psychology from Howard University while renting a third-floor room in a stately Columbia Heights row house owned by the mother of her cousin, Asha Machel. She then bounced around from 16th Street in Adams Morgan to purchasing a small row house on Sherman Avenue and the property she currently lives in near New York Avenue and Florida Avenue, in the shadow of the XM/Sirius building in Eckington. As a single woman without children, she has more options than many women her age. As a result of moving to D.C. in the mid-1980s, Thompson has a sense of how much the city has changed.

You have these people that come in usually like one or two, then it get to be three or four, then you go over there and there's a whole bunch of Europeans over there and there ain't no Black people. Ok? That changes the whole thing, and I found a metamorphosis of that in Adams Morgan. Adams Morgan used to be the joint. Remember back in the day when they had the festival and …some band would be there? Some go-go bands, it was just a beautiful thing. And now it's got to be so commercialized and it's like back in the day I used to complain to the ANC well you're turning this into a mini Georgetown. And what's going to happen is you're going to have an increased crime rate, we're going to have a lot of people flocking here from other jurisdictions and it's going to be a situation.

Thompson then went on to say it was precisely because of these changes that she left Adams Morgan:

> I got tired of [it]…they are seriously racist over there. They're dog-eat-dog. Now I'm on a community board over there. Blatant stuff over there, OK, and I literally got into some arguments with those people. And what I find a lot of times is that people, the Black people, are generally sometimes intimidated by Europeans[16] or they don't know how to manage them. And they really care about what they think. I don't care what they think. I know how to manage, and you're not going to step to me, and if you step to me you do it correctly. So I think a lot of times that really affects what goes on at the micro level in this community, because they come in and make all these suggestions.

Among other subthemes, Thompson's comments about gentrification and race relations point to sensitivities African American have expressed about White authority. Her attitude also reflects a hostility that views, assesses, and then "others" White Americans.

Representations of White Americans in the African American imagination have generated ambivalence in U.S. public discourse historically (Hooks, 1998). Lynching and other forms of violent punishment were perpetrated against Blacks in retaliation for real or perceived instances of eyeballing Whites. As recently as the last century, Blacks were opting to minimize problematic outcomes by "casting the gaze downward so as not to appear uppity," internalizing the understanding that looking "directly was an assertion of subjectivity, equality" because "safety resided in the pretense of invisibility" (Hooks, p. 42). This survival strategy was accompanied by other forms of masking and enacted because power was central to the evaluative beholding of the racialized (and gendered) body.

The passage of time and the aftermath of social movements have offered new sets of options that challenge the status quo and provide more space for women and ethnic, sexual, and racialized minorities to openly observe and put forward their assessments of dominant groups. As a conduit for this, gentrification is fostering uncharted circumstances for African American appraisals of White Americans to occur. Examples of both interracial conflict and cooperation stemming from gentrification in the District were observed in the field. These are discussed further along but a key query this chapter also considers, as it explores questions of "whose D.C. is it?" is how African Americans have socially constructed race in general and Whiteness more specifically as these forms of demographic change occur around

---

16   For clarity, Thompson frequently refers to White Americans as Europeans.

them. This question is explored incorporating analysis and discussion of the broader political economic context in which urban restructuring has taken place.

These macro-level, contextual factors are local, national, and global in scope. In a contracting economy U.S. populations of color are disproportionately vulnerable due to the legacy of racism. The opposing sets of spending cuts proposed by President Obama and his Republican counterparts during the debt ceiling debates of July and August 2011, for example, were projected to have a devastating impact on African American and Latino households. *The New York Times* recently held an online forum that examined how proposed cuts to the public sector will affect college-educated Blacks who are professionally-employed as a part of its "Room for Debate" series.[17] In her contribution, Pattillo (2007) maintained these members of the black middle class are disproportionately among public sector employees and the consumers of public sector produced goods. The sociologist also stated that:

> According to census data, Black children are more likely than White children to be enrolled in public schools, and the gap is largest between White and Black families making $25,000 to $35,000 per year. When state and local budgets are slashed, and teachers are laid off, the children of lower middle class Black families, whose prospects define the future of the Black middle class, are disproportionately hurt.

> The story is repeated across the various services the public sector workers provide. In health care, Blacks are more likely than Whites to use public hospitals, no matter their income. In public safety, higher earning Blacks have victimization rates comparable to lower income Whites. Cuts to public budgets will mean fewer police, and more important, fewer jobs programs; that is fewer alternatives to crime. These cuts will sting more acutely for middle class Blacks.

> The final domino falls within African American families. My research with Professor Colleen Heflin of the University of Missouri shows that middle class Blacks are more than three times as likely as middle class Whites to have a poor sibling. Public sector job loss and the resulting drop in public sector services means that already fragile middle class families will be less able to lend a helping hand just as the needs of their extended family members rise.

It must also be acknowledged that, across the country, these same minorities groups have been hit hard by the recession and housing foreclosures. Moreover, studies of race and wealth accumulation in the U.S. over time show the detrimental effects of deindustrialization, globalization, and "Reaganomics" on the shifting of resources

---

17 This excerpt is taken from an online forum hosted by *The New York Times* in which seven social scientists debate the impact of proposed budget cuts on the Black middle class on 25 July 2011. http://www.nytimes.com/roomfordebate/2011/07/25/how-budget-cuts-will-change-the-black-middle-class.

from the bottom and middle to the top. One report on the escalating wealth gap between Whites, Latinos, and African Americans implies that these unequal conditions are not solely the result of neoliberal economic project implementation (Taylor, Kochhar, Fry, Velasco, and Motel, 2011). This study also documents the byproducts of racism over time and reinforces the findings from previous studies and scholarship (Rivera, Huezo, Kasica, and Muhammad 2009; Shapiro, 2004).

Gentrification is not only occurring within this context, it is also an outgrowth of job loss, downward mobility, and wealth inequality in the United States. Ideological factors are also added to the equation. Moreover, the coded and outwardly racist discourse of the right wing and the equivocation or absence of broad-based resistance to this has chipped away at the important work done to repair the damage of racial upheavals and racism.

Some African American responses to these actions come in the form of disparaging sentiments directed toward White Americans as shown by my conversations with Bernadette Thompson. Added strains of CWS encouraged me to look beyond *othering* as the sole framework through which the Black imaginative of Whiteness is recognized. The validity of Hooks' assertion that casting an unmitigated Black gaze at the dominant group constitutes acts of resistance against the racial hierarchy complicates our understanding of these processes.

The range of my observations that connect gentrification and demographic change to African American constructions of Whiteness are thorny and at times convoluted. While the content may vary, these racialized notions can be offered up for immediate public debate with the use of social media. This is precisely what Akua Templeton did after she encountered a confrontation between a two women in downtown D.C. She tweeted followers after witnessing a Black woman become incensed when she saw a White woman's leashed dog urinate on the lawn of an African American church. Meaning is ascribed to symbols and in the minds of some African Americans, bike lanes, dogs and their play-spaces and bike lanes have become the marks of colonizers who have claimed the land for their work and recreational needs. In this context, White newcomers, the young in particular, can be viewed as self-indulgent, happy-go-lucky intruders who are also unencumbered by the legacy of class and race hierarchies Blacks negotiate. These ideas are circulating as African American residents of Washington, D.C. struggle, to varying degrees, with unemployment, underemployment, health challenges, ravaged kin networks, inadequate child care and educational resources, transportation woes, environmental hazards, foreclosures, and the stress these problems can generate.

There are other examples, like the discussion above, that reinforce how societal position shapes perspective. When an off-duty African American detective brandished his gun at a crowd after his SUV was pelted by snowball-throwing White winter revelers at 14th and U Streets during the winter of 2009, the act was covered by local newspapers and on the Internet. A cell phone videotape surfaced on YouTube documenting the detective's actions and subsequent acts that transpired; discussions ensued about race, privilege, and gentrification in D.C. This incident, juxtaposed against (Whites only?) no-pants subway rides in D.C.

celebrated by the media while African American youth face criminalization for wearing sagging pants (Koppel, 2007), highlights the ironies and dichotomies of racialized urban experiences. In the context of a rapidly changing D.C. and its growing social inequalities, the perspectives of residents can vary widely along the lines of race and class.

The irate, gun-wielding detective wildly overreacted and brandished his weapon without concern for community safety. From the outlook of some African Americans, however, adults throwing snowballs at cars is not only unacceptable behavior it also calls to mind the many unarmed African American males, the late Brian Hundley and Deonte Rawlings among them, who did not even survive unprovoked interactions with off duty officers in the District. The criminalization of Black youth, along with the shrinking spaces in which they can gather, moreover, further underscores the double standards with which poor, young residents of color wrestle.

Samuel Hallowell admitted he and his friends threw snowballs at cars when they were children. He also said

> We had enough sense to haul ass if a car stopped because we knew we were
> wrong and nobody wanted to get jacked.

Some African Americans see young White Washingtonians as an undifferentiated population that displays their privilege as the appearance of the landscape bends for them through policy and in accordance with the vicissitudes of neoliberal urban restructuring. Activist Bobby Jaminson adamantly offered a counter to this idea when I interviewed him at a tent-city encampment. Activists were squatting on a lot on Rhode Island Avenue, NW in protest of inadequate affordable housing in Washington, D.C. Jaminson maintained that White youths from middle class backgrounds were also being economically stretched in the District, sharing housing with other youths as well as cutting corners on food and entertainment spending. He was not equating the challenges of middle class White youth with what the poor were confronting but he did want to provide another lens through which to see White youth other than the "rich White kids whose parents purchase a condo for them the heart of the city" model.

Stereotypical constructs of whiteness are associated with discussions and conflicts connected to gentrification. These include warnings that White Americans are unclean and unrestrained, inherently dismissive of the African American presence in this city, or predictably racist and domineering. In discussions with interlocutors about issues of race and space, I also heard very contextualized considerations of how White privilege has historically functioned in U.S. society and the ways in which it is linked to gentrification.[18]

African American politicians were included in the subject matter of this race talk and also discursively implicated in gentrification. An upcoming chapter will take a closer look at policy issues. For the moment, suffice it to say that more than half of interlocutors viewed former mayors Anthony Williams and Adrian Fenty as smoothing the way for gentrification to take hold in D.C. and decried the men as inauthentic African Americans who lacked concern for the well-being of Black communities. Current city leadership did not escape scrutiny or evade criticism. Two project participants described Mayor Vincent Gray as an old-school Washingtonian who will cater to the light-skinned, elite old guard of D.C. The impact of his proposed budget cuts on the poor and vulnerable of the District have provoked anger and suspicion on the part of progressive D.C. activists as well. My e-mail inbox is filled with saved announcements of marches and other forms of protest initiated by African Americans against the current mayor and members of the city council.

This chapter described contestations over spatial belonging that have occurred among neighbors and friends, become part of public discourse via journalists, or are initiated as a consequence of public policy or the work of community organizations. I found that African American engagement in debates was often informed by physical and ideological interconnections between historical memory and geographic origin, as well as the socioeconomic challenges faced by individuals and people in their social networks. While conducting fieldwork I also learned that the present and past actions of White Americans were never far from the minds of many.

18 Checking in with project participants during this last week of July in 2011 involved discussions of the recently released Pew Research study on the escalating wealth gaps between White Americans and people of color in the United States. Interlocutors were aware of the connection between foreclosures, gentrification, and the overall declining economic status of African Americans and other racialized minorities in the U.S.

Chapter 5
Race, Class, and the Individual Dynamics of Gentrification

The event occurred on the campus of Howard University and was organized around the documentary *There Goes the Neighborhood.*[1] The crowd was small, consisting of filmmakers, students, activists, academics, and residents who had gathered to see the movie and hear a panel discussion on its topic, gentrification in Washington, D.C. At the conclusion of the event, as attendees moved about to disperse or informally converse in small groups, an elderly Afro-Caribbean woman asked, seemingly of no one in particular, "Why won't they say good morning to me?" Her query referred to the young White people she encounters on the street who have recently moved into her neighborhood. No one in the room had an answer for her.

The woman left after asking the question, but this wasn't the first time issues of civility and the acknowledgement of others had been raised in connection with African American concerns about the impact of gentrification. I had heard variations on these themes and was told by a Black resident of Columbia Heights that it took the White people in her neighborhood more than "10 years to realize Black people actually spoke to each other in their communities."

Working from earlier discussions of arrival and attachment, this chapter delves more deeply into African American perceptions of gentrification. The emphasis on what residents say about their direct experiences with gentrification is rounded out by a consideration of the conditions, policies, and practices that contribute to this demographic change. Additional consideration is shown to how population shifts have influenced relationships across the boundaries of race and class. Cross-cultural interactions are as layered and complex as the populations I came to know while conducting field research. Relations are also shaped, in part, by history and the political and economic context African American residents have had to contend with over time.

It is important to reiterate that demographic change has been a constant in the history of Washington, D.C. This book has already shown that people have come, gone, and moved about from the earliest moments in the history of this city and that race and class have been inexorable aspects of these shifts. This means, by extension, that power relations have figured into these changes because race and class have come to exist only through the formation of hierarchies. Similarly, gentrification

---

1   This documentary was directed by Rebecca Kaufman and depicts myriad struggles with gentrification in various corners of Washington, D.C. The film won Black Entertainment Television's award for best documentary in 2011.

is, by its very definition, tied to and dependent on social inequalities (Glass, 1964). The ethnographic data presented here highlight processes that support this theory without minimizing the fact that the interactions, responses, and constructions I heard recounted or observed also reflect a complexity of experience.

Relations and conditions are made all the more intricate given African American Washingtonians' familiarity with the contradictions of racism and the silences of class oppression. Living with these understandings and the legacies of unfairness fosters varying degrees of differential, racialized standpoints among African Americans. This supposition is supported by my data and this assertion has also been validated by various quantitative studies including a phone survey of 3,086 people conducted by the Pew Research Center in conjunction with National Public Radio (2007). It revealed that, compared to Whites, African Americans held distinctively different views about a number of race-related issues, including the pace of Black progress and a growing gulf between the African American poor and middle classes. This same study also showed that gaps separating Latino, White and African American views about how these different racial-ethnic groups were getting along with each other had increased (2007).

Qualitatively-discerned patterns in African American responses to gentrification and demographic change can augment statistical data on racial attitudes. These findings can also advance understandings of how history, structure, and current-day experiences coalesce to shape a wide-ranging, African American urban culture. This assertion is demonstrated in the stories shared by the women and men who participated in this project.

African Americans Framing Gentrification: From the Grassroots to Elected Officialdom

It would have been easy for Deborah Peterson to follow the example of her siblings and move from the District to Maryland or Virginia. She certainly had the resources and there were a lot of folks within her social circles poised to validate this choice if she decided to relocate to the suburbs.

Prince George's County (PGC) in Maryland has received many of the African Americans migrating out of Washington, D.C. The county's Black population has increased by 10 percent over the last decade with African Americans now constituting 64 percent of its population (D.C. Neighborhood Info, 2011). Hillcrest Heights, Seat Pleasant, and Suitland were common destinations during the 1970s and Bowie, Chillum, Upper Marlboro, and Mitchellville have sizable African American populations today. In 2010 the 7th Council District reached 91 percent, the highest African American population of that county (D.C. Neighborhood Info, 2011).

Peterson was an upper-level manager in the administrations of mayors Marion Barry and Anthony Williams. She conveyed that she was always aware of her choices and had given relocation some thought. In the end her views about her home town were unwavering:

I could have bought a home out in P.G. County. I didn't want it. I never wanted to live out there, period. And that had as much to do with not only my love for the District of Columbia, but also you know I've seen those homes out there, they are beautiful homes. You know great model homes. But the quality of them could never compare to the older homes here in the District.

A portion of the Black outmigration she described was motivated by people's desires for a larger home and more backyard. Petersen did not begrudge anyone their personal tastes, even if she did not like to see so many African Americans leaving the District. However, what did gave her pause were the patterns of demographic change that became evident during the 1990s, decades after the shifts associated with the post-King assassination period. In her estimation, these were deliberate and more nefarious than African Americans simply pursuing the American dream of a suburban lifestyle. Petersen thought the present-day changes were redolent of "The Plan," the conspiracy theory which dates back to the year 1979 and has been attributed to Afro American newspaper writer Lillian Wiggins (Jaffe, 2009).

The idea of The Plan is embraced by an unknown number of African Americans and scoffed at by others. The notion posits the existence of clandestine, long-term efforts to remove African Americans from D.C. over time in response to the establishment of home rule. Wiggins wrote that Marion Barry would be the last African American mayor of D.C. because of the threat posed by African Americans' increasing political autonomy (Jaffe, 2009).

Placing The Plan within a social context is more instructive than validating or disproving the soundness of the idea. Attempts to understand this notion necessitate a closer consideration of local history and policy implementation, as well as the racialization of reasoning as connected to both.

Toward that end, this book has already pointed out specific cases of African American displacement in Washington, D.C., including the removal of African Americans from Georgetown, Old Southwest, and alley communities across the city. These are stark examples that numerous middle-aged and elderly African Americans in D.C. are undoubtedly familiar with. There are Black residents living today who were present during heightened urban renewal and the upheaval this caused. These individuals witnessed the dismantling of communities and the displacement of residents who were forced into vulnerable living positions because of highway construction and other developments. Distrust of top-down "improvements" has been nurtured in vulnerable communities where residents have seen the converging, profit-driven efforts of politicians, developers, and banks in their midst. First-hand.

I had discussions with two elder residents who have been active in the local politics of housing and urban development for many decades. Lamond Riggs resident, Lolita Waymons, was born in Tampa, Florida in 1931 and moved to D.C. in 1950. She attributed her political drive to her mother, who implored her children do for others, not as a show of goodness and concern, but because it was the right thing to do. Her mother's example motivated Waymons to co-found or join numerous

Democratic clubs, committees, and federations over the years. She also served two mayors, consecutively, leading commissions on food, nutrition, and health.

Waymons met me at a library on South Dakota Avenue NE during the heat wave of 2012. I was surprised to find out she walked more than three blocks to meet with me, and I drove her home when the interview was over. When I asked her opinion on gentrification, she mentioned urban renewal and gave me the patented, "it wasn't urban renewal it was urban removal." I nodded with familiarity.

Gentrification is preceded by disinvestment, and the following comments indicate Waymons was clear that this is what occurred in Washington, D.C.:

> Because after the riots—after the '68 riots those places that housed Black people like in the inner city and all over in Northwest, people used to live down in, might be a store downstairs and they lived upstairs and vice-versa. After the riots, when those places were burned, who was displaced? Nobody tried to hurry up and replace the buildings and they stayed like that for a many, many, many. I remember Congressman Walter Fauntroy pleading with people that owned property to put it back on the market and those that could, buy property. He went to churches and asked them to buy as much around them as possible so they could begin to redevelop. It took a long time and only a few churches did that. Like Bible Way was one of the ones that bought into that. You had several others. Some Catholic churches over there in Ward 1, they did it.

Her analysis did not cease at the structural, however; she also blamed African Americans in D.C. for selling their property and chastised them for being, in her words, short-sighted and lazy.

Sterling Tucker made history by heading the D.C. City Council after the establishment of home rule. A large portion of his career in public life has been spent working at the front lines of desegregation efforts and housing debates. Tucker, 88 at the time of our meeting, also served as assistant secretary of Housing and Urban Development, after losing a mayoral election to Marion Barry in 1979.

I met with him at his home and solicited his thoughts on gentrification, urban renewal, and the concept of The Plan. As the following quotes reveal, the responses I received were complicated. Tucker gave no credence to The Plan and expressed the view that alley dwellings and other dilapidated housing stock just simply were not viable in key downtown locations:

> Dislocating was easier. Just get out. Relocating them was more difficult. That challenge was not easily accepted or developed. They tried developing, you know, if you're going to have some market-based housing you've got to have some subsidized housing, and did some of that in Southwest. That was kind of a big thing there. We had to fight through all of that, with the Urban League we had to fight through all of that, with the developers, with the city government with the private developers. It was a big fight every step of the way. People

were, I remember holding public meetings down there and people were crying, 'no place to go.' But still, the area needed to be renewed because people had out houses still in some places.

The following exchange occurred when I asked Tucker where people went who were displaced through urban renewal projects:

Tucker: Barry Farms was out there. Most of them went to far Southeast, to Southeast and some of them in Northeast. But many of them—most of them went to Southeast. Some spilled over into Princes George's County. That's where many of them went. That was a very, very difficult thing, not only in Washington but all over the country. People called it Black removal.

Prince: Yeah, that's true. How do you respond to people who say that it was some kind of conspiracy going on? It wasn't really about helping but it was more about removing. How do you respond to that?

Tucker: I don't believe a lot in conspiracy theories. There's a lot of very practical issues there. I do believe, however, that people saw Southwest as very valuable land. It's very close to downtown. A lot of people didn't want those shanties and all that appearance to be so close to the nation's capital, the capital buildings and so forth. So where'd they go? They didn't come up this way. They didn't go to Ward 3. They didn't go to Ward 5. Where'd they go? Where the poor people moved, the poorest people were, in Ward 8, the people most disadvantaged and least able to fight back. But that was the easiest way to do it.

I was receiving mixed messages from Tucker and pressed him on the question of deliberate plans to remove African Americans from the land, to which he responded:

When I say I don't believe in conspiracy theories, I don't believe the purpose was just to dislocate Black people. I think the purpose was, it was to gain control of land that was valuable for other development purposes. White people just had to be on the land. I don't think they were trying to run the Blacks out of the city. They didn't care where they went.

In other words, I don't think the city itself had a plan. I think the real estate community did ... the city would not be above that in terms of the people who controlled us before... but the city would not be involved in a plan to deliberately dislocate the people from their land, except that there was some planning, kind of a total plan involved.

For Tucker, developments around urban renewal marked the early stages of gentrification and, like Waymons, he places partial blame on African Americans for leaving their communities. He said the message he conveyed to people during that time was, "Don't sell, then they can't run you out. Don't sell your house. They want to buy out, if you want to go that's your choice." Tucker also added more depth to the discussion of Black outmigration by positing that the conditions in public schools, a lack of confidence in the city's ability to recover from the riots, concerns about crime, and the need to protect their investment were four key contextual elements motivating significant numbers of African Americans to leave the city for surrounding suburban communities.

I would add vulnerability to Tucker's list of push factors as an aspect of the human condition that connects these past events to similar processes occurring today. Whereas White residents fell prey to blockbusters who stoked fears of invading Negroes and plummeting housing values during the 1950s, African Americans confronted more-than-imagined difficulties in neighborhoods after the 1968 riots.

For too many working and middle-class Blacks, fears about their family's futures were growing as fast as bars on windows and doors were being installed. Scant confidence in law enforcement, following decades of experience with police misconduct, combined with the economic reality that, in comparison with Whites, greater portion of their wealth tied up in their homes (Oliver and Shapiro, 1997), African Americans were susceptible to financial insecurity and physical violence in ways only they, apparently, could appreciate. Research documents the disproportionate impacts violence has had on African Americans, particularly young males (Harrell, 2007) and after the introduction of crack cocaine in the 1980s, these vulnerabilities worsened.

Brenda Duke and Lorraine West could bear witness to the changes described above. I visited the couple at their home in Columbia Heights NW on an unseasonably warm spring day in 2012. I stayed for over two hours listening to stories about encounters with neighbors, changes in the availability of services, and the causes for gentrification as they saw it. The women bought their house in 1987, before the larger waves of gentrification that would follow during the late 1990s. When I asked about amenities that have been brought into the neighborhood in association with the recent demographic shifts, our conversation turned to policing. Both women talked about crime and what they viewed as the lack of cooperation they received from the Metropolitan Police Department (MPD) before the present wave of development and gentrification when neighbors banded together to eradicate crack-cocaine selling from their streets and alleyways. Duke shared the following description about what occurred in their community:

> We had a lot of crack houses in the neighborhood, and we knew where they were, but we couldn't get our police to do a doggone thing about it. The park police had to come to do what we wanted to close those things down. And the prostitution that was going on in these alleys was exploiting young Black women. Because people have garages that have fallen into disrepair as people who live in the neighborhood get older. And kids are looking at making money the wrong kind of way and it was a climate and a culture in the 80s.

West added:

> Again, it is a lovely neighborhood at this point but the police let us suffer with having to call them, them getting here, us having community meetings, them telling us "please call us." It's just like me telling you oh please read—or something you already do. We have been calling but y'all ain't doing nothing but pointing things out. Nothing is happening but I noticed down there where the Reeves Center is I remember it was crawling with drug addicts if you remember 14th street and that corner. But once the Reeves Center got there y'all managed to clean that shit up. We have a whole lot less here but y'all can't... (inaudible)

> So we would sit out on that corner with the people who were concerned and would sit out on that corner of 13th street with little notebooks maybe writing down license plates and taking our lives in our hands quote unquote.

The concerns expressed by both women about their community's battle with illegal drug sales drew attention to what I call the law enforcement abuse/neglect dichotomy that is not uncommon among African American experiences. The social phenomenon is so recognizable that Black comics, Dave Chappelle most effectively,[2] have tackled the subject in stand-up routines. In this particular Columbia Heights instance, Black residents felt their concerns were not taken seriously enough by the MPD until the percentage of White residents grew in the community, at which time, according to these residents, a police presence increased.

I heard this same refrain from Barbara Best, the former co-director of the grassroots advocacy organization D.C. First. Best moved to Columbia Heights in 2003 after living in downtown Washington and also in Shaw. She concurred with Duke and West and supported her validation of their assessment based on her direct experience. Best then recounted having verbal altercations with sex workers and drug dealers in front of her past residences and receiving what she felt was inadequate attention and cooperation from the MPD.

Duke and West are politically savvy women who were also keenly attuned to D.C. politics and the tensions that play out between local and federal governments. At the end of this particular discussion, I brought the line of questioning around to The Plan. West was a native New Yorker who had been living in D.C. since the late 70s. She was not familiar with the idea, and I declined to elaborate to avoid tainting their responses with my point of view. Duke, on the other hand, had extensive roots in the city—she was born in D.C. in 1951 and expressed a definite position. She quickly gave her opinion about The Plan:

---

2   Chappelle did this bit as a part of a larger 2007 performance entitled *Killing Them Softly*. The video can be accessed through this link and the specific piece on the police is located around the 10:40 marker http://www.youtube.com/watch?v=9SUiIqmKahM.

It means that the trilateral commission has evolved through the years into a new kind of urban plan. It used to be more local but now since the economy has gone more global you have all these institutional think tanks that are sponsored by enormous amount of money that will never be traced. These people are coming up with a concept of five, 10, 15, 20, hundreds of years of where they want things to be at and that is not inclusive of the people who don't look like them.

Additional comments made by both women reveal combined critiques of White supremacy and the U.S. class structure. As we continued to talk, West made a comment about the children of the 1 percent[3] whose parents, she argued, have the financial means to secure housing for their offspring. Duke retorted with criticisms of oligarchies and divide-and-conquer strategies. Campaign finance also came up in the conversation and was linked to patterns that reflect how far down ordinary citizens rank in the setting of priorities for improving the lives of D.C. residents.

The language of the occupy Wall Street movement seeped into my discussion with West, who mentioned banks as exemplifying the forces undermining local self-rule:

> I remember at one point unless you were a DC bank you couldn't be in DC. Then Charlene Drew Jarvis goes off and gets crazy with some guy from Citibank and the next thing you know she is writing the banking bills and is the chairman of the banking committee to change the rules and so that some out of state bank could come in here and rewrite the rules and become a part of the DC banking group. It didn't help the residents at all.

I recorded Akua Templeton's views on demographic change in 2009 as we sat around her dining room table in NE and she shared opinions forged at the intersections of her multiple positionalities and accomplishments. Templeton is a west coast native who holds a doctorate in economics. She also runs a non-governmental organization (NGO) located in NW that works with local and national agencies, institutions, and organizations to build healthy communities across the U.S. Her organization's website describes their take on the existence of health inequality in American society and posits that difficulties to thrive are

---

3   As this book was being written, activists took over a park in lower Manhattan to protest social inequality and corporate malfeasance. These actions dovetailed the Arab spring movements that spread across a number of countries in the Middle East. While mainstream media pundits diminished the efforts, in the U.S., of what came to be called the occupy Wall Street movement (OWS) by labeling it as discordant and limited in swaying political developments, the language of these activists influenced the public discourse of journalists and politicians. One aspect of their impact on our lexicon was the use of phrases like the 1 percent and the 99 percent to distinguish between the wealthy minority and the majority of U.S. citizens.

linked to systemic and institutional problems which appear in the form of disease, poverty and injustice on a global scale.

Since 2005, Templeton and her family have rented the three-bedroom house in a part of Brookland where, she says, the renters are Black and the new homeowners are White. It is one of the communities I grew up alongside, and she described it as:

> a neighborhood in transition. Brookland has always been a multiracial neighborhood. So I think that's important to say. And for the old-timers, a number of people have been here since the 50s and 60s. That's very important to them, and that's a very important part of their identity. Some of them have to do with Catholic [University] clearly. Catholic's here. So whenever, [*sic*] then you add Black people, it's at least bi-racial if nothing else. But it's becoming more, a little more diverse than Black and White. But it is, it is a heritage that people are proud of.

From her perspective, demographic change in D.C. is fomented by the extreme income inequality in this city. It is her assessment that:

> The housing crisis has created a tremendous pressure. The thing about D.C. is there's this sort of strange two tracks. You have people who are lobbyists and all who can spend a tremendous amount of money on houses and feel that that kind of stuff is important. And that pushes people out. And then, and then that raises the taxes. And so you have a tremendous amount of people in DC lose their homes for $3000 or $4000 in taxes. I mean I went through looking at the rolls, you know and one of the things that a number of groups like DC First are trying to do was to approach then Mayor Anthony Williams to provide some amnesty for people around taxes. And interestingly enough that was one of the things Fenty promised when he ran.

She also added that former mayor, Adrian Fenty, did not honor the promise to secure amnesty for the vulnerable:

> you know you had all these seniors. So you go, you go up and down, like take a street like Harvard. Once you cross Georgia Avenue, that area between say 11th going down to Sherman across the pretty wide swath, you have houses going way up and down, new people buying on those blocks. And you see it. And you saw the houses, the houses that were all fly and hooked up, ready for HGTV and the people with the green astro turf and the striped awnings, struggling there and getting jammed up on code violations, no support. So and then you had policies that purposely promoted newcomers to get support. You had money for people who were first-time, so called first-time homebuyers in DC who should have been really people who were trying to move up the ladder from rental to buying homes. Right? It could have been constructed in a way where you could really privilege those people. Not just anybody who had any kind of money through

whatever. But then folks who you know had vacancies in their homes, who were paying taxes sixty years. There was no fund for them to have money to be able to catch up on their bad taxes. Or to do some kind of amnesty or to be able to fix up their houses so they can get more value for their house you know.

Deborah Petersen summed up former D.C. mayor Adrian Fenty as an agent for "the agenda of the wealthy and the rich and the White pretty much." Some interlocutors accused Fenty of orchestrating a racialized transformation of D.C. by using the real estate development, zoning practices, schools, public sector jobs, and law enforcement to create an urban landscape that would attract and sustain a larger White presence in the District. The former mayor was such a lightning rod for the tensions that proliferated in the wake of heightened gentrification and the apprehensions that played out around the mayoral election that unseated him were so tangible that his primary opponent, former Councilman Vincent Gray, emphasized unity with his "One City" campaign slogan. Gray emerged as the victor following an election in which White residents overwhelmingly voted for Fenty (Schwartzman and Jenks, 2010).

Duke and West referenced the plans of both the Adrian Fenty and Anthony Williams administrations to bring in 100,000 new residents into Washington, D.C. Duke specifically mentioned programs that helped first-time home buyers purchase property. When I asserted that African Americans were just as able to avail themselves of these programs, the following exchange ensued:

> Duke: And there was a tax credit going on in the end of 1998 and 1998.
>
> West: And anyone could have taken advantage of that.
>
> Duke: But they didn't because Black people weren't getting educated. White people knew about it but Black people didn't know about it.
>
> Prince: How do people learn about things?
>
> Duke: They tell each other. They don't tell everybody. It stays within the classes and the races.

At the crux of the above exchange is hierarchies and the flow of strategic information through individual social networks. Two project participants, Asha Machel and Charles Potter, became property owners by participating in programs oriented toward helping moderate income, first-time home owners. Machel applied to the Neighborhood Assistance Corporation of America (NACA) and when I asked how she initially discovered the agency, she shared:

> My co-worker told me about it. What I found is a lot of the non-profit organizations who are charged with getting the information and processing

people for a lot of these government programs, they often—for maybe lack of resources or whatever—they just have difficulty getting the message to the people who can most take advantage of it. Now that being said, if you want to know and you say to yourself, "I want a home," you can find out. It's not hidden. It's just that homeownership, if you've never done it, like I'm a first-homeowner, so I qualified for several programs. My union helped me. They helped me with down payment money.

Machel said the assistance she received was invaluable but the process was arduous. Involvement with the program starts with first-time homeowner training. Machel described herself as a person who didn't hesitate to call the agency in search of clarification on any number of issues related to the extensive amount of paperwork she had to keep on top of, as well as numerous rules and regulations. She complained that her calls were frequently not returned and the counselors she spoke with during the preliminary stages often could not locate the information they needed to validate her identity.

On one particular occasion, after having put a contract on the condominium she currently owns, Machel called the agency for a random check-in with her counselor. She was shocked to be told that her NACA application for subsidized assistance was about to expire in a week. She shared with me the following to convey how the conversation with her counselor transpired:

> I said, "Yeah, but I already have my contract on my place." She said, "No, what I mean is next week it will expire. You will no longer qualify for HPAP, which meant I wouldn't have that $10,000 down payment, all that other stuff would go away. We did an emergency—all kinds of calling around

> Every time I would call the first housing organization that actually processes your application, they never knew who I was. I even talked to the director of their program because I was right in the crux, and I just wasn't getting anywhere. They would say, "Oh, it's gonna be another 30 days. We can't get you an appointment to get this certificate so you can go on." I just said, "I'm really feeling like I don't matter." I said, "I'm missing deadlines. I don't know what's going on. Every time I talk to somebody I have to start all over again with who I am, what I want." I said, "You all have my most intimate, private personal financial information, and you don't know who I am when I call?" I talked to like four or five different people.

Machel was also sympathetic about the limitations she surmised these organizations contended with as nonprofits. She described one representative as apologetic about the process being so cumbersome and difficult and Machel also attributed NACA's problems to the volume of applicants being processed. The organization requested feedback and Machel suggested they use a numbering or ID system. "I shouldn't have to repeat an entire page of information every time I call here," she conveyed to the counselor.

First-time homebuyer and second-generation Washingtonian Charles Potter also participated in the NACA program. He found out about it through a close personal friend who directs a nonprofit organization that assists people living with HIV and AIDS. Potter was very satisfied with his experience working with NACA and indicated he would recommend the program to anyone who wants to purchase a home for the first time. He and his partner purchased a three bedroom row house in Lamond Riggs, NE approximately three years ago. Potter said he liked the process because:

> They do preliminary budgeting with you. They are there for the long haul; it is not just a few weeks or a month and then they let you go. We were active in that program for at least 2 years; a least a year and a half. They look at your credit rating. They ask you; they have like forms and a process that helps you evaluate the size of the home you want. What you want out of your home in terms of bedrooms bathrooms etc. They provide an analysis of the market and how much it would cost to get the kind of home you want and then they instruct you financially about want you need to have in place in order to get the home you want. It's an excellent program.

Machel and Potter had drastically different takes on the process of working with NACA but aspects of their scenarios did overlap. Both individuals shared becoming first-time homeowners in their mid-fifties and each is currently employed in an administrative capacity in Washington, D.C. In addition, Machel and Potter also discovered the program through their connections to social networks that include middle-class professional people and other homeowners. "NACA operates by word of mouth," says Potter about how the information gets disseminated and he has helped spread the news among his social network. When I asked if he has told anyone else about it he responded, "Yes, my voice coach. He wants to get a condo close to the 14th/U Street corridor." It may be that the word of mouth emphasis severely limits the amount of participation of people who are in tremendous need for this key resource. Potter described the other assistance he and his partner received from the NACA program:

> Their arrangement is that they automatically give you a certain number of points below the current interest rate and they pay your closing costs. Whatever the interest rate is you are guaranteed you home mortgage rate would be a few points below

The organization offers this type of support in association with their work stabilizing communities and as a part of their advocacy for low-to-moderate income members of society. Potter elaborated on where the financial aid provided by NACA comes from:

> The reason why they are able to do that is because they have a direct pipeline to the money they had to pay due to predatory lending practices. Several

banks were found by the U.S. government to have practiced discriminatory lending practices ... either cutting people of color out. They had a billion dollar penalty that they had to pay and NACA is able to use that money. They have a relationship with the government to assist first time home owners. That is how they are able to get rid of your closing costs and get your points down. They are using that money up.

As he points out, the organization is able to offer what their website admittedly describes as a program that "sounds too good to be true"[4] because of groundbreaking litigation against banks found guilty of engaging in illegal practices that harmed working families. The same website provides a timeline of events, beginning in 1988, that set the stage for Signet, Fleet, First Union, and other lending institutions to provide billions of dollars to atone for their engagement in second mortgage scams, and charging steep interest rates, balloon payments, and other inflated fees.

"The government doesn't advertise," says Lolita Waymons, the ardent Democrat whose life-long political efforts have focused on training female leaders, getting women more actively involved in the Democratic Party, and advocating for vulnerable populations in the District. During our conversation she demonstrated a keen knowledge of party politics along with some narrow-minded views about Latinos and gay men and women. I asked what she thought about the availability of services working-class residents can take advantage of to help with pursuing home ownership. Waymons laughed in agreement at the view that this important information was being kept closely under wraps.

The most debated issue among interlocutors was not whether African Americans were experiencing dislocation in D.C., but whether displacement was forced or incidental. Tension between viewing these processes as intentional or inadvertent was pervasive. Another way to describe this is that some equivocated on the why but were adamant about the what – which was informed by their own observations.

The following dialogue was recorded during a women over 40 group interview and exemplifies a more radical and unequivocal use of language:

> Comment: ... basically we are at ... we're at a neo-colonial model now, whereby ... what is driving everyone is the economic imperative. And the economic imperative supersedes ... people are so fixated ... and this is the neo-colonial model.

> Response: Well I think it's ... it's a dual process... It think it's something more sinister than just the economic imperative ... cause there's also cultural imperialism where they take the essence of what you have and transform it and then sell it back to you? Is that integration?

Deborah Petersen also expressed specific views about the efforts she felt politicians were making to remove African Americans from the city. She pointed to the

---

4   https://www.naca.com/nacaWeb/about_naca/timeLine.aspx?language=undefined.

creation of the manager supervisory services (MSS) category among public sector employees as an attempt to decrease the number of African Americans among this cohort. Petersen says that advocates for this change:

> said that they were creating this in order to create accountability and to attract top rate managers into the district government, and so they created that. And they made it at will and authorized terminations with or without cause. Well the fact of the matter is that Fenty came in and Williams did a bit of it but not much. Not much for anybody to really raise hay over. Fenty came in and his administration fired people left and right that had nothing to do with their performance. Do you understand what I'm trying to say?

I asked Councilmember Tucker about Petersen's viewpoint and his response was:

> I don't know anything about it. I know that's happening at lots of agencies now, at-will. The reason—and to some degree I believe in it but you have to create a climate where people think you're being fair. I don't believe in last hired and first fired and all that. I don't believe seniority should be the number one thing to cause to keep a job. Seniority, that kind of policy can make you lazy. I do believe in at-will, but they have to have a good reason for letting you go. I don't think it's just to get rid of Blacks, I think it's getting rid of incompetent people.

As the differences between Petersen and Tucker show, viewpoints are individualized but connected through a critique of power. It has also been the case that a small number of political appointees who have been placed into key positions of power in D.C. government who are not African American. This is a notable shift from what became the norm after home rule was ushered in almost three decades ago and Blacks began to fill key city government posts. Given this history many African Americans have come to assume that other Blacks would head these important agencies particularly in a majority African American city.[5]

* * *

Of course this idea is not without its problems but the move away from majority-Black leadership has reinforced for many the notion that the city has been taken over by White outsiders. This suspicion is partly fueled by anti-White bigotry but it is also stoked by the distrust many from these African American communities hold for leaders perceived as responsible for the declining numbers of Blacks in the city.

---

5   As discussed in Chapter 4, and per interlocutor input, this ascendance of local African American leadership went part and parcel with the concept of Chocolate City. The idea grew as Blacks escaped the political and economic confines of Jim Crow and embraced the possibilities of greater opportunity and autonomy. Many of the women and men I spoke with said the CC concept was about a new-found pride.

Opposing views about competence and entitlement are intertwined in these discussions and further racialized. The belief that Blacks should predominate in all top positions in local governance is unrealistic at the outset and is made even more so given the rapidly changing demographics of Washington, D.C.

Housing, Gentrification, and Demographic Change

Housing is central to the scale and impact of gentrification. As Washington, D.C. has increased in population and reputation, the costs for housing have severely affected the needs of moderate to low income households. Remarkable statistics verify this change.

Research conducted by the D.C. Fiscal Policy Institute (DCFPI) has noted sharp increases in rents and house values since 2000 (Reed, 2012). During this period, half of low-cost rental units have been lost while the number of high-cost units has tripled. This is occurring at a time when the incomes for 40 percent of D.C. households have not kept pace with the cost of living (Reed, 2012). As a result, what the report refers to as "the typical low income D.C. renter" (p. 6) spends the majority of their income on housing. These are conditions that put a severe strain on households, perpetuating stress and preventing such residents from accumulating any surpluses.

Nowhere To Go (Lazere, 2010), another report issued by DCFPI, noted that a fifth of households in Washington were facing "severe housing cost burdens" that are yet to be abated. Increases in the provision of subsidized housing have not kept pace with the rising number of low-income residents in the District. Ironically, the dire indicators for low-income renters are being documented at the same time practices such as the eschewing of past architectural traditions by overturning The Heights of Buildings Act[6] and improving infrastructure to make the city more welcoming to middle and higher income residents are also taking place. Examples of the latter include establishing dog parks and bike paths along city streets.

Dominic Moulden is a housing activist who lives in the community of Shaw. Shaw has seen significant gentrification and Moulden spoke with me about the neighborhood's problems as he sees them unfold:

> There's a building several blocks from here called Washington Apartment. In one summer, the one-bedrooms went from $400 a month to $1,500 a month.

---

6   This Act, initially introduced to Congress in 1899, put limits on how tall newly-constructed buildings can be. These restrictions were based on safety concerns but local lore posits that such limits on the heights of new structures is related to the desire to not have other buildings exceed the height of such key local landmarks such as the Capitol Building and The Washington Monument. There are debates currently taking place between those who want to maintain the ceilings imposed by the Act and those who feel these thresholds are a hindrance to economic development.

Every week, almost every day, there was a new sign saying now they're renting for $500, now they're renting for $800, now they're renting for $900. Once they got to hit by $1,100, they took the sign down. Forty-two families got displaced from that development. But if you go down there, you won't see most the people of color, you'll see the new folks, but let's go down there five years from now see what it looks like. Or like in my block. I live around the corner. In my block, they've sold properties less than 1,100 square feet for $450,000 dollars. There was one property on my block for $800,000, and another for $600,000. So we're saying if our hard-working people, like in this neighborhood, the median income for people of color in this neighborhood is about $25,000 dollars. The median income of the new residents is about $52,000.

Policy implementation related to the conversion of apartment buildings to condominiums is another housing issue fostering Black vulnerability and outmigration in D.C. Approximately 32 years ago, members of the City Council wrote a law, under the leadership of David Clark and Hilda Mason, that was designed to protect renters. These laws made it mandatory for residents to determine, by majority vote, if they wanted their building to become a condominium. The law also stipulated that vacant buildings could be transformed without any consent required from residents for obvious reasons.

In relation to this law, a *Washington Post* investigative report (Cenziper and Cohen, 2008) found a huge number of tenant's rights violations coupled with deplorable rates of enforcement by the Department of Consumer and Regulatory Affairs (DCRA). Although the DCRA is responsible for the protection of renters in the District, the *Post* report found that the agency was not enforcing housing codes or responding to emergency complaints within 48 hours. DCRA was also failing to attend court hearings and collect fines from landlords who violate tenants' rights by stalling on repairs and other maintenance issues. The meager performance of the agency has resulted in huge profits for property owners. As residents flee from suspicious fires, rodent and insect infestations, power outages, and inadequate water and sewage conditions, buildings are renovated and converted into condominiums.

While households struggle economically, the budget current Mayor Vincent Gray has put forth at this writing calls for cuts in affordable housing and public assistance for low income residents of the District (D.C. Fiscal Policy Institute, 2012). These are proposed policies that portend to increase the vulnerability of residents from low to moderate income backgrounds. When households reach a threshold wherein they are no longer able to handle their economic burdens, foreclosure or eviction and homelessness ensues. Foreclosures in the District result in doubling-up in the homes, apartments, and rooms of friends and kin and, if these are not options, street and shelters.

Christine Elwell notes that turning to the outdoors is always the last resort for those who do not have a home (2008). In D.C. history "discrimination, gentrification and displacement stemming from the elimination of affordable housing contributed to the sudden appearance of large numbers of street dwellers"

(2008, p. 40). While homelessness already constitutes an increasing problem for D.C. households, shelters for the homeless have been targeted for closure by local authorities. The crises generated by a lack of intervention on affordable housing are broadly felt throughout communities. These conditions represent an implementation of neoliberal policies that privilege market-driven processes over protecting vulnerable populations.

Homelessness can be preceded by the loss of a home through foreclosure. An Urban Institute report sounds the alarm on rates in the District with a specific focus on the impact of residential instability upon the District's children. *Where Kids Go: The Foreclosure Crisis and Mobility in Washington, D.C.* indicates that children living in foreclosed buildings move more frequently and experience greater amounts of school switching, which has also been connected to poor academic performance and behavioral development (Comey and Grosz, 2011). This is particularly bad news for D.C. because foreclosure rates in this city, although fluctuating, are high (Comey and Grosz, 2011). The percentage of households that have been foreclosed upon after first receiving notice of intent to foreclose by banks has increased from 14 percent in 2005 to 44 percent in 2008 and this affected over a thousand students during that same year (NeighborhoodInfo DC, 2011). African Americans students have been disproportionately affected by foreclosures and Latino youth have not fared much better (Comey and Grosz, 2011).

The amount of suffering poor children experience in the District is occurring at the same time D.C. is being touted as a great American boomtown (Lowrey, 2013). As these shifts occur and additional changes are contemplated, the social indicators for working-class households lag and racial disparities continue to unfold. The large number of people not positioned to benefit from approaches to urban redevelopment that privilege the middle class points to the necessity for a long term, broad based response that emphasizes sustainability. Unfortunately, low-income households are not prioritized in this arrangement unless they are perpetuating violence or involved in other problematic or tragic events with consequences that bleed outside of their communities. Additionally troubling, proposed cuts in the mayor's budget that decrease services to the poor will, if passed, isolate this populace. When considered in combination with an erasure of the perspective of the poor from critical writings on gentrification this becomes even more problematic. An example of this is illustrated in the following excerpt from an Atlantic Monthly article on gentrification in Washington. In the piece its author discusses the end result of public housing demolition:

> That was reserved for SE, where the crime-ridden, rat-infested Capitol Gateway and Arthur Capper and Carrollsburg Dwellings housing projects were razed in 2005 an effort to break up concentrated poverty in the District and reduce crime. (It worked.)[7]

---

7   Franke-Ruta, Garance, The Politics of the Urban Comeback: Politics and Gentrification in Washington, D.C. *The Atlantic Monthly*, August, 2012.

I cannot gauge the writer's familiarity with the housing project she referred to in this quote but I am certain residents would not blithely dismiss their former neighborhood as "crime-ridden" and "rat-infested" nor concur that their dispersal and the simultaneous destruction of their community "worked." The perspectives of those most directly affected by gentrification should be taken into account in considerations of its affects.

Why Can't We All Just Get Along?

In a *City Paper* cover story, "A Guide for the Responsible Gentrifier," "little restaurants in Petworth [and] big Whole Foods stores in Logan Circle" are unequivocally marked as community amenities (Schaffer, 2012, p. 19). Although the article acknowledged some of the race-based economic disparities at work, much of it was written as if the author didn't know that the commercial needs and desires of young newcomers, who he congratulates for gentrifying the city, do not neatly coincide with those of long-term community members.

The number of *Yes* organic health food stores that have popped up in, Anacostia, Petworth, and Columbia Heights, for example, are no equals for the larger grocery stores that carried the familiar brands and more affordable foods that residents who do not reside in food deserts[8] have been familiar with. The Brookland *Yes* at 12th and Quincy Streets, NE, for example, is much smaller than the Safeway it replaced. Although the previous store sold a greater variety of items, nearby residents elders who no longer drive, like 87-year-old Nathaniel Potter, only purchases staples from *Yes* because it is the sole grocery store within walking distance of his home. When he can get a ride from a neighbor or one of his adult children, he can travel to the Giant on Michigan Avenue or the Giant on Riggs Road, NE.

It is a glaring race and place-related error to assume that the replacement of large and well-established grocery stores with small, upscale organic markets constitutes an improvement for the majority of residents. Although this option is better than no access to food and fresh vegetables at all, such stores are not ideal when considering the needs of the entire local populace – that is unless one subscribes to the belief that the low income, elderly, and uninitiated should simply adjust to the broader ramifications of demographic change by familiarizing themselves with the food preparation and consumption habits that will make the products being offered in upscale food stores more appealing.

Samuel Hallowell expressed concern that this is an ideological, public health-related trend in the United States that is fueled by the resentment of obese, low

---

8   Food deserts are areas where residents do not have good access to affordable foods that are necessary for maintaining a healthy diet. Residing in food deserts contribute to chronic disease according to the Center for Disease Control. See http://www.cdc.gov/features/fooddeserts/ for additional discussion of this issue.

income people. Sizism is a common form of prejudice and obesity rates are higher among African Americans. It is likely the combined impact of these two factors have shaped the perspective of this interlocutor (Farrell, 2011).

To further contextualize in relation to consumption, intra-racial social variables such as age, class, and place of origin differentiate tastes and habits. Consequently there are instances where middle-class Blacks may appreciate certain commodities not desired by working class African Americans. It has also been observed that members of the White middle class all too often view themselves through an ideological prism that renders their palates and penchants as universal (Bonilla-Silva, Goar, and Embrick, 2006).

It should shock no one that communities facing gentrification are not encouraged by ideas and policy implementations that ignore their needs, unique experiences, and identities. These are not new developments—populations have seen these attitudes before. We can harken back decades to the displacement of thousands through urban renewal in SW or step back a few years to consider the hundreds dislocated through HOPE VI Federal Housing Program demolitions. The record of multicultural experiences shows that the perspectives of the vulnerable are not always taken into consideration so the historical record must be attended to before a full analysis can occur. Where communities are labeled as crime-ridden and dilapidated, residents use different terms to describe their home places. These opposing points of view illustrate the connections between authorized structural changes that cost people their homes on the one hand, and ideas about people and places that are shared by policy makers and gentrifying populations on the other.

Some stories of interpersonal conflict involve micro-aggressions around issues of greeting or respecting neighbors as seen in the example of the elder African-Caribbean woman's complaint from this chapter's opening. I heard other examples reflecting these types of grievances. During my visit with Duke and West I heard a humorous tale about their new, next door neighbor and how his practice of ignoring the couple came to a head one summer afternoon. West described a scenario in which she was puttering about in her small backyard garden at the same time her White, male neighbor was working on his vehicle. He was crouched and out of her line of vision as he worked on the car which was parked in their alley behind their homes. His housemate came out into the backyard as West recalled, saw her but did not acknowledge her presence as was his usual practice. When the neighbor behind his car engaged his housemate in conversation by making disparaging remarks about African Americans, the man who was standing turned to looked at West with an embarrassed expression. We laughed heartily as she described returning his sheepish expression with a shrug of her shoulders and a look that implied a clichéd combination of *what are you going to do* and *that's the way the cookie crumbles*. She then explained to me why she responded as she did:

> I don't want you to think that you can live next door in a pretend world that
> I don't know what is really going on here and it is OK because I can tell you
> somebody is trying to break into your house, I can tell you your house in on fire,

I don't care if you don't like me I will still do it but you know what he was not ready for that. Ha ha ha

The women laughed off the insult but the take away is that too many new residents show their hostility by snubbing the working class and residents of color in gentrifying neighborhoods. My discussion with Duke and West revealed their sense of what it means to be neighborly. This was based on a foundation of mutual respect or, at the very least, acknowledgement but the couple also believed that members of the same community can be helpful to each other.

I recorded additional cases that stemmed from African Americans' concerns about gentrification threatening their way of life. Edna Simmons had a few examples of this being an issue in her NW community vis-à-vis what she described as a penchant for newcomers to align and conspire to remake neighborhoods. As a resident of a predominantly African American neighborhood composed of stately homes near Rock Creek Park, Simmons described her community as one in which, in the past, everyone "got along." Throughout our conversation, she pointed in the directions of the homes of the various neighbors she has known for a long time. In doing so, she mentioned single women of various racial/ethnic backgrounds, an interracial couple, and a White gay man whose porch she would sit, laugh, and have a cocktail or two with. The picture she painted contrasted significantly with what has transpired with the recent trends in demographic change.

Simmons described conflicts that arose between newcomers and long- term residents which escalated in one instance and resulted in the police were called and a neighbor being arrested on Mother's Day. Tensions on the block were first fomented around the violation of a tacit consensus about the use of parking space on the block. Simmons told me:

> There's some understood things when you come into a neighborhood. There's some things that are understood. If the neighborhood is accustomed to everybody parking in front of their own homes then that's what you do.

When one newcomer, a young White female, began parking in front of the homes of an elderly and an infirmed neighbor's house, agitation ensued. Simmons engaged the "culprit" and reported to me that:

> She moved it, kind of, [*sic*] ugh ... it's a public street and then she says, I'm not even adhering to that. I said, *****, this is what has worked for this neighborhood and nobody has a problem with it but you. You need to do what the rest of the neighbors do. And it protects your space in front of your house. But she just decided that it's a free country and a free street and all that kind of stuff

The new neighbor later relented and moved her car but this became an issue later when a different neighbor had her hip replaced. Simmons, who was block captain for many years, had to tell her "don't park in front of, in ***** space. We've got plenty of spaces. There are plenty of spaces for you able-bodied people who can walk to get to your house."

Simmons conveyed other examples of interactions that were more directly racialized and galling. Donna Stetson, another White female newcomer, used poor judgment very early in her arrival to the neighborhood, by commenting to Simmons that the neighbors should be grateful to Stetson for renovating her home and raising the property values on the block. Stetson then began complaining about the music her next door neighbor Karen Oliphant's teenage daughter played as she cleaned her room on Saturday afternoons. Oliphant had lived there for over 30 years, and she and her daughter Ebony, who Simmons described as the community baby, were loved by their neighbors. Simmons described Oliphant as approachable, intelligent, and loud. "It's a cultural thing," Simmons stated in her description of the working-class family who inherited the home from grandparents. The conflict began because Stetson:

> Would knock on Oliphant's door and say, could you ask your daughter to turn her music down ... but first of all, you don't ask somebody with a house full of teenagers to turn their music down on Saturday afternoon.

Stetson felt differently about this and went as far as to offer Ebony an iPod so her music could be listened to quietly. After knocking on the door a few weekends in a row, Stetson shared her view with a White resident close to Simmons that Ebony and her mother were "ghetto elements" that did not belong in this community. Around this same time Oliphant summarily cursed out Stetson and told Stetson not to ever come on her front porch again. In the weeks that followed this confrontation, Oliphant was handcuffed and taken away on Mother's Day because Stetson and another White newcomer on the block neighbor told the police they felt threatened by Oliphant. Simmons said she confronted Stetson about her behavior and shared:

> She said, well I didn't know it was going to go that far. I said, where did you think it was going to go?

> She was telling her, the officer, she did threaten me. I said, what did she say she was going to do? She said, I was afraid for my children. I said, ****** has never did anything about your children. She's a child-person. She would never do anything to your kids. I said a lot of this is cultural but because you think your way is the right way, you didn't even want to bother to come to me, who you have an open conversation, who you have open dialog with, to find out how to handle it. But she walked and knocked on her door. It wasn't vice versa. That's like the Trayvon Martin thing, it's like you can't say you're defending yourself when you want to screw with someone. I know. So that's the story that happened in this neighborhood.

Simmons said the arrest angered members of what had purportedly been a tight-knit community. She also reported that Stetson called child services after having Oliphant arrested and reported there were unsupervised, underage children in the home, not knowing that the children's grandmother was also a resident of the household.

Simmons' assessment was that Stetson was an arrogant usurper who had no real desire to become a neighbor because she just wanted to quickly renovate and resell the house; a practice known as "flipping". Making matters worse, because Stetson did not view members of the Oliphant family as her equals, she did not make any credible attempts to resolve her conflict with this family. Simmons characterized this behavior as a display of Whiteness in the racialized conceit and lack of consideration Stetson and her ally showed for what would happen to Oliphant with their involvement of law enforcement.

Oliphant was an immigrant from the Caribbean. She has had legal run-ins with immigration services because of the charges brought against her, but, in time, and with added expense, these matters were straightened out. Stetson incurred the wrath of her neighbors and eventually moved away. Race and class played obviously roles in fomenting this dispute between households. Labeling a person and/or place as ghetto is code for Black and poor, and flipping properties is a practice associated with the upwardly mobile. The concept of a moral geography, applied in another ethnography of Washington, D.C., is also analytically relevant (Modan, 2007). In this instance Simmons attempted to reinforce the idea that belonging to this community was about adhering to what had been deemed traditionally acceptable by neighbors, showing concern for the well-being of those living among them.

Another way whiteness was invoked by those who viewed gentrification unfavorably was through the labeling of these processes as colonization. Simmons' critique carried this implication and while the colonizer description may reflect a degree of racial generalization for some, in other instances this description resulted from what many long-time residents saw as a dishonoring of community history and the ideological monopolization of community needs.

There were other examples of this specific problem that came to my attention in the field. Columbia Heights resident Morgan Shackleford and anthropologist Kalfani Ture both spoke of mural wars being waged in connection with gentrification in different parts of D.C. Ture was completing his ethnography on a SE neighborhood and imparted the following on the significance of murals and other forms of art in gentrifying neighborhoods and some of the contradictory processes that are currently taking place:

> There is this introduction of what might appear to be sort of socially critical art, but at the same time there is this erasure of art that the indigenous folk are used to seeing and are familiar with, the indigenous expressions that, at least cultural expressions, that sort of portray their life and their community life. These were cultural markers for these people.

I remember somebody saying when they went by the Uniontown Bar & Grill saying, "Oh, that used to be such-and-such shop, and man, whatever happened to that mural?" Obviously the mural was painted, and they're aware that it was painted, but they're sort of letting you know that this used to be a different space. I think in that question it also suggests it's registering some disorientation to this sort of new space that's happening.

Further exploring paradoxes Ture discussed the significance of expurgation:

There is this erasure of sort of the indigenous expressions, and there is this denial, on the other hand, of indigenous expressions. There's erasure of what exists, but then there's also a denial of sort of recognizing what's there on the sort of off-beaten path like the memorials and the graffiti and stuff like that as being sort of legitimate, as being authentic, and certainly is not part of how we're marketing the area.

Related examples are cases where new, White residents attempt to drive out African American businesses that are not seen as appropriate or upscale enough to belong in changing neighborhoods (Schwartzman, 2006). A *Washington Post* article focused in on the vagaries of race, class, and interpersonal relations in another community hit by the 1968 riots (Brown, 2007). Along the H Street corridor in NE, in another rapidly gentrifying area, the mere existence of a Black-run, Cluck U Chicken restaurant caused an African American business owner to become besieged by views and apprehensions normally seething just beneath the surface. The author of the piece wrote that:

Change bringing with it newcomers, who want to fix things, change them into their own image. Bringing issues: stratification, generalizations, classism, police presence, rising rent, rising taxes, two-way streets becoming one-way, an invisible squeeze on loiterers, pushing them gently but insistently until they are no more. And the new neighbors push for a "quality of life" ban on single-sell alcohol, and the request turns into a discussion about race. And someone is complaining about Cluck-U Chicken, arguing it was not the kind of sit down restaurant they wanted. Some neighbors say war has been declared on Black Washington.

This is the same article in which a then 27-year-old African American bartender Courtney Rae Rawls recounted being held back from assaulting a White patron who became irate after hearing Rawls repeatedly warn young White patrons to stop writing on the table. The patron became annoyed and yelled, directing her comment at the young Black waitress "You ought to be glad I bought a $500,000 house in your Black ghetto neighborhood" (2007). Shades of what Simmons encountered on her street by Stetson, the newcomer who similarly commented she is contributing to the neighborhood by her mere presence. Ironically, the majority of the people on their block did not view Stetson as an asset to the community she apparently sided against.

A similar comment was made by Donna Petersen, whose friend complained about a White neighbor's audacity to walk across the street to discuss how the African American person's home was in need of improvement or out of code in some way. This is starkly divergent from what Edna Simmons has observed taking place. She described a scenario which unfolded in her middle-class and predominantly Black neighborhood, that involved her White and male next-door neighbor. He avoided being fined for not conforming to regulations governing his home renovations, even though an unsightly tarp partially covered his roof for weeks and incessantly irked his neighbors. Although the neighbor took what Simmons and others on the street considered a long time to complete exterior improvements to his home, no one made a formal complaint against him. Simmons maintained:

> If he had lived in a White neighborhood, they would have fined him by now. Now, I'm serious because Black people don't call the po-po [police]. You understand? We don't call the po-po on that kind of stuff because we know that the po-po comes then everybody is subject to deal with, got to deal with the po-po ... so the Black lady across the street, down the street, who can't afford to get her house fixed because the back of her house is like it's falling off.. So, they take advantage of that benevolence ... because he would never, they would never get away with that on Capitol Hill or ... or anywhere like that.

I came across additional examples that conveyed a divide that did not bode well for the promise of cross-cultural understandings in gentrifying neighborhoods. Although these findings were not quantified, these ethnographic findings remain invaluable grassroots indicators. That being said, neither tenuousness nor vitriol encompassed the entire story of Black/White relations in changing, D.C. communities. Despite the stories of conflict that she related, Simmons reported having great relationships with the minority of White neighbors who were not new to the community. Templeton had similar comments to make about the long-term White residents she knew in Brookland and these are data that beg questions for future research. What are the myriad analytical and experiential processes that differentiate relations across class and race? What is the impact of political—economic context upon these developments, and how conscious are residents of underlying tensions and their potential to emerge in day-to-day interactions?

The next chapter examines the work of activists who are lending a hand to populations adversely affected by gentrification. In the process of carrying out community work some of these folks are also bringing to light ideas and practices that are at the forefront of the battle for social justice and cross cultural understandings in D.C.

Gentrification and the Intra-racial Interplay of Race and Class

Socioeconomic differentiation within African American communities has been a component to Black life in the U.S. from the outset. There is an extensive body of literature that shows how class has altered the ways African Americans experience their racialized lives and how race differentiates the ways populations of various socioeconomic strata experience their status (Feagin and Sikes, 1995; Royster, 2003).[9] Complexities notwithstanding, I approached this project with the belief that households headed by African American professionals would have more housing options available to them than those of the poor due to dissimilarities in income and assets.

While gentrification is rooted in the flow of money, resources, and people stemming from class inequality, it remains almost impossible to disentangle discussions of economics and social relations from those on race and ethnicity in the this country. The interplay of these and other variables creates a panoply of statuses, standpoints, and experiences that resist being separated into neat categories. In other words, there are gradations and that was apparent in the discoveries I made while talking with people and collecting the data for this book.

Areas of nuance undermine misconceptions about race, class, and gentrification. For example, African Americans are also engaged in processes of demographic change as gentrifiers. Some of these women and men are newcomers, but others are natives, or individuals who have lived in D.C. for decades like Bernadette Thomas who resides in Eckington. Native Washingtonian Brenda Duke bought in Columbia Heights during the late 1980s when very few of her neighbors were college-educated professionals.

A section of the city that has seen concerted inroads in African American gentrification has been the community of Anacostia. Anacostia owes its name to the indigenous peoples who first called this area home (Humphrey and Chambers, 1977). The area is located east of the river with which it shares a name and although gentrification is taking place with more racial homogeneity in Anacostia, population shifts there have not been without controversy.

The *Washington City Paper* published a cover story entitled "East of the River or River East" that looked at some of the contemporary outcomes of gentrification in Anacostia of SE Washington (Lewis, 2010). Contrasted against what has transpired in other parts of D.C., its author writes that Anacostia is one of the final frontiers for gentrification. The area is geographically set apart by a river and has been stigmatized due to comparatively higher rates of poverty and unemployment

---

9 Space doesn't allow a thorough citation of the extensive list of useful references on the specific subject of how race and class differentiates the ways African Americans experience their socioeconomic status and racialized selves so only an abbreviated list of the sources available to researchers is offered here. These two books I refer to look at the experiences of the Black middle class and African American male workers in the skilled trades respectively.

that plague much of Wards 7 and 8. Less focused on, Anacostia is also affected by environmental racism and the negative health indicators associated with this (Williams, 2001).

Anacostia appears to be the primary site for African American gentrification because so many other areas have become cost prohibitive to purchase into. Although the area's mainstream reputation has been built around negative themes, its core populace has always consisted of working and middle-class residents who care about their community. Anacostia is also attractive to those who appreciate its quiet, apartness, and housing that holds the potential to shine in instances where good bones are in need of renovation.

Anacostia was 94 percent African American in 2010[10] and given this statistic it should not be surprising to know that skirmishes around gentrification are not strictly oriented along racial lines. The author of the *City Paper* piece says that:

> battles in Wards 7 and 8 break down largely along class and generational lines: a set of ambitious and largely Black newcomers versus a Black working class that abhors high-priced condos and new urbanist branding schemes.

The phrase *new urbanist branding schemes* in the quote above refers to the practice of renaming the area. Communities located across the Anacostia River have been commonly referred to as existing "east of the river." In his piece, Lewis writes about the movement of some African American gentrifiers to foster an unsullied image of Anacostia by rebranding the area with the new moniker River East (2010). The article was written when Lewis was an undergraduate attending American University. His piece resulted in a flurry of angry emails and Internet postings. Readers took issue with the way it portrayed Black professional gentrifiers as insensitive usurpers and accusations about Lewis taking people out of context and being unaware of the facts were heard in the weeks following publication of his piece.

Lewis' piece raised questions about cross-class tensions among Black people and this is a subject African Americans are still learning to have meaningful conversations about. Complexities were found in the views of professional people who critiqued gentrification but offered unique perspectives on what they found essentially problematic about urban restructuring. That is what I gleaned from comments made by Edna Simmons, who told me:

> And sometimes, and I'm not mad about gentrification because gentrification does bring, on some level I am, but it does bring resources to the area. But, that's the shame of it, to me. That White folks have to be here before they'll put resources into a neighborhood. That's the way I see it.

This same perspective was echoed over and over. More examples came from Lorraine West a self-employed visual artist, who said:

---

10   http://www.neighborhoodinfodc.org/wards/nbr_prof_wrd8.html#sec_1_race.

The biggest impact that I have seen city services have [*sic*] on every corner on instead of a liquor store there is a restaurant. And the difference is that maybe I don't have as many parking spaces, but on the other hand I do like taking my client up to the restaurant on the corner. So there is a good side and a bad side to it.

Class is apparent in this description above. West has clients to amass and impress as well as the discretionary income to patronize the new watering holes that have popped up. The analyses shared by these women reveal a sophisticated understanding of race, place, economics, and history. They grasp the contradictions and the macroeconomic requirements but do not want to push the working class and vulnerable under the bus of urban development.

Mixed feelings were not only expressed from middle class African Americans. Asha Machel describes herself as a member of the working class. She is also a former teen mother with two adult daughters and the proud grandmother of three. She earns a moderate income and because she obtained a Master's degree from the University of the District of Columbia (UDC) last year I would describe her as upwardly mobile. Machel has also made key sacrifices and meticulous plans to arrive at this point and getting here was not by way of a smooth path. Her viewpoints are forged at the interstices of the harrowing gendered, raced and classed challenges of her past including work experiences ranging from office support staff to a researcher of contemporary urban redevelopment and change at UDC.

She expressed the following sentiments about gentrification in Washington, D.C.:

I would define it as a class of people who have the means to go anywhere they want, and absolutely transform it. They have the resources to purchase quality homes at a low price. They have the ability to sit on their assets and their money so that when those opportunities come they can jump on it. Which I mean is buy low and sell high. They will watch a neighborhood that's gone to pieces, but they might see something that's really valuable. One thing that's valuable is living in a city. Not using fossil fuels and cars to drive to and from work hours on end. Being in the city next to culture.

If you're a privileged person and you want that you can take it, and you can take this person's house, that person's house, and you can do it through several ways. You can do it by limiting other people's access to things. You go after some of the strong pieces of that community. Maybe it's the church, maybe it's another institution. You actually increase the value of your house just by mere fact that you increasing the value of the house, you might have a couple of homeowners, but then their taxes go up, and then they're strapped. You're dealing with people with different resources. They just don't have the resources to keep up. That's how I see it.

Project participants raised the issue of how African American socioeconomic differentiation contributed to gentrification and demographic change in indirect ways – not just in response to specific questions about intra-racial hierarchies among Blacks in D.C. For example, when I asked David Robinson what he thought D.C. would look like in the future given the current pace of change, he said middle-class Blacks would fare fine. Robinson also attributed the suffering of the more vulnerable among African Americans to intra-racial selfishness. He said, "In the next 10 to 20 years look for more of the same with a smattering of young Black professionals moving in with having Obama in the White House. But for some reasons some Black folks don't like to spread the wealth; they say 'I got mine … you get yours' … sad commentary on our race."

Machel came to the District during her teen years and early on she discovered that calling carbonated drinks pop instead of soda wasn't the only difference she encountered after making D.C. her home. During one conversation we had in her Brightwood condominium I asked for an elaboration on the impact of African American class differences in Washington as she sees it. She he admitted that Black Washingtonians always seemed stuffy to her. In her response were echoes of Gatewood (1990) and Higgenbotham (1993) on the politics of respectability:

> That's a really touchy subject, because Washington DC, to me —cause you know I wasn't born here—has always—I've always sensed and seen and have experienced a very strong conservative Black middle class, whose ideas may have been more similar to White middle class. When I say ideas I mean what they thought was proper. For example, loud talking is, oh, no—they're conservative, they wanna live a certain way. You have to be dressed a certain way all the time. A lot of them were very educated.

> This new wave of gentrification, I see it a couple of ways. I see people pointing to them and saying that we don't need to [*sic*] anything. We don't need to address issues of race because, as you can see, these guys are doing exactly what we do, so there is no racial issue here. It's an issue of class. Well, if they can do it then you can do it, and isn't it better for everybody if the entire—what's wrong with people trying to improve the values of their homes? What's wrong with them trying to live the way they want to live? That's true, but do you just dump your people who don't have anything? What do you with them? Or do you care? That's the question I have.

Reading between the lines, Machel sees a connection between African American class differentiation and the promotion of gentrification by policy makers. Her words also summarize the quintessential social justice concerns this book centers upon.

This chapter looked at the intersections, nuances, and contradictions associated with interactions within and across race and class boundaries. Generally, interlocutors agree that gentrification is unfair and problematic even if they saw conveniences associated with the shifts. There were also varied opinions on what was causing gentrification to occur and who the changes benefit.

The final data chapter uses information I gathered while participant observing with advocacy groups in D.C. Chapter six examines the ideas embraced collectively by the members of two organizations working to empower and assist vulnerable D.C. residents. In addition to showing some of the connections between individual and group stances, it also reveals that new forms of inequality and innovative ways to fight against unfairness emerge where neoliberalism intersects with the unfairness of class and race-based disparities.

Chapter 6
Race, Class, and the Dynamics of Collective Responses to Gentrification

Collective responses to gentrification are just as wide-ranging as those uttered and acted out by individuals. This chapter turns its attention to my experiences observing and collaborating with members of community-based organizations in Washington, D.C. Data on the strategies and ideas activists utilize and express when mobilizing support for people threatened by gentrification offer important evidence of the harm these changes cause. These impacts can be seen at the grassroots level and include sadness, displacement, alienation, homelessness, and even death.

The ideas, actions, and goals of two groups are represented by some of the individuals who compose their membership. By looking at the work of organizations operating in two different quadrants of the city and considering their strategies, goals, and challenges, we can learn about race, class, community, and the future of a city facing massive urban restructuring. This chapter explores related questions and concerns.

The Homesteaders Action Committee

The performance ended and, once again, a D.C. audience was left riveted as the slight and unassuming Zahira Kahlo took her bows, switched gears, and began to address those present as her earnest self rather than the assortment of identities she assumes in her one-woman play about urban dislocation in Washington, D.C. As mandated by the humanities grant funding this event, I was introduced by Kahlo and followed her on stage after she thanked the people who helped make the evening possible. Indeed, bringing this production of *The Homes* to fruition required a coming together of a few disparate entities.

This particular performance, and four others that took place in different locations across the District, was funded by the Humanities Council of Washington, D.C.[1] The grant and the modest production it supported all stemmed from Kahlo's work with the Homestead Action Committee (HAC). The HAC was a collective formed

---

1   The Humanities Council of Washinton, D.C. is a local organization that is supported through the Mayor's budget. It funds such projects that enhance understanding of D.C. history and culture. I have been a selected as Humanities Scholar on three distinct community-based research projects. In the case of *The Home*, funding was awarded to the head of an African American-run theater company because eligibility applies to an organization and not individuals.

under the co-leadership of native-born Washingtonian, Mu-Tem-Uwa and other activists who lived at former SE public housing complex The Homestead Houses before it was demolished through the federal government's Housing Opportunities for People Everywhere (HOPE VI) program.[2]

Administered by the Housing and Urban Development agency (HUD), the stated goal of HOPE VI was to come to the aid of municipalities and their management of public housing properties by providing agencies with funds to purchase sites for new construction. Funds could also be directed toward the eradication or rehabilitation of existing public housing. Monetary awards could also be used to assist people who faced relocation because their residences were being renovated or destroyed.[3] One of the selling points of the program is its promise to create a mixed-income community where people of different socioeconomic backgrounds will be able to live together and share a host of neighborhood conveniences.

The selling, implementation, and impact of HOPE VI have been complicated affairs. Most people prefer to live in safe, clean, and spacious housing. It is not surprising, then, to witness low-income residents showing enthusiasm at the promise of having their domiciles extensively improved. Residents of The Homestead Houses were no different in this regard. Many also shared a robust appreciation for the positive characteristics of their neighborhood that too often go unrecognized by people who live outside of low-income communities.

Where advocates for gentrification see only blight, crime, and danger, former residents describe Homestead as a place where important social relationships were maintained. I can already hear the scoffs that this borders on a cliché romanticizing of the poor but I heard similar expressions of neighborly support and community involvement in the field and observed examples of it too. I also did lengthy, open-ended interviews with two former residents of The Homestead Houses who discussed appreciating their old community. They described the priceless value knowing neighbors having them looking out for each other amounted to.

Robin Jeffries is another founding member of the HAC. Together with Mu-Tem-Uwa the two women recounted the story of Miss Rose, an elderly woman in their complex facing eviction, to explain how residents would rally to support neighbors in need:

---

2   I do not use the actual names of this housing complex or the activists discussed in this chapter. Kahlo gave me permission to use her real name but I declined her offer. I explained to her that making what efforts I could to maintain her anonymity would loosen any constraints which may prevent her and those she has associated with over the years from speaking candidly. Confidentiality may also shield her from inadvertently damaging some of her relationships as well.

3   http://portal.hud.gov/hudportal/HUD?src=/program_offices/public_indian_housing/programs/ph/hope6/about.

Robin Jeffries: We had an incident where the lady was getting ready to get put out of her home. Well, everybody in the community refused for her to get put out of her place. They had the truck out there.

Mu-Tem-Uwa: Yep, we found out this evening, and we found out she was gonna move tomorrow. Next I know, everybody was on the phone. They said they gonna be out there. People come evict you before the morning. Eight or nine in the morning, the drug dealers across the street was lined up. Our social service support agencies came. Me and Miss Rose was there. Afternoon, we were posting up in front of the house there.

Robin Jeffries: My grandbaby, I had my grandbaby. I said, "Ain't nobody coming in here until we find out what's going on." I go into her house, now just find out her son's locked up. Now, she has a stack of Oodles of Noodles on her table, and that's all she's eating. Guess what? They check on her.

Every day one of them fellas—"Miss Rose, you alright? You need something from the store? What you need?" They don't ask her for no money. They go in their pocket and they help this lady. When we found out that she was getting ready to get evicted, guess what? She had the money. She had the checks, but didn't know who to pay the checks to because her son—

Mu-Tem-Uwa: Her son used to do it.

Robin Jeffries: was locked up.

Miss Rose was eventually relocated by HUD but in the process she lost the protective social networks that filled the gap in seeing to her needs. In the weeks following the move her dead body was discovered. The elderly woman had passed away alone and in a community that was foreign to her. She was an elder and her passing could have come at any time. With her son incarcerated and no acquaintances nearby to look in on her, procure medicines and groceries, or meet the other needs she may have had, Miss Rose's body went undiscovered for three days until neighbors complained about the stench. The manner in which this former member of their community died symbolized the powerlessness and neglect associated with the unraveling of their community and the dispossession left in its wake.

HOPE VI did away with the continuity so many valued and sought. When housing authorities were advocating for the program, residents had a simmering suspicion that all of their neighbors would not be easily incorporated into the new, mixed-income community. The dubious among residents were not surprised by the problems that arose in relocating residents who were promised with the right to return. This wariness and concern prompted residents to organize and form HAC in order to monitor outcomes and ensure that the many promises made by HUD and the D.C. Housing Commissioner's office would be kept. Their motto became "400 out, 400 in," an echo of the reassurances given by local officials that all displaced residents would be welcomed back into the new and improved properties that would replace their previous homes.

The provision of inadequate amounts of space for "temporarily displaced" families and the placement of residents into communities where they felt unsafe and/or cut off from their social networks were among the problems associated with transitioning occupants into the housing that would become their homes during the period of renovation. Miss Rose's outcome, however, stressed that the realities of the life cycle predetermined some of the elderly residents would no longer be alive at the end of reconstruction.

Residents complained when barriers to their relocation discovered in the fine print became apparent. Hindrances to taking up residence in the new mixed income community included limits connected to poor credit or the arrest records of children, grandchildren, and other family members. Residents began concluding that proponents of HOPE VI exaggerated the ease with which they would become reincorporated in order to minimize the amount of resistance they would receive from the community.

After The Homestead Homes were totally demolished, housing was built for low-income seniors at the Navy Yard. Of the remaining majority of residents, Robin Jeffries was the first and, for quite a while, only low-income former resident to realize what was promised by the officials promoting the HOPE VI program and the return to the neighborhood. Jeffries became a seasoned activist by advocating for herself and her neighbors. At the time of writing, she and her close and equally savvy friend, Mu-Tem-Uwa, are reaping the rewards of being optimistic, exceptional, diligent, and lucky self-advocates.

Through displacement these women have learned how to make full use of the resources local and federal governmental agencies have in place to help low-income people find affordable housing. At the same time they also lament the onerousness of the process and the difficulty other low-income residents will have attempting to model their actions. While Jeffries and Mu-Tem-Uwa were both persistent and fortunate, their triumphs point to another problem: Residents should not have to be extraordinary to acquire affordable housing. However, the experiences of Jeffries and Mu-Tem-Uwa show that the search for affordable housing for low-income residents is rife with unfairness and instability.

One of the barriers these employed, low-income women discussed was a lack of transparency on the part of the administrators and developers charged with transitioning dislocated residents into new housing. This was a complaint I also heard from advocates for Ivy City residents. In both cases, residents discerned authorities' proclivity toward skirting the requirements that housing activists and sympathetic elected officials fought for years earlier. These are obligations that compel agencies and developers to keep affected populations informed by holding a requisite number of information sessions that detail anticipated impacts and allow residents to have their questions answered. These mandatory meetings were intended to empower communities but HAC members noted passive-aggressive instances of noncompliance acted out through small attempts to minimize information-session attendance. Holding meetings when most residents were working or offering late notice to meetings negatively affected the ability of wage workers to attend and limited any opposition policymakers might have to contend with.

Without flexibility at work, Jeffries' ability to meet the conditions for incorporation into the redeveloped property was dependent on the kindness of a supervisor and the fortuitous support of family and friends. It was a huge challenge but because of the breaks and bits of assistance she received, Jeffries did not have to jeopardize her employment in order to fulfill the many requirements. There was an abundance of paperwork that had to be received in the mail, completed, and returned in a timely fashion. These bureaucratic hurdles would pose serious difficulty for individuals with tenuous housing and shifting addresses.

Mu-Tem-Uwa discussed another problem confronted by former Homestead residents. The implementation of an income-based cost scale for the Homestead replacement housing was designed to put builders in compliance with the mixed housing mandate. Dislocated residents earning $25,000-$30,000 annually were told they could purchase one- and two-bedroom units at below-market rates when construction was finished. Mu-Tem-Uwa shared what ultimately transpired but to set the stage, she first stated:

> Let's call it working poor because the structure they did set up for us was - you would be able to purchase. We have money set aside, lots of pots, DC first-time homebuyers, HPAP money. Nobody touches HPAP money, you have to be special, special to get, HPAP money, and then whatever your income was. So they gave us some structures at that time the numbers were a whole lot smaller when we moved out, but if you were making up to $25,000 you'd be able to afford to buy a unit.

> We since come in to discover what a tall tale that was as a function of the way the market changed. Although we heard from people that—from other developments, that when we first got in we were able to buy a two bedroom for $150,000, the first ones on the list. Then two years later they went to $200,000; three years later they're $400,000.

It seemed that the market was determining the prices rather than the agreement set in place by HOPE VI administrators. Mu-Tem-Uwa then took a number of forward and backward steps on her journey to obtaining a unit in a new and upscale building located close to her former home and just a stone's throw from the D.C. baseball team's Nationals Stadium. The building has complimentary Wi-Fi, free weekly yoga lessons, proximity to public transportation, restaurants, and entertainment. She talked about the pressure she experienced to use the dislocation housing voucher she received before it expired. Before moving into this building Mu-Tem-Uwa was living with her adult daughter and grandson in Bloomingdale. Her daughter's plans to move to Atlanta jeopardized Mu-Tem-Uwa's ability to pay her rent so she began searching for more affordable options, having already experienced multiple eviction notices and landlord evasion. It was her daughter who heard about the new building before construction was complete. As Mu-Tem-Uwa says:

> I came and checked, and looked, and got the tour, and saw the stuff and saw that this developer here, Forest City, had a commitment to subsidized housing. So much so, I found out later, that even clauses in the lease even have—those spaces would say we pay a lease, or if you are an affordable housing client. They had a commitment to do part of this development as affordable housing, subsidized housing units. There is also a D.C. law that very seldom gets enforced that says if you have new development ... some percentage has to be affordable housing.

Mu-Tem-Uwa capitalized on inclusionary zoning and described her success obtaining the unit as heavily dependent upon her networking skills and the contacts she had made over the years as a seasoned activist. The lengthy excerpt below is presented to document the extent to which she worked within the system to gain decent, affordable housing:

> I'm looking, I'm doing, I'm scrambling. Then, I'm reminded as I'm talking to everybody now; I'm talking to Housing Authority folks, and they're saying why aren't you coming back. I'm saying bah, bah, bah, but still keeping my fingers in quarterly meetings that they're having, still advocating for residents. Still making sure that they're choosing only returning residents to come back to that property. Then one of the directors of the program, the housing phase, said, "Oh, you know, Ms. ***** Forrest City owns that property:" I'm like, "Oh, okay."
>
> I'm remembering some of the boards and the meetings we've been on, and they've mentioned to me, like I know that the builder at EYA and the Forrest City builder, we've been in negotiations. They say, "Oh, they remember you." I'm like, "Okay." I made a call up to the head dog, to the big guy, and said, "You remember me, I'm *****." He agrees, and we also had the Housing Authority people call him first and tell him if I'm gonna get in, how I'm gonna get in. I'm trying to get in here and make something work.
>
> They made some calls, and I made the call, and we went back and forth, and back and forth, and back and forth with Housing Authority and leasing over what are we gonna do, and are we gonna do then, blalala, and have me use on the left and whatever, whatever, ever. Anyway, from networking, from organizing for those years and years of going to meetings with developers, I shamelessly, *[laugh]* shamelessly greased lots of wheels and called and made some big folks tell these little folks, approve her application and say nutting else.

Given the scenario painted above, Mu-Tem-Uwa was able to exceed the expectations her fellow low-income residents may have held as a result of who she knew. Another key takeaway from the experiences of these two activists is that, even though both women currently have the housing of their dreams, they have not ceased their agitation for affordable housing. Jeffries and Mu-Tem-Uwa continue to advocate for other former residents of The Homestead Homes who do not have the skills needed for navigating the pitfalls of D.C. housing bureaucracies. In doing so they confronted the apathy of residents but kept pushing. The excerpt below describes what happens when she works to organize returning residents:

> Three people showed up because they've been so disappointed and so been lied to so much about different things. Then they are just so disappointed in how they are reentering these people back into this community. The units, they're brand new. They're brand spanking new. Nobody has lived in these units but us, so who wouldn't want to come back to a brand new unit?
>
> I think the stipulation of them coming back is what's peeling them off and making them disappointed, and making them not want to come. Then when you go and sit in front of one of the resident managers she's really snobbish. They don't want to be bothered with it. They'd rather go ahead and just stay in the projects or wherever they at and not be bothered with it at all.

In the case of Jeffries, residing in the location where her former public housing complex once stood has been a mixed blessing. Overall she is satisfied, particularly with her individual unit, which is new, clean, and brightly lit. Her apprehension stems from concerns over the many difficulties she and Mu-Tem-Uwa have had in organizing the heads of other low-income households. Jeffries is also troubled by the poor quality of interpersonal relations in the new neighborhood. This sense of a missing key element in her life makes her ill at ease, and this eroded sense of belonging is exacerbated by the absence of any remnants of the old community in the form of people or landmarks.

As one of only a handful of former residents to return to the renovated properties, Jeffries says she is looked upon by her higher income earning neighbors as "that low-income person." Mu-Tem-Uwa elaborated on this point by recounting an incident where she was locked out of her apartment and reached out to her next-door neighbor so she could call a family member for help. She described the humiliation she felt dealing with the inhospitable attitude of her neighbor, who did not conceal his distrust of her request. The reformulation of the neighborhood has brought many more White residents into the community, and both women commented that the Black professionals that have also moved in are no friendlier than their White counterparts. Distrust and contempt for the Black poor are not the sole preserve of White Americans, as these women observed.[4] Class and race intersect to influence the kind of responses Jeffries and Mu-Tem-Uwa receive from newcomers.

Jeffries doesn't feel close to anyone in her surroundings and notes the absence of children playing and people like her to interact with. She also finds aspects of the built environment wanting and a dearth of businesses that catered to her interests and tastes:

> How can we build our community back like we had it, with knowing that Ms. Robertson down the hall right here has somebody checking on her, or there's a lady that needs to go up to work. Can she get somebody to babysit for her, or somebody that says, "Okay, my phone is out. Can I use somebody's phone?" We so discombobulated and so disconnected, we don't even know our neighbors. We don't even—when the children can't stand on the corner; it's not a time that I have came [*sic*] through my neighborhood and seen a child play. I have not seen—I have seen the dogs barking, pooping, and stuff. It's nowhere for our children to go around there…

Here is an exchange between the two friends and co-activists:

> Robin Jeffries: In the new space, they promise us a recreation [center]. I've been down there three years now, but they keep saying something about money, money, money. I notice they have money for other things. They have this big—Big and Ready put this big park down the street, Canal Park, which has a—is gonna be a new restaurants and an ice skating rink. I don't ice skate.

Mu-Tem-Uwa sarcastically replied to Jeffries' description, "that's what every Black person dreams about" in response to the prospect of using an ice skating rink.

Commentary on the type of food available for purchase reflects palates more accustomed to *soul food* or African American southern cuisine, as well as more limited budgets. This is apparent in another exchange between the two women:

> Mu-Tem-Uwa: We used to go hang out on 8th Street. If you get some three chicken wings and some fries, some fried rice, and something. Only one more community place that you can afford is there, which is pizza.

> Robin Jeffries: It's very busy over there.

---

4   DeSena's writing on boundary-work in Greenpoint, Brooklyn is instructive here. In *Segregation Begins at Home* (2012) she advances this concept to describe the cultural practices that residents in gentrifying neighborhoods engage in to maintain social distance between the classes.

Mu-Tem-Uwa: Give me an order of fries to go. We're just thinking...there's nobody—there's the Potbelly. There's a Subway and a Five Guys. You know, some good old community greasy food or a corner store.

Robin Jeffries: Starbucks. They have Starbucks, five dollar coffee.

Sarcasm, again, this time reflecting the diverging impact of social class in gentrifying communities. Both women are witnessing and responding to the physical transformation of their surroundings. Changes in the built environment reflect the shifts of ethnicity, class, and culture associated with the impacts of gentrification in cities. These are very real transformations that affect ordinary citizens and that also have visually apparent repercussions (Krase, 2012).

The stated impetus for the relocation of public housing residents that inspired the formation of HAC was the refurbishment of "crumbling" public housing and the reduction of poverty concentration. By replacing the units of Mu-Tem-Uwa, Robin Jeffries, and their neighbors with renovated, spacious town homes, middle-income earners would be attracted to the area and the pitfalls of concentrating poor populations would be avoided.

Mixed income housing has been advanced as solution in the promotion of gentrification. It is certain and without much debate that the practice of concentrating poor people, particularly in high rise public structures, was a tremendous misstep in the practice of urban housing development (Atlas and Dreier, 1994). Although progress in redressing the consequences of centralizing low-income households by attracting middle-income residents has led to some types of improvement in reformulated communities, the specific and tangible policies required to lift households out of poverty are not addressed by this strategy.

One fault D.C. housing activist Brenda Best has found with the emphasis on building mixed-income communities is that the focus overlooks the diversity that exists among low-income African American individuals. The poor are conveniently lumped together in an impoverished heap but Best sees the range that exists in D.C. neighborhoods. Ethnographic studies of other U.S. cities validate this view by contradicting simplistic portrayals. Sociologist Mary Pattillo looks at gentrification in Chicago and writes that the older, low income residents in a changing neighborhood her research has focused on "are not a monolith-young families and senior citizens; a majority of renters and a minority of home owners-they are disproportionately poor and working class" (2007, p. 84). These same dissimilarities in age, gender, employment and marital status, and income are also represented among Washingtonians who are poor. The combination of these social variables has a huge impact on how poverty is experienced by members of households with different compositions.

The apparent invisibility of this pre-existing mixture is also relevant for race relations. It reflects a dismissal of the poor and the equally common stereotyping of Black Americans, particularly poor Black people. It is chiefly important to note that establishing mixed-income communities does little to alleviate actual poverty. Instead, the visibility of the poor becomes diminished as these populations are removed from the sight of the general or non-poor public.[5] The erasure of the poor makes their former spaces more marketable, but where do those who must make way for the coming middle class go, and what becomes of their condition? Based on what the Homestead Houses case reveals, with few exceptions, the poor do not experience upward mobility or improved housing. Displacement generally causes disruption which can easily make these populations more vulnerable than before.

The changes described above come under the rubric of a nonstructural policy intervention (Pattillo, 2007). Various types of passive mediation have been promoted over the last decade. One group of urban theorists makes a social capital argument maintaining that by establishing mix income communities the low-income residents experience betterment through more social control in their communities; the sharing of key resources through new, class-diverse social networks; and the overall political sophistication of their middle-class neighbors who will fight for improved community conditions (Joseph et al., 2007).

These hypotheticals sound good; however, I learned from gathering ethnographic data in Central and West Harlem that the promises of class heterogeneity can be undercut by realities on the ground (Prince, 2004). Having professionals in the vicinity does not automatically lead to close community ties or the lack of conflict within a community and this has been verified by other ethnographic studies (Boyd, 2008; Davila, 2004; Patillo, 2007). This is a false and misleading assumption that informs policy.

It is also important to acknowledge that the mixed-income focus implies ancillary benefits that are not intended to directly ameliorate the conditions that have been determined to cause or reproduce poverty and central among these causes is unemployment (Austin, 2011). Despite the need to shore up the tax base, key resources and programs such as child care, early childhood education, living wages, affordable housing, and job training have not accompanied the investment in mixed-income communities.

A cadre of critical urban theorists has pointed out additional problems with market-oriented solutions to poverty in cities. As neoliberalism continues to expand its reach, the "state-market boundary" has been eroded and "needs-based aid for

---

5   In Brazil, South Africa, India, and other countries the bulldozing of "slums" for the Olympics, World Cup soccer competition, and general urban revitalization projects has displaced thousands of poor people globally. In *Cities With Slums*, Huchzermeyer argues that the United Nations call to improve conditions for people living in these areas as been used as the impetus for governments to eradicate communities of the urban poor (2011). In the book *Shanghai Gone: Domicide and Defiance in a Chinese Megacity* (2013), ethnographer Qin Shao advances the concept of domicide to describe the destruction of residential areas for the poor that preceded the tremendous high-rise construction that Shanghai has become admired for.

the poor has been retrofitted as a market transaction" (Soss, Fording, and Schram, 2011, p. 177). Ruben observes that "neoliberal economic development continues a long standing tradition of uneven development with regard to cities, in which the urban poor have been bypassed by funding and strategies intended to promote growth and prosperity" (2001, p. 445). These are the precise challenges that the activists I researched in D.C. are addressing and attempting to draw attention to.

What happened to residents of The Homestead Homes is instructive because it highlights the flawed promises of gentrification and the detrimental impacts these developments have on low-income people. This case also highlights what can happen when people who are organizing to prevent displacement turn toward the artistic realm to build awareness around their housing struggles. For the HAC, this openness to new strategies has involved expanding their battle beyond the immediate community to form coalitions with other communities and join forces with residents across the divisions of race and class. This final section looks more closely at the implications of HAC endeavors combining social justice work with the arts.

Race, Class, *The Home,* and The HAC

The arts have had a vibrant history in D.C. and Washingtonians are easily moved to praise native-born performers whose fame has pushed the city onto the international stage. The images and names of Edward "Duke" Ellington, Marvin Gaye, Roberta Flack, and others appear at the entrances to parks and on mural walls across the city to honor those native sons and daughters who remind the rest of the country that D.C. is more than home to governmental power brokers. Washingtonians have also been quick to claim non-natives who were one-time residents as their own. Among these honorary-natives are such groundbreaking artists as Gil Scott Heron, Shirley Horn, the members of Sweet Honey in the Rock, musician/educator Donald Byrd, and horn-playing siblings Antoine and Wallace Roney. This practice of adoption could not be more perfectly illustrated than by the example of Chuck Brown, The Godfather of the District's indigenous Go-Go music.

Chuck Brown is the quintessential example of a non-native being transformed into a native son. The love African American residents of D.C. have for the man and the music was aptly on display at one of his concerts at The Warner Theater. The Parliament All Stars were playing Flashlight when they were practically run off the stage by audience members yelling "wind 'em up Chuck," a joyful chant that could be heard during any of his performances. North Carolina born and bred, Brown passed away in the summer of 2012, but the driving beat of his musical hits will always be associated with the city he called home.

A powerful means for expressing local identity, the arts also reflect the social hierarchies that exist across the city today. Vocalist Edna Simmons knows something about this. Her husband Samuel is a musician and jazz instructor at a city high school and together the couple runs a foundation that provides encouragement and support for young musicians. Some of the young people they have helped come from desperate economic situations. Simmons feels D.C. is not living up to its illustrious musical history:

> Absolutely, because there's so many luminary artists who have come from this town, as well. It's really terrible that …Washingtonians have to go somewhere else to make their fortune. You know, it really is. A lot of people didn't even know Sonny Stitt lived here, you know.

It is also Simmons view that too many African American musicians are locked out of performing at well-paying venues because they don't have the necessary connections or union affiliations. She elaborates on this point saying:

> Washington is still a, artistically in my estimation, is still on some level, kind of wants to be highbrow. The establishment wants to be highbrow. There's a very private jazz community. There's been this big fight with the musicians, the local musicians; the Black musicians are like, why the hell should I join the union? They haven't done a damn thing for me. They don't call me for any of those, all those gigs, those theater gigs and stuff, there are cliques.

> You know, there are a few people, a few Black folks who are in that mix but they don't have any power. They just get called by the White boy because they know them and they know they work and they're really making them look good. So the Kennedy Center, the National Opera, the big venues, like the Warner Theater pit crew. And it depends on what music group comes in, but you know, there are a couple of Black contacts who call people. My husband winds up working at some of those places, and he's done some plays and stuff, but in general those are reserved for the people that the White people know.

These were harsh words expressed by Simmons but she was also hopeful about the role musicians can potentially play to minimize racial animus. On the subject of what role the arts could be used to address inequalities and impact politics in a progressive way, she answered:

> I believe there's that possibility because artists have a different frame of mind. We don't think Black and White ordinarily when we're in our art. We don't think Black and White, it's art. It's art. It's like the fulfillment of your work. You know, it's not like, Whiteness or Blackness … artists just don't think that way.

> Now, I live in D.C. so I have other thoughts about stuff that goes around my 'hood but, I mean, in terms of artistically I don't think artists think that way.

> And most artists have all kinds of people in their mix. My regular band, my piano player's White. This is a guy who I trust and it's my music, he's played my piano for me, is White. We have another bassist that we use who's White, sometimes …

> I never think when I'm booking musicians for a gig. Hmm, it's a Black gig. My
> White pianist has played in my Black church many, many, many, many times.

Simmons is friends with visual artists and Columbia Heights residents Lorraine West and Brenda Duke. Both of these women are connected to a network of artists who use filmmaking, poetry, and music as their mediums for creative expression. Among these artists with a local connection I am personally connected to differing degrees with filmmaker Michelle Parkerson, painter Wayson Jones, comedienne Robin Montague, jazz musicians Marc Cary, Naser Abadey and Janelle Gill, the late poet Essex Hemphill, my brother, singer/songwriter/actor/poet Christopher Prince and others. These individuals work locally and some have achieved a fair amount of fame on the national stage.

Working among this diverse group of artists are those who orient their creativity toward addressing the inequalities faced by communities of color and the poor in D.C. Local rapper and activist Head-Roc has been using his considerable talents as a lyricist to speak about issues like racism, class inequality, and gentrification. Sociolinguist Gabrielle Modan's study of gentrification and conflict in the Mount Pleasant neighborhood included a focus on actor and playwright Quique Aviles by engaging in a textual analysis of his play *Chaos Standing*, which explores the marginalization of Latino men in this changing NW neighborhood (Modan, 2007).

As an artist and HAC member Zahira Kahlo also straddled these categories. An actor and playwright, she is a current D.C. resident who was recognized as artist of the year by the D.C. Mayor's office. Kahlo's work has been covered by major media, including local television stations and *The Washington Post,* and she has received periodic financial support for her writing and performing.

As these accomplishments suggest, Kahlo has received key measures of respect from mainstream theatrical and funding institutions but lives an economically unstable life and essentially remains an underground performer. This is, in part, due to her love/hate relationship with the idea of becoming successful and famous. It appears her commitment to social justice combined with her impatience with White privilege are characteristics that put her at odds with some of the influential persons in the arts who have become familiar with her work over the years. Limited roles for radical thespians of color notwithstanding, Kahlo has such exceeding talent and notable comedic timing, she is impossible to overlook.

In *The Home*, Kahlo convincingly alters her tone, body language, and facial expressions. No costumes or props are used when she transforms herself into characters representing Black children, elders, women, and men, depictions inspired by real people she interacted with as a volunteer and activist working at Homestead Homes. Kahlo made her way to D.C. after graduating from college and traveling to Brazil, India, and South Africa on a Watson Fellowship grant. Her visits to these countries were done to complete research into street theater in low-income communities around the world. This research focus reflected her concern with inequality and ways she could merge her interest in the arts with her drive to seeking social justice for people living in poverty.

Kahlo did not go into community work in DC with the intention to write a play about dislocation. She ended up on this path as a result of her work with the children attending the recreation center at The Homestead Homes. She told me:

> I decided on my own that I was gonna go to the recreation center as this kind of emissary from the ***** and just start hanging out and getting to know people there. The young people were not connected to this group that identified themselves of *******. They were just a group of youth that happened to go to the rec center, and I built relationships with them.

The young people came to the center to play basketball or just hang out after school. Kahlo got the children to express their feelings with poetry, doing work that influenced her path as an activist because it put her in closer contact with people of more diverse backgrounds.

Kahlo did not share the same racial/ethnic or socioeconomic status as the people she worked with on the HAC. Most of these individuals were working-class African Americans descended from multiple generations of U.S.-born Blacks - like her friends Robin Jeffries and Mu-Tem-Uwa. Kahlo was born and raised in Kansas. Her father immigrated to the United States from India during the 1960s to obtain a Ph.D. in engineering from The University of Iowa, later sending for his wife. The regional and immigration-related aspects of her background added to the cultural differences between Kahlo and the activists she worked with.

The actor/playwright reflected on these social variables and whatever sway they had over her relationships in The Homestead Homes. I also asked what responses she received when she first began visiting the neighborhood that would become like a second home to her. The following exchange is an example of the small yet significant interactions she began to have visiting the housing complex:

> Kahlo: Some people thought I was Spanish. Some people didn't really know what I was, but they didn't really—like, I sounded White. The way I talk is White, so they just were like, "You're just not from here." Some people didn't seem to really care what I was; they just knew I wasn't Black. Some people thought I was mixed and some people thought I was Ethiopian, which meant I wasn't Black. [laughs]
>
> Prince: Anybody ever tell you you had good hair?
>
> Kahlo: Yeah. Every—oh god, the girls were just like, "I love your hair," you know? "I love your hair." Yeah. Yeah.
>
> Prince: How did I know that? [laughs] I was a Black girl once.
>
> Kahlo: Yeah. [laughs]

Her initial impressions of the community were:

> I think—I remember when I first came to the neighborhood and I remember
> walking down and I was like, "Wow, I feel like I am walking in a favela in
> Brazil," because of the—just the picture—the immediate picture I got when I
> started walking in the neighborhood, and the lack of social services available for
> the public spaces. Like things weren't picked up or something. People's houses
> were fine, but you could tell there was not a lot of money being put into this
> neighborhood.

> What I was really looking for was I wanted to find a place that was a working
> class slash poor area or neighborhood or community where people—there was
> some issue going on and it was an opportunity to organize. Actually, I didn't
> care what the racial makeup of it was—if it was ... Latino community or if it was
> poor White Appalachian, you know, but just where I was, it just so happened
> that I came to D.C.

The above excerpt reveals much about Kahlo's motivation and character. She is
a passionate social justice advocate who is highly motivated by a concern for
low-income people wherever they may be located. Her arrival to Washington,
D.C. was largely coincidental. The move was initiated at the suggestion of her
activist acquaintance Terry Agee, who was the only other non-Black member of
the HAC. It is because of this overall make up of HAC—a Black-run organization
whose goals were geared toward aiding this same population—that Kahlo did not
consider it to be a multiracial organization. One Indian American and a white
American did not meet her criteria for multiracial but their collective work still
had implications for the consideration of interracial relations.

While collecting data for this book I began seeing anti-gentrification activism
as a conduit for softening race and class based barriers. I discussed my view that
fighting for social justice in the face of gentrification was emerging as a sustainable
means for bringing people together across key differences with Kahlo and she
agreed. She said that she and Robin Jeffries once concluded they would never
have become friends had it not been for the advocacy work they engaged in on
behalf of the displaced residents of The Homestead Homes. Ironically, and as I
have shown elsewhere in this chapter and based on other research, rather than the
establishment of mixed-income communities it is the activism against this that has
led to building of relationships across these boundaries.

There were instances where community work around *The Home* had a direct
effect on relationships and conditions shaped by racism and class inequality. One
is demonstrated by the following sentiments Kahlo shared with me during an
October 2012 interview in which she observed:

> It was just interesting when I took the play to Michigan. Every now and then
> when I'd gotten an opportunity to perform, I made sure that the people that I was

in touch with, which were really like three or four people max, "Do you wanna come?" When I went to Michigan, that was first time Rose had been on a college campus, and it was a really cool experience to be there together with her. It was just really cool to be with her in that environment and see how these college students, some of whom were White and middle class, and how she learned from some of these students and they learned tremendously from her. It was a very powerful experience

These types of opportunities made possible through *The Home* helped open the eyes of many participants. In the instance described above Robin Jeffries gained novel experiences that could potentially change her life forever. Kahlo also saw that exposing predominantly middle-class White students to people like Rose could cause affirmative results on the campus as well.

This kind of *race work* is something Kahlo is uniquely equipped to undertake. With a degree in history and a distinctive personal story, Kahlo had a heightened level of awareness and she attributed this in part to her relationship to racism in the United States:

> I'm Indian heritage. I'm not White. I'm not Black. In this country, there's racism towards people of African heritage. The way racism is targeted towards people of African heritage is different than the way it's targeted toward people that look like me.

Kahlo rightfully demonstrated a keen sensitivity about community sentiments concerning her depictions of their members. By her direction, the performances funded by the Humanities Council of Washinto, D.C. grant all took place in settings that were easily accessible to low-income and working-class people. Kahlo wanted to see dialogue fostered and indicated that as the primary reason she was involved in this project in the first place was so she could bring people together. However Kahlo also encountered instances in which the politics of representation overshadowed her attempts to convey a message about the duplicity of HOPE VI administrators and the vulnerability of public housing residents. The following excerpts demonstrate how she dealt with the disapproval she periodically encountered during performances:

> Once I did the play at SEEDS School and I did excerpts of it. Because of that, it wasn't the full context so a couple of the pieces were more on the lighter humorous side, but because I'm doing it about gentrification, because I'm doing it about these people that are moving—being forced from their homes and I'm not Black, and here I'm doing a funny monologue about it. One guy, he got upset about that. I appreciated—I talked to him. I asked him questions, and he was like, "It's not funny," and I'm like, "Yeah, you're right." I needed to have included more of the play so that he could see that.

In another instance Kahlo performed *The Home* at the National Low Income Housing Coalition Conference:

> Everybody gave me a standing ovation. In the middle of the performance though, there was a few people in the back and they were pissed. They started talking and talking back to me during the show, so then, as a character, I was like, "Just let me finish and we'll talk. Let me say my piece. Then you can say your piece, okay?"

> At the end, I got all this flack for, like, you know, "Shaniqua's such a stereotypical name." It was like, "Yeah, sure, but that's the name of somebody I knew, so what are you trying to say? Are you ashamed of that name? Should you be?" He's like, "I'm a doctor. I live in public housing. What about that story?" Like, you just had people that don't have education." I was like, "Well, this isn't your story. This is about the people that I knew here." The thing that would've helped, I think, is if Robin or Mu-Tem-Uwa or whatever had been there, because it gives it that validation, you know?

> Yeah. I did get a bit of flack, but not much. I really fully expected more. 'Cause when you're dancing on these lines, it's like, "Sure."

Kahlo is acquainted with a retired, African American schoolteacher who migrated to D.C. from the south during the 1960s. After she saw the play for the first time, she responded that Kahlo should be depicting Indian people in her plays, not Blacks. The conclusion Kahlo reached, facing the realization that her depictions of Homestead Homes residents were not resonating with all of the people who saw the play, was that middle-class African Americans were the primary individuals who took issue with the play. Kahlo attributed this indifference to the internalized oppression of the Black middle class. It remains her view that Black professionals were demonstrating shame when they attack her for depicting the experiences of the low-income African Americans.

Stumbling blocks like these notwithstanding, *The Home* helped build awareness about urban dislocation and bridge gaps across a host of relational differences. The play also led to personal growth on the parts of numerous HAC participants including Kahlo who grew in unanticipated ways. She ultimately realized that despite her good intentions, she was substituting involvement in this project for investing her own heritage and the baggage she carries from her past. She had some epiphanies about how she was processing her own personal history through her involvement in this project:

> I felt this moment of like I was trying to seek community with a group of people that are not like my home. It's like I'm running. I felt like I was running away from the people who are a part of my home community or whatever because of whatever pain in my own family and here I was trying to have a sense of

community, but it was too painful to actually go directly to the people that are my community, you know what I mean?

In that moment—I don't know. Ever since then, I've been doing some more work and looking at what gets really hard about being around other Indian people—Indian-American people who are the bastions of assimilation, you know? Like, we've been sold on this —a lot of people sold on the idea—I guess it's across the board of, like, going to this country and going to a country that's been built on the backs of the exploitation and the genocide and da da da. Then come here, "You can make it and then we're gonna treat you kinda shitty, but we're gonna treat you better than we treat Black people or whatever." There's just this—anyway, so I've been thinking a lot about that.

I'm in this moment where I'm really thinking about representation and I would love for other people to perform *The Home*. I don't know if I would do it. Then, what do I do? I go to India and I perform *The Home* there because there's a community that is going through the exact same thing.

Through their activism HAC members Robin Jeffries and Mu-Tem-Uwa secured improved housing for themselves and began making connections between their experiences and similar struggles taking place in other D.C. communities. Anthropologist Kalfani Ture is currently writing up his observations working with the residents of Barry Farms who are also confronting pending dislocation. There are other examples of activists attempting to connect the dots. Wrapping up a phone conversation with Mu-Tem-Uwa I said I was on my way to a community meeting in Ivy City, NE, convened to discuss the D.C. government's plans to build a bus depot on the grounds of the famed Alexander Crummell Elementary School. Mu-Tem-Uwa asked me to convey to Ivy City residents that the members of the HAC support them in their struggle. Fighting alongside those Ivy City residents opposed to this project was the Shaw-based advocacy group D.C. First. This chapter's final section examines this organization's campaigns to push back against gentrification in working-class African American communities.

D.C. First

A multiracial group milled about on the upper floor of The Sumner School. The building was a majestic edifice located at 17th and M Streets, NW and named after the emboldened, anti-racist and champion for African American rights, Senator Charles Sumner.[6] Sumner was one of the District's earliest schools open to African

---

6   Charles Sumner (1811–1874) was born in Massachusetts as the son of an abolitionist who also grew to despise the enslavement of African Americans. Sumner was a Harvard-educated attorney who served in the U.S. Senate from 1865–1871. In addition to opposing

American elementary and high-school aged students. Today it is made available for nonprofit and community-based organizations to hold meetings there at no cost.[7] On this night the historical site was teeming with the twin energies of people poised for celebration and catching up with folks they have not seen in a while.

The event was enlivened by the presence of children. Some were running about in inimitable childlike fashion, while others were in the process of being ushered off by members of the childcare collective to a separate room. A few of the youngsters were scanning the offerings of the potluck at the back of the meeting room. The budget for carrying out this event was modest. Most of the food was purchased by organizers but a small portion was contributed by members and local residents.

This particular gathering marked the culmination of another year's work for D.C. First (DCF), a grassroots organization run by seasoned African American housing activist Barbara Best and Miriam Khan, an Iranian American from suburban Maryland whose activism began through environmentalism. Khan was born in 1976, and Best, the older of the two, migrated to D.C. from Florida in 1980. These women, who were more than 25 years apart in age, ran an organization that was primarily staffed by women of color. Their roles as co-directors lasted until the summer of 2012 when Best joined another local organization that focuses on the housing needs of the very lowest income residents in D.C.

DCF staff and membership intended to use this event to recount collective accomplishments, bear witness to challenges, and share their vision for future growth. Occasions like these were also used to recruit volunteers and solicit ideas from the membership about future campaigns. DCF thrives on the energy of its members, and although that may not be unique for a nonprofit, this outlook is ingrained into the organization's operating philosophy.

The concept of self-advocacy is at the center of all the work done by DCF. The organization's work on educational equity, affordable housing, childcare for working people, and the preservation of public resources, space, and property is joined with a focus on finding and nurturing people willing to take on the mantle of community leadership. Meeting this challenge is the thread that links these four campaigns together, and with this specific mission DCF members attempt to affect sustainable change in struggling communities.

---

slavery, Sumner advocated for radical socioeconomic reform during Reconstruction based on his view that African American equality had to be based on access to resources and not just emancipation. After a prolonged caning by a pro-slavery southerner, Sumner suffered severe injuries to his head and back. He died two years later in Washington, D.C. His life is documented in David Herbert Donald's two volume biography, *Charles Sumner* (1996).

7   The building housed the very first institution to train Black teachers in the city. The school was called Myrtilla Miner's Normal School and later became known as D.C. Teacher's College or DCT. Today, the building is run by The National Park Service houses the archives of the D.C Public School system. This link to a National Park service website provides additional information about the establishment of the Sumner School and Charles Sumner http://www.nps.gov/history/nr/travel/wash/dc58.htm.

Among the tools DCF uses to achieve the goal of cultivating local leadership are workshops they organize called empowerment circles. These gatherings are used to foster a sense of political awareness and competence among the people that DCF members and staff work with.[8] Examples include the periodic offering of workshops on the structure of the D.C. local government and the various ways residents can have a lasting impact on the decisions of elected officials. One such event provided a training session on Advisory Neighborhood Commissions, or ANCs, which are described on a D.C. government website as that portion of the local government that has "the closest official ties to the people in a neighborhood."[9]

Events like the ANC teach-in are intended to demystify government and break down barriers in order to inspire residents to get involved in local politics. DCF has convened similar types of events to show attendees how the Mayor's budget is formulated and how ordinary citizens can lobby members of the City Council. Empowerment is the legacy members try to create in the communities they work with. As they carry out the sometimes, gruelling work of knocking on doors and attempting to motivate often tired and disaffected residents, DCF members also communicate their unequivocal views regarding their individual and collective battles against gentrification. Best and Khan have determined, for example, that gentrification has not only not assuaged the economic struggles of poor and working class people from any of the households they interacted with, it may in fact have exacerbated them.

The word gentrification appears as a subheading at the top of the organization's website under the category of housing. Historically, advocating for affordable housing has been the foundational concern for DCF. This is because it emerged in 2003 from the ashes of another grassroots organization that was founded in 1978. Khan says, about this DCF forerunner-organization:

> [It] grew through the '80's and early '90's into an organization that played a major role in housing, in particular, and tenants' rights laws in D.C., laws that we have now, like the tenant first right to purchase, things like that. Then they also, at some point in the '90's, started developing housing. They were the only organization in D.C. that was developing limited equity cooperatives

---

8   The organization has also begun a grassroots media project which teaches audio and video production to residents and DCF members. The media focus, which includes using film and radio documentation to preserve the histories of communities, is a part of the empowerment orientation. Now members do not have to wait for mainstream media to follow their campaigns. In addition to recording their own actions, residents working with DCF use their equipment to capture the words and deeds of elected officials and hold them accountable for the policies they promote. Political actions and short documentaries are placed on the organization's website or recorded on DVDs and distributed to interested parties.

9   http://www.dccouncil.washington.dc.us/offices/office-of-the-advisory-neighborhood-commissions

with the tenants in place, so instead of taking a vacant building and making it into a cooperative, they were actually helping the tenants organize, exercise the first right to purchase, buy the building, renovate the building, and run it as a cooperative.

Khan says the organization fell apart in the 1990s after "they lost some funding and some poor decisions were made, in terms of not paying payroll taxes." The entire staff was laid off after debt was incurred with the Internal Revenue Service. Today DCF carries on and expands the work of that now-defunct organization and as such their active membership see housing as a basic human right that must be protected for D.C. residents.

Informed by her views about the unfavorable impact gentrification has on the right and access to housing for the working class, Best wants local officials to redirect incentives to bring single, child-free people into the city. This was a strategy first openly advocated by Anthony Williams when he was the mayor of D.C. from 1999 to 2007 (Swarns, 2006).[10] Best, however, along with other advocates for the poor, want his plans revamped so that all proposals for growth incorporate rather than overlook long-time, working-class, and minority residents in the District. Best also maintains that these absences reflect the low regard with which city officials hold poor Washingtonians and this is an assessment that she directs to the administrations of Mayors Fenty, Williams, and, more recently, Gray.

During our most recent conversation, Best noted how programs such as HUD's Choice Neighborhoods are "an insult" to low-income people. She elaborated:

> To say that I have to be someplace else which is considered a choice neighborhood to have opportunities to move up. No, what we have to say [*sic*] and that it is all about trying to create strong organization. My neighborhood is a choice neighborhood. We want you to make the housing better where I am now. Put the resources into making the neighborhood better. Whatever crime exists, get rid of it. Do what you have to do to make my neighborhood a better choice. Don't tell me I have to move to some other neighborhood.

The issues Best raises above reflect the social justice concerns I have raised throughout this book. She is adamant about the rights of the poor to exist and have their needs prioritized. Her thoughts also address the idea promoted by some gentrification advocates that this particular form of urban development will foster diversity in communities. To that point she offers:

---

10   As current senior strategic advisor and consultant with the international law firm McKenna Long & Aldridge LLP and a member of the secretive but influential Federal City Council, former D.C. mayor Anthony Williams remains an influential local figure. He has left his stamp on the course of urban development in Washington, D.C.

> Even when we move into so-called mixed neighborhoods we don't mix. White people stick with White people, Black people stick with Black people, poor people stick with poor people. We don't speak, communicate, or socialize. That is another one of those myths.

Unprompted and without my anticipating it, Best spoke plainly to another of my research foci: the building of relations across the boundaries of status, perspective, and identity. The notion of gentrification as a path to multicultural interaction was not validated by observations I made in the field. I also did not find this idea embraced by any of the activists I spoke with over the years. I would also argue that individuals like Best have a lot of credibility in this area of concern. As an activist from the south who was born in the early 1950s, she has had direct experience with racism and classism and can boast about her decades-long track record of working closely with people from different racial/ethnic and immigrant backgrounds.

I also asked for Khan's thoughts on this view that gentrification is a conduit for diversity. Her answer was also emphatic:

> I think it's a lie. I think that gentrification does not foster relationships and relationships are the only thing that would foster multiculturalism. Gentrification, from what I've seen, has promoted segregation just as much as anything else. There is no space in a gentrified community for the very lowest income people, and when they say they're building mixed income, of course, they exclude the lowest income from that strata.

> Gentrification does nothing to promote relationships. In fact, it drives a wedge that puts people against each other, that makes it appear—I mean, the saddest thing; I remember years ago, 'cause our office is in the U Street area, which is totally out of reach now. These houses around here are a million dollars. I remember being down the street, and there was a house that had been renovated and it was for sale. A young girl and her mom were walking down the street, and the young girl was like, "Oh, look at that. That's a nice house," and her mom was like, "That's not for us."

> I mean, I'm a newcomer, and that hurts me. I can't imagine what it feels like to be a third generation or whatever, a native born or whatever; you've grown up here your whole life, and then you're seeing these things around you being finally improved. Like the vacant buildings, "Oh they're being renovated. Oh, isn't that nice. Oh, yeah, but it's not for you."

In her views on the social relations of gentrification, Khan described herself as a community organizer and defined the difference between activism and community organizing. Her response to this question appears below and reflects her belief that her work revolves around the bonds established among people rather than accomplishing a particular set of goals. In her words:

The fundamental piece of organizing that people miss is that it's all about relationships. Most of the time, people take action because somebody asked them to, somebody who they trusted or who they felt would have their back or who they felt was being supportive in some way. Somebody provided them with an opportunity, maybe, to do something that they, somewhere in their heart or mind, saw themselves, wanted to be; like somebody thought of themselves in some way, like, "One day, I would love to testify at City Council or speak to the media," but they didn't even know that that would ever happen or that there would be the opportunity.

The staff and membership of DCF and the HAC symbolically typifies individuals coming together across race, class, gender, and other alleged lines of demarcation.[11] In this instance it is to work for social justice in D.C. on behalf of the poor and other vulnerable populations. Diversity at DCF extends to the staff, membership, steering committee, and base of volunteers, which includes women and men of African, Asian, European, and Latin American descent, as well as immigrants and native-born people of various ages working with persons from low and middle-income backgrounds. I reiterate that women are well represented in positions of authority and there is some non-work-related socializing that occurs across these lines as well. Khan commented on her organization's prospects for helping to mend societal divisions, in response to my assessment that acknowledging inequality can lay the foundation for transformative relationships across the barriers of race and class.

Yeah; yeah, I agree, and I think when you say activism, I include in that, for instance, tenants coming together in a building that has Latino residents and African American residents, and understanding what the common ground is, and working together around a shared goal. Now the work around really understanding each other's backgrounds and experiences and having respect for the different challenges of an immigrant versus an African American, that stuff doesn't always happen, even in that setting.

I think it comes out. There's [*sic*] groups that do that in a group setting, talking about oppression, talking about racism, but I think, again, the individual relationships that people form are probably the best teachers for people. I mean, we can do workshops and stuff, but until you have somebody, a White person, saying to you, "I acknowledge that White dominance and White supremacy and racism have had a huge impact on the lives of African Americans, and I want to work to understand, and also help rectify the situation." Until you've had a person say that to you, you can know about White power and all this

---

11   I did not hear heterosexism advocated by any representative of DCF and I also did not knowingly interact with activists who were from LGBT communities. For this reason I cannot include sexuality as one of the social variables I list here. For the sake of clarity, both Best and Khan have spoken out against homophobia.

stuff. You're still gonna distrust White people, as you should, to a certain extent, [laughs] but it's the relationship that can transform that, right?

It doesn't always have to even be spoken in that way. It could be spoken in another way. It could be somebody just showing love and respect, but to be honest, [laughs] the work that we do, in some ways, is engaging a lot of people who've been hurt in different ways. We're hurt, even the fact that this type of system that oppresses people exists, hurts us, even those of us who are not directly impacted by the need for affordable housing or education. When we see it happen to other people, we feel connected and it hurts us. That's not the world that we want to live in. We believe in something else, and so we have to find a way that we can build relationships that address, not just the "isms" and all of that, but also that can help heal each other. There's a lot of work to be done there.

As her comments suggest, mending the kind of divides Khan and I discussed is not an automatic process, regardless of the political persuasion of the individuals involved.

As they fight their battles, DCF members and staff use a collection of strategies. Working to increase services for members and their communities and halt or reverse the effects of privatization and gentrification call for range and flexibility. I have witnessed and worked directly with DCF to do public outreach, fundraising, membership updates, educational workshops, protests, research, grant writing, and interface with public officials. As an amateur photographer I have also donated framed prints to be sold in silent auctions. Staff and members also tap into the ideologies and strategies of past social justice warriors in order to glean lessons from their experiences and familiarize community members with these important historical forerunners. Through DCF's efforts in Ivy City, residents have learned more about people like Perry Carson[12] and the better-known Alexander Crummell whom I discussed in an earlier section of this book. Both Best and Khan have recognized how a sense of continuity can fortify collective belonging and the organization's fight against gentrification and one way they have tried to achieve this idea of mutual reliability is by seeking information local histories.

DCF's works are shored up by an ideology that privileges poor and working class households and conceptualizes inequality as a force that caused by overlapping forces. One of DCF's most recent triumphs epitomizes this tactic and connects their fight against gentrification to battles for environmental justice in

---

12   Perry Carson (1842–1909) was an advocate for Washington's Black working class populace who lived in Ivy City at the time of his death. Born in Princess Anne County, Maryland and dubbed "the tall black oak of the Potomac" and "the Black boss of Washington," Carson was a Republican delegate to the National Convention three times (Kraft, 2004). His Afro American Newspaper obituary stated over 3,000 people attended his funeral at the Metropolitan Church (November 6, 1909).

Washington, D.C. This is a campaign I learned about in July of 2012 after receiving a flyer announcing a community meeting at the Trinity Baptist Church in Ivy City. Advertised around the motto "Job Training Not Bus Parking at Crummell," the event was intended to provide residents and other interested parties with an opportunity to learn more about D.C. Mayor Gray's decision to award a contract to The Union Station Redevelopment Corporation (USRC) for the construction of a bus depot on the grounds of the historic elementary school. The facility was to temporarily house up to 60–70 buses while the normal staging area in Union Station gets renovated, but residents organized to thwart the progress of this project based on a number of concerns.

The account of the city's plan for the school lot and the conflict it engendered presented here are based on my observations attending this first, large-scale meeting in July, email updates sent through the DCF listserv and the information I recorded during an interview with Khan. Approximately 100 people crowded into a meeting room of the church that summer evening. Supporters were asked to express their solidarity with those opposed to the project by wearing red, black, and green D.C. First T-shirts. The meeting was organized to provide residents and other interested parties with an opportunity to directly question representatives from the mayor's economic development office and the Department of Transportation (DOT). It was facilitated by Alicia Swanson-Canty, vice president of the Ivy City Civic Association, and also attended by Khan and other DCF staff as well as advocates for job training, affordable housing, environmental justice and legal representation for the poor.

The atmosphere in the room was charged and the two officials representing the DOT and Mayor Gray were defensive in the face of accusations that their offices did not take the proper steps to inform the community of proposed construction. Activists, NGO representatives, and residents expressed alarm over the prospect buses with idling engines releasing toxic fumes into the community. This vision would spur future protestors to organize holding banners which read, "Don't Dump on Ivy City." At the meeting DCF went on the record with their, already initiated, plans to establish a job training center at the boarded up school and when Khan announced their organization was poised to file a lawsuit against Mayor Gray and the USRC the crowd cheered.

DCF followed through on their pledge to sue the Gray administration and on December 10, 2012, Judge Judith Macaluso called for a halt to the construction on the grounds that the mayor violated D.C. law by not informing the Advisory Neighborhood Commission about this project and disregarding considerations of the environmental impact of the buses. The Judge also determined the USRC presented misleading information on intake forms about what opposing forces saw as callous disregard for the respiratory health of Ivy City residents. The mayor's office appealed Judge Macaluso's decision later in December of 2012 and DCF currently continues to marshal their forces against this plan for the historic school, demanding that the mayor "Let Ivy City Breathe."

The case against the proposed bus parking lot constituted new territory for DCF but the effort did grow out of the organization's already-existing anti-privatization campaign. Privatization is one of the lynchpins of neoliberalism, and DCF has devoted significant resources and attention toward stopping the flow of public properties, services, and/or assets into the hands of private entities and reclaiming that which has already been leased or sold.

As further evidence of their appreciation for the power of intersecting inequalities, gendered oppression has also been confronted at DCF. The organization has taken direct steps to promote issues that are relevant to women. For example, the Child Care For All campaign focuses on an overwhelmingly female constituency. The organization has also worked with other local groups to promote issues that are not directly related to their campaigns, such as capital punishment and domestic violence. One evening I caught a glimpse of Best among a crowd in Columbia Heights who were protesting the death sentence of Troy Davis.[13] On another occasion, I joined a multiracial group of DCF members who had gathered on the corner of 14th and U Streets to draw attention to the dangers of domestic violence. Under the watchful eye of a handful of police officers, men and women took to the microphone to speak about the perils of intimate partner abuse and the need for more action on this issue. These detours from their core issues reflect the broad approach to fighting for social justice that both Best and Khan engage in.

Approximately two years later I would walk along the historic U Street corridor with Khan in search of a late-night watering hole. It was the summer of 2012 after we had just had unleashed upon us the uniquely-combined social commentary and stand-up comedy of Dick Gregory at the newly renovated Howard Theater. We detoured from our linear trajectory to peruse Ethiopian restaurants on 9th and then doubled back to turn left onto U and continue in the direction of our previous path. We passed a handful of new eateries and the long-standing Caribbean restaurant *The Islander* to eventually sit at the bar of a tavern-like establishment owned by her acquaintance, Iranian immigrant who served a multitude of beer varieties.

During that evening's conversation Khan and I talked about cross-class relations, charter schools, gentrification and topics unrelated to my research or her political work. Sadly, I was not in a mode to collect data and could not record any of the ideas we exchanged during a lively conversation that was very pertinent to my research. Months later Khan and I would meet in her office under conditions where I would record our conversation for the first time since making her acquaintance more than five years ago and after engaging in significant amounts of participant observation.

---

13 Troy Davis was executed by the state of Georgia on September 21, 2011 after spending 19 years on death row. Davis was convicted for the murder of a police officer in Savannah, Georgia. His case drew worldwide attention because of the many inconsistencies involved in his case. The execution of Davis came to symbolize what opponents of the death penalty in the U.S. find so egregious about this practice.

Over the years I have observed Khan, Best, and DCF work with a host of local NGOs and grassroots organizations. An admirable record in coalition work notwithstanding, Khan shared that a central responsibility of the organizing efforts DCF does is to help residents push back against gentrification. Khan said the following regarding this issue:

> D.C. First's fundamental role is to assist the people who are directly impacted by gentrification and its related issues with being confident and capable in advocating for themselves, and then joining forces with others that are concerned about the same kinds of issues and forming an action plan and carrying them out. For us, no matter what issue we work on, we care about the issue, but even more, we care about what we think is the building block of social change, which is the individual people [*sic*] who are directly impacted, who have not been politicized, or who have not felt confident being involved, transforming into somebody who is confident and involved. Sometimes I call it transforming the soft-spoken to the outspoken, and I say that because I've seen it happen here.
>
> No matter what your educational background is, your income background is, whatever, there is something about having a supportive relationship with somebody, just like people say about mentors in general, or with kids in school or whatever, having a supportive relationship with somebody that gives you support in understanding things that are impacting you; understanding that it's not your fault, that it's a systemic problem and it's a systemic problem that has roots, oftentimes, in things like racism or economic, class isolation or whatever, classism.

Khan also elaborated on her view of what gentrification is and shares a view which falls in line with the definitions put forth by numerous scholars including Ruth Glass (1964), the British sociologist who popularized the term many decades ago:

> My sense of what gentrification is, is a many decades long process that has been going for a very long time. It's not just something that just happened in 2000, that began with divestment; that began with planned blight, intentional blight in communities, largely on the part of the government itself or private landowners; basically, like absentee landowners who, when seeing that it was mostly African American people or lower income people who were residing there, stopped investing in uplifting, improving, maintaining, and waited to the point where there was an influx of higher income people, gentry, whatever, who were interested again, in order to cash in. I think that the District government has played probably as large a role in gentrification as any kind of private developer. I say this for a couple of reasons. One example is that, look at the schools. The schools have been allowed to deteriorate, particularly in African American communities.

The schools that have been closed—not just the ones that were closed in 2008, but the ones that have been closed over the years—have been turned over to private developers and used to promote gentrification. For instance, and this is what we dealt with the People's Property Campaign, is that there's a whole list of historic schools that were built around 1900, 1911, and all that, that were closed, that are now condos.

They're not just condos. They're the highest cost condos in the city, and many of them were in strategic places that were among the first properties in those areas to kind of usher in gentrification.

This work of DCF undercuts the arguments of people who want to minimize the impacts of gentrification and neoliberalism in neighborhoods across D.C. Taking a closer look at the ways communities are responding to the force of power in their midst uncovers current ideological trends and myriad connections to the past. This work also shows that some community members are not passive or disinterested in improving their surroundings. Knowing and seeing what people are doing mitigates the invisibility of cogent activism. People are pushing back against neoliberalism and advanced predatory capitalism and these actions are crucial—particularly as DC has become infused with capital in ways that, social justice advocates feel, overshadows the needs, values, and well-being of working class communities.

Chapter 7
Furthering an Anthropology
of Gentrification in D.C.

The Peace Ball was pulsating with color and sound. Mos Def was the final musical performer of the evening and as my shoes dangled from my wrist I looked toward the stage and saw Angela Davis vigorously hand-dancing with restaurateur and event-organizer, Andy Shallal.[1] The backgrounds and ages of the people surrounding me were eclectic. This was my second time attending the Peace Ball and, again, the event was organized around the themes of "Hope and Resistance" and coincided with the inauguration of President Barack Obama. For his re-election, instead of the Postal Museum, the affair was held in the large and multi-tiered lobby of the Arena Stage Theater in SW Washington.

Moving about and taking in the scene, I walked past W. Kamau Bell who was interviewing political science professor and MSNBC-host Melissa Harris Perry. I recognized the faces of other journalists and politicos and also chatted with the personal acquaintances I ran into. I saw friends Katea Stitt and Verna Avery-Brown and also ran into a woman I had known since elementary school who moves in Pan Africanist circles. Later in the evening I said hey to Joseph Munch, a local music-industry entrepreneur and president of Hedrush Inc. A few years earlier he was the DJ for 50th birthday parties thrown consecutively for my husband and myself.

As was the case with 2008, men and women in tuxedos and gowns danced alongside those wearing traditional African clothing and other less formal styles of dress. One young man was sporting a cobalt blue, spaghetti-strapped ball gown and a tiara. I heard an assortment of languages and accents among the people and I also noticed that African Americans were well represented among the Peace Ball-revelers. The gathering was organized around themes and speakers linked

---

1   Shallal is the proprietor of the Busboys and Poets restaurant chain which has become very popular within progressive circles and with young patrons. The restaurant first opened at 14th and V Streets, NW and, since that time, Shallal has opened locations in Alexandria, Virginia, Hyattsville, Maryland and another D.C. address at 5th and K Streets, NW. The restaurants all have a social justice motif as symbolized by the art depicting photographs of Malcolm X, Cesar Chavez, Rosa Parks and other social justice activists on the walls. Each establishment also has an additional business within it subcontracting to a bookseller, fair trade goods dealer and art supply vendor at respective locations. Events are also held Busboys during monthly discussions on race or in spaces such as The Howard Zinn Room at the Hyattsville location.

to progressive political causes like anti-racism, environmentalism, and economic equality. It was also extensively advertised on WPFW, a Pacifica Radio Network station with ample Black listenership.

I took a moment to bask in the visual and auditory delights of the evening. There was a lot of diversity on display but, given the $135 cost for the tickets, I had to assume socioeconomic variation was not represented the same extent to which differences in nationality, gender, race, age, and sexuality appeared to be. The composition of this, seemingly, class homogeneous gathering symbolically resonated with the implications of my study of gentrification. The food, drink, and entertainment consumed in the relative opulence of a newly-restored theater corresponded to the resources the middle class have access to through the urban restructuring and development associated with gentrification. Among the people eluding the cost prohibitions of The Peace Ball were, more than likely, some of the same folks who could also avail themselves of the goods and services the market, now, offers in communities where these were previously more restricted.

Like having the means to attend lavish balls, gentrification proliferates through the disparities of class. However, disentangling socioeconomics from that which is racial and ethnic is a difficult task, particularly in this geographic setting. The bond between the two is fortified by the impact of structural racism on wealth accumulation, housing procurement, and other uneven outcomes connected to gentrification. Symbiosis is also nurtured by the alienation and urban neglect that preceded these political economic and population shifts. Consequently, gentrification reproduces inequality and foments racial resentment.

It is also the case that the poor are too often at the conceptual and participatory margins of discussions about gentrification. One set of arguments disputes the supposition that gentrification causes displacement (Freeman and Branconi, 2004) and others posit low income residents will derive secondary advantages from associated of changes (Vigdor, 2002). There are also pro-gentrification writers who have admitted that urban dislocation will undoubtedly stem from development strategies they support. Ehrenhalt, for example, argues that negative consequences may be unavoidable but that the hardships some people experience could, in the scheme of things, be dwarfed in importance by the overall gains made by other populations (2012). The assumption here is that the economic activity of the middle classes will elevate the conditions for a larger populace in time.

This book doesn't minimize gentrification's impact on vulnerable populations in D.C. Neither does it find the practice of relegating the needs of the poor and working classes to the sidelines as an acceptable approach to sustainable urban development. The pressures on low income households through burgeoning housing costs can worsen as a result of the housing market boom in Washington, D.C. According to Real Estate Business Intelligence (REBI), the median cost for homes is $421,000, up 12.27 percent from last year.[2] While it is assumed profits from home sales may be accrued by working class families, more data are needed

---

2   http://www.rbintel.com/statistics/washington-dc.

on the extent to which this is the case. As it relates to this point, housing activists have raised concerns about what type of replacement-housing sellers are able to purchase after closing - an issue to which I return momentarily.

African Americans and Gentrification in Washington, D.C. uses gentrification to contextualize an exploration of the contemporary experiences and thoughts of Black people in the Nation's Capital. As such, it contributes to discussions of city life today by sharing the views and experiences I have heard and observed in face-to-face interviews and through participant observation. This book also amplifies the concerns of critical urban theorists by placing the ideas and actions of African Americans who are responding to gentrification within a structural context. These wider circumstances should, not only, account for the larger backdrop of racialization and class formation in D.C. history. It also encompasses any impacts upon households that are affected by developments occurring in the overall U.S. economy during this period of heightened gentrification.

Because D.C. is a federal city, for example, both the great recession and potential budgetary assaults on the federal government could pack a powerful punch in this region. African Americans make up 17.6 percent of the federal workforce, compared to the 10 percent employed in the private sector.[3] As Edsall notes, Black employees are also well represented in the agencies and departments Republicans want to cut funding for such as Health and Human Services, Housing and Urban Development, the Department of Education, and the Equal Employment Opportunity Commission (2012). These assorted economic threats are being posed at a time when African Americans are witnessing roll backs in voting rights, the valorization of excessive policing and pseudo-law enforcement tactics, and vehemently racist attacks lobbed against the President, and sometimes his entire family. Moreover these verbal attacks are not solely emanating from fringe elements. All these factors are part and parcel of an economic and social climate in the U.S. that is loaded with uncertainty and contradiction.

Contextualizing contemporary urban shifts can also help build awareness around the formation of Black ideologies and patterns which may be associated with fueling or allaying of discord rooted in difference. Relatedly, this book also advances work in critical Whiteness studies (CWS) by documenting the urban, economic legacy of White supremacy and its relationship to gentrification. Cashin writes that, since the late 1940s, the federal government spent three billion dollars to implement urban renewal projects that destroyed approximately 400,000 units of affordable housing and displaced about one million people (2004). Half of the people dislocated were African Americans who were funneled into "existing ghetto neighborhoods or into racially-segregated public housing" (Cashin, 2004, p. 116).

Today, gentrification tests these past demographic patterns. White and higher income populations are moving into areas that were formally, rigidly segregated.

---

3   U.S. Office of Personnel Management. 2007. Federal Civilian Workforce Statistics, The Fact Book. Washington, D.C., accessed 31 March 2001, available at http://www.eeoc. gov/federal/reports/fsp2009/profles.cfm.

As this White, urban rediscovery is taking place and fostering change, there is also demographic consistency. Research indicates that White Americans still "place a premium on homogeneity" (Cashin, 2004, p. 10). This is verified by a study that concludes members of this population will pay a 13 percent increase to live in a predominantly White neighborhood (Calmore, 1998).

What are the implications of these findings for conditions and relationships in rapidly changing urban neighborhoods across the U.S.? Perhaps the tensions born out of these inconsistencies are at the root of micro aggressions and other community-level conflicts? A yearning to live in the city and in closer proximity to work may not align with a longing to avoid localities with populations that are deemed undesirable. At the other end of the spectrum is documentation that some gentrifiers want to reside in culturally heterogeneous communities and that this is a part of what is driving their embrace of urban life (Modan, 2007). How many White residents does it take to foster a sense of comfort with new urban surroundings? How do the different waves of gentrification differ from each other and lead to varied outcomes? As it pertains to D.C., answers to these questions would be edifying. I contend, however, that the view of White newcomers as colonizers of communities of color is, in part, fostered by the view that dominance rather than integration is the desired outcome of these demographic shifts.

Of course conflicts occur among people within racial-ethnic groups as well as during interactions across the boundaries of standpoint and identity. Mollifying cross-cultural tensions does not trump addressing inequality but addressing these problems can yield constructive outcomes. Case in point, my project participants encompassed those who have been at the center of these kinds of clashes and those with ties to diverse social networks at the same time.[4] In addition to the examples provided in previous chapters, four of the 44 people with whom I interacted directly were involved in interracial marriages or relationships. Others discussed having friends of different racial-ethnic backgrounds[5] and this description includes activists who work closely and sometimes under stressful conditions among populations with whom they do not share a racial-ethnic identity.

Activism that occurs in multiracial settings and is done on behalf of low to moderate income residents is important work to observe. Casting light on how relationships are maintained and the ways conflicts are addressed or averted can

---

4   Interlocutors for this project include gay and straight African Americans who also range from being very low income to individuals who have attended college and are professionals. I can only count one occasion where xenophobia and heterosexism dripped from the responses of one person, an African American elder who felt comfortable not masking his/her prejudices during our conversation. These remarks were irrational, anti-immigrant, and anti-gay.

5   As further indicators of close, cross-cultural interaction, I observed in the field, interlocutors Miriam Khan and Zahira Kahlo are two Asian-American women project participants who either have been or currently are involved in relationships with African American men.

offer a keener understanding of what standpoints and strategies are needed to meet organizational goals and build a congenial workplace atmosphere at the same time. It is possible that where pretenses about White privilege and White supremacy are stripped bare, stronger bonds can be fostered among different kinds of people working together to eradicate barriers to equality.

These are questions I ponder, not only as an urban anthropologist and social justice advocate, but also as a native Washingtonian who has worked in diverse and White-led, progressive organizations. Racial understanding is a possibility but not an inevitability, even in a work settings with an openly, anti-racist orientation. I base this on my experience seeing discomfort, anger, and denial intensify when sensitive issues of race and class are broached among well-meaning people who are inexperienced with having, what can amount to, difficult conversations.[6]

Even when all appears congenial, frictions may rage below the surface because incendiary beliefs and practices may have not been delineated from the minefield of racial-ethnic relations. My field data show that familiarity, as represented by the relationships of diverse neighbors who have lived together for years, or strong effort, and not the rote call for cross-cultural dialogue, is what mends sociocultural fissures. Talking is no substitute for social justice activism, particularly when discussions are bereft of context. These types of racial-ethnic dynamics also vary from the settings where women of color were in high ranking positions compared to work environs where only the administrative-support staff consists of Black women. These nuances can lead to qualitatively distinct conditions and should be attended to in ethnographic inquiry.

This book continues what was initiated decades ago by pioneers in D.C. ethnography working to examine race and class and, in their own way, advance social justice concerns (Hannerz, 1969; Liebow, 1967). It has already been stated that the body of anthropological literature on D.C. is not as extensive as it should be. Slow progress has been made with a select number of significant ethnographies emerging which examine history and sociocultural relations in the contemporary Nation's Capital (Modan, 2007; Williams, 1988, 2004). Doctoral students and newly-milted Ph.D.'s have conducted qualitative research in D.C. but few have published monographs at this time. At any rate, my research differs considerably from the conversations the other anthropologists work to promote.

African Americans and Gentrification in Washington, D.C. looks at Black residents across a socioeconomic range. As the, sometimes, lengthy interview

---

6 During the summer of 2012, my 20 year old daughter worked with a progressive non-profit organization that had an entirely White staff. Oblivious to the need for praxis in fostering diversity up to that point, upon accepting the internship over the phone my daughter was asked to conduct weekly workshops with staff members on the impact of White privilege in U.S. society at large and workplaces like their Dupont Circle location in particular. She reported experiencing some push-back, particularly from older White men and she also carried the burden of "teaching" White people about racism alone since none of her colleagues could assist her with the related tasks.

excerpts I have included in this book's data chapters indicate, it has also been important for me to allow the candid and heartfelt viewpoints of my interlocutors to appear as plentifully as possible. These women and men have a lot to say, and while I make no argument that these findings are definitive or statistically-representative, my data expose frameworks of racialized and political ideologies to shed light on how these are formed. Readers can also glean what I learned from talking with African Americans who are regularly confronting or constructing gentrification in D.C. The value of these discoveries notwithstanding, additional areas of gentrification-related inquiry remain that I did not tackle but which are ripe for examination.

For example, this book is not about one neighborhood in the District. However, studies that focus on one community have made important contributions to urban anthropology and the study of race and politics (Gregory, 1998; Sanjek, 1998). *African Americans and Gentrification in Washington, D.C.* casts a wider net which informs readers about what is going on in a variety of neighborhoods as well as city-wide dynamics. This book offers a broader survey of conditions and events, but ethnographic studies of specific parts of cities are necessary and can provide additional details for persons who are keen on knowing more about D.C. culture, life, and history.

One overlooked subtopic in published ethnographies of gentrification in Washington, D.C. is the impact of gender relations. Bondi maintains that divisions of labor and other factors related to sexual difference are crucial for any analyses of gentrification (1990). Taking intersectionality into account is particularly important in a city like D.C. where more than half of the residents are African American and Latino and the poor in this metropolitan area are predominantly from these communities of color. Female headed households are central components to these low income populations. Validating Bondi's observations is research showing that Black women living in cities are disproportionately affected by evictions (Desmond, 2012). This research prompted poverty-blogger Megan Cottrell to write, citing Desmond's study on Milwaukee, Wisconsin, "Eviction is For Black Women What Incarceration is to Black Men" (2010). How are women and men differently affected by gentrification and what are the key patterns associated with individualized and collective responses to gendered processes?

It is also important to hear from Washingtonians belonging to a range of racial-ethnic groups about how they perceive, are affected by, and responding to gentrification. Like African Americans, Latino populations have also been on the losing end of gentrification. There is much more to know about the specific experiences within a multifaceted grouping that includes peoples of Caribbean and South and Central American descent. These are folks of different phenotypes who straddle racial categories and may also speak English as a second language. As a result, Latinos face varied forms of discrimination which may emanate from the nativism of African Americans or the legacy of White supremacy, among other sources. Numerous questions remain about how these diverse populations fit into the experience of gentrification in Washington, D.C.

Long term White residents constitute another segment of the D.C. population about whom much more ethnographic data are needed. The Chocolate City paradigm has its relevance but it should not be relied upon to essentialize notions of belonging in the Nation's Capital. That my research is rooted in the study of African American life and culture requires no justification, but interested anthropologists should take a close look at the viewpoints and experiences of White households; those who are new to the area and those with extensive roots in Washington, D.C. as well. These data can generate much needed perspectives on racial conflict by getting at a standpoint unattainable from the individuals *African Americans and Gentrification in Washington, D.C.* has focused on. Such a focus may also get at the prejudices some White residents have faced as a result of bigotry harbored by African Americans.

A list of issues remain uncovered in published, qualitative studies of Washington, D.C. Some of these topics are discussed, albeit briefly, in this book but there is much more to know about the experiences of gay Black Washingtonians, members of the African American middle class populations, the role of the arts in social justice movements, and development of Pan African thought and activism in this city.[7] These subtopics come together in the documentary *A Different Kind of Black Man* in which anthropologist Sheila Wise profiles "accomplished" African American gay men living in Washington, D.C. (2001). One interlocutor for the Wise film was Melvin Deal, a Pan Africanist gay man who is also the founding director of African Heritage Dancers and Drummers.[8] African Heritage is an award winning company that has performed across the country and around the world while also being credited with helping to inspire and train local youth. As the costs for performance and rehearsal spaces increase, organizations like Deal's also face challenges surviving and maintaining a presence in D.C.

Finally, incarceration and education are topics which relate to gentrification and the displacement in Washington, D.C. Both of these issues are in need of in depth, qualitative examinations that look at related concerns such as the plethora of charters schools now operating in the District and the school-to-prison pipeline (Bahena, Cooc, Carrie-Rubin, Kuttner and Ng, 2012; Rios, 2011). This book has shown that rising housing-costs are one manner through which vulnerable populations experience urban dislocation. What we have too little of are the details about where displaced people are finding housing and the specific types of challenges they are facing once they lose their home-places. An increased focus on these questions can assist the work of policy makers and settle key debates about

---

7   In 2013, anthropologist Michelle Chatman completed her doctoral dissertation that explored how African Americans in the District see themselves related to Africa. Her field data were collected through participant observation at African-centered schools and among African American adherents to African religious or belief systems.

8   Sheila Wise. 2001. *A Different Kind of Black Man* (15 minutes). San Francisco: Frameline Films. The documentary can be purchased by visiting http://cart.frameline.org/productdetails.asp?productcode=t525.

the benefits of gentrification. *African Americans and Gentrification in Washington, D.C.* is only one step in that direction. Adhering to calls for greater transparency, inclusion and compassion in budgetary decisions and urban planning will help promote the well-being and staying power of residents from varied socioeconomic backgrounds. The future of the city is dependent upon government and citizens meeting an assortment of responsibilities. Gentrification has already wielded powerful impacts, but by attending to the needs of vulnerable populations for affordable housing and other vital resources and services D.C. can become a city for all to thrive in and enjoy. It is certain that local advocates for housing and social justice will not cease their collective efforts until this possibility is realized.

Bibliography

Abrams, A. 2011. Where We Live: Truxton Circle in Northeast D.C., Reclaiming its Identity. *The Washington Post*, 27 May.

Aguirre Jr., A., and Baker, D.V. 2008. *Structured Inequality in the United States: Critical Discussions on the Continuing Significance of Race, Ethnicity, and Gender*. Upper Saddle River: Pearson Education.

Aizeman, N.C. 2007. D.C. May Be Losing Status as a Majority Black City. *The Washington Post*, 17 May.

Alexander, M. 2012. *The New Jim Crow*. New York: The New Press.

Apidta, T. 1995. *The Hidden History of Washington, D.C.: A Guide for Black Folks*. Washington, D.C.: The Reclamation Project.

Atlas, J., and P. Drier. September/October 1994. Public Housing: What Went Wrong? Shelterforce. Issue #74, Montclair, N.J.: National Housing Institute. http://www.nhi.org/online/issues/77/pubhsg.html.

Bahena, S.A, North C., Carrie-Rubin, R., Kuttner, P. and Ng, M. 2012. *Disrupting the School-to-Prison Pipeline*. Cambridge: Harvard Educational Review.

Baker, L.D. 1998. *From Savage to Negro: Anthropology and the Construction of Race, 1896–1954*. Los Angeles: University of California Press.

Balkin, J.M. (Ed.). 2001. *What Brown vs. the Board of Education Should Have Said*. New York: New York University Press.

Bay, M. 2000. *The White Image in the Black Mind: African American Ideas About White People, 1830–1925*. New York: Oxford University Press.

Blackmon, D. 2008. *Slavery by Another Name: The Re-Enslavement of African Americans From the Civil War to World War II*. New York: Doubleday.

Bloom, A. 1988. *The Closing of the American Mind*. New York: Simon and Shuster.

Bobo, L. 2011. Somewhere Between Jim Crow and Post-Racialism: Reflections on the Racial Divide in American Today. *Daedalus, the Journal of the American Academy of Arts and Sciences* 140(2): 11–35.

Bondi, L. 1991. Gender Divisions and Gentrification: A Critique. *Transactions of the Institute of British Geographers* 16(2): 190–98.

Bonilla Silva, E. 2010. *Racism without Racists: Color-Blind Racism and the Persistence of Racial Inequality in the United States*. Lanham: Rowan and Littlefield.

Bonilla Silva, E., Goar, C. and Embrick, D.G. 2006. When Whites Flock Together: The Social Psychology of White Habitus. *Critical Sociology* 32(2–3): 229–53.

Borchert, J. 1980. *Alley Life in Washington: Family, Community, Religion, and Folklife in the City, 1850–1970*. Urbana: University of Illinois Press.

Boyd M. 2008. *Jim Crow Nostalgia: Restructuring Race in Bronzeville.* Minneapolis: University of Minnesota Press.

Boyer, B.D. 1973. *Cities Destroyed for Cash: The FHA Scandal at HUD.* Chicago: Follett Publishing Company.

Brenner, N., Marcuse, P. and Mayer, M. (Eds.). 2012. *Cities for People, Not for Profit: Critical Urban Theory and the Right to the City.* New York and London: Routledge.

Brodkin, K. 1994. *How Jews Became White Folks in Race.* New Brunswick: Rutgers University Press.

Brookings Institution Center on Urban and Metropolitan Policy. 1999. *A Region Divided: The State of Growth in Greater Washington, D.C.* Washington, D.C.: The Brookings Institution.

Brown, DeN. 2007. U-Turn on H Street. *The Washington Post*, 18 March.

Brown, M.K., Carnoy, M., Currie, E., Duster, T., Oppenheimer, D.B., Schultz, M.M. and Wellman, D. 2005. *Whitewashing Race: The Myth of a Color-Blind Society.* Berkeley and Los Angeles: University of California Press.

Cacho, L.M. 2012. *Social Death: Racialized Rightlessness and the Criminalization of the Unprotected.* New York: New York University Press.

Calmore, J.O. 1998. Race/ism Lost and Found: The Fair Housing Act at Thirty. *University of Miami Law Review* 52: 1067–1101.

Cashin, S.L. 2004. *The Failures of Integration: How Race and Class are Undermining the American Dream.* New York: Public Affairs.

Centers for Disease Control, A Look Inside Food Deserts, http://www.cdc.gov/features/fooddeserts/.

Cenziper, D. and Cohen, S. 2008. Forced Out: A Washington Post Investigation into the Casualties of the District's Real Estate Boom.

Chatman, M.C. 2013. *Beyond Kente Cloth and Kwanzaa: Interrogating African-Centered Identity in Washington, D.C.* Unpublished Doctoral Dissertation, Department of Anthropology, American University, Washington, D.C.

Chow, E.N. 1996. From Pennsylvania Avenue to H Street, W: The Transformation of Washington's Chinatown in *Urban Odyssey: A Multicultural History of Washington, D.C.*, edited by F. Curro Cary. Washington, D.C.: Smithsonian Institution Press.

Clark-Lewis, E. (Ed.). 2002. *First Freed: Washington, D.C. in the Emancipation Era.* Washington, D.C.: Howard University Press.

Clarke, K.M. 2004. Mapping Yoruba Networks: Power and Agency in the Making of Transnational Communities. Durham: Duke University Press.

Clarke, K.M. and Thomas, D.A. (Eds.). 2006. *Globalization and Race: Transformations in the Cultural Production of Blackness.* Durham: Duke University Press.

Comey, J. and Grosz, M. 2011. *Where Kids Go: The Foreclosure Crisis and Mobility in Washington, D.C.* Washington, D.C.: The Urban Institute.

Congressional Digest. May 2007. District of Columbia Self Government, History of Home Rule.

Conrad, E. 2010. A City Divided: Race, Class and Inequality in Washington, D.C. General Honor's Capstone, American University. Last accessed on 14 March 2013 at http://aladinrc.wrlc.org/bitstream/handle/1961/9255/Conrad%2c%20 Emily%20-%20Spring%20%2710%20%28P%29.pdf?sequence=1.

Cooper, A.J. 1892. *A Voice From the South*. Xenia, Ohio: The Aldine Printing House. C326 C769v (North Carolina Collection, University of North Carolina at Chapel Hill).

Corrigan, M.B. 2001–2002. Imaginary Cruelties? A History of the Slave Trade in Washington, D.C. *Washington History* 13(2): 4–27.

Cosby, B. and Poussaint, A.F. 2009. *Come on People: On the Path from Victims to Victors*. Nashville: Thomas Nelson.

Cottrell, M. 2010. Eviction Is to Black Women What Incarceration Is to Black Men. http://trueslant.com/megancottrell/2010/01/27/eviction-is-for-black-women-what-incarceration-is-to-black-men/.

Davila, A. 2004. *Barrio Dreams: Puerto Ricans, Latinos, and the Neoliberal City*. Berkeley: University of California Press.

Davis, D. 2013. Border Crossings: Intimacy and Feminist Activist Ethnography in the Age of Neoliberalism in *Feminist Activist Ethnography: Counterpoints to Neoliberalism in North America*, edited by C. Craven and D. Davis. Lanham: Lexington Books.

Dawson, M. 2001. *Black Visions: The Roots of Contemporary African American Political Ideologies*. Chicago: University of Chicago Press.

D.C. Agenda. 2004. Issue Scan. Washington, D.C.: D.C. Agenda.

D.C. Fiscal Policy Institute. 2010. *Nowhere to Go: As D.C. Housing Costs Rise, Residents are Left with Fewer Affordable Housing Options*. Washington, D.C.: D.C. Fiscal Policy Institute.

D.C. Fiscal Policy Institute. 2012. *What's In the Mayor's Fiscal Year 2013 Budget Request?* Washington, D.C.: D.C. Fiscal Policy Institute.

D.C. Office of Planning. 2005. *Northeast Gateway: Many Neighborhoods, One Community, A Revitalization Strategy and Implementation Plan Featuring Ivy City*. Washington, D.C.: D.C. Office of Planning.

D.C. Hunger Solutions and Social Impact. 2010. *When Healthy Food is Out of Reach: An Analysis of the Grocery Gap in the District of Columbia*. Washington, D.C.: D.C. Hunger Solutions.

Delgado, R. and Stefancic, J. 1997. *Critical White Studies: Looking Behind the Mirror*. Philadelphia: Temple University Press.

DeSena, J.N. 2012. Segregation Begins at Home: Gentrification and the Accomplishment of Boundary Work. *Urbanites*, Vol. 2(2): 4–24.

Desmond, M. 2012. Eviction and the Reproduction of Urban Poverty. *American Journal of Sociology* 118 (1): 88–133.

Donald, D.H. 1996. *Charles Sumner*. New York: De Capo Press.

D'Souza, D. 1995. *The End of Racism: Principles for a Multiracial Society*. New York: The Free Press.

DuBois, W.E.B. 1897. Strivings of the Negro People. *The Atlantic Monthly*, August.

Dyson, M.E. 1993. *Beyond Essentialism: Expanding African American Cultural Criticism, in Reflecting Black: African American Cultural Criticism*. Minneapolis: University of Minnesota Press.

Edsall, T.B. 2012. *The Age of Austerity: How Scarcity Will Remake American Politics*. New York: Doubleday.

Edsall, T.B. September 2012. Is Poverty a Kind of Robbery? http://campaignstops. blogs.nytimes.com/2012/09/16/is-poverty-a-kind-of-robbery/.

Ehrenhalt, A. 2012. *The Great Inversion and the Future of the American City*. New York: Alfred F. Knopf.

Ellwell, C. 2008. *From Political Protest to Bureaucratic Service: The Transformation of Homeless Advocacy in the Nation's Capital and the Eclipse of Political Discourse*. Unpublished Doctoral Dissertation, Department of Anthropology, American University, Washington, D.C.

Farrell, A.E. 2011. *Fat Shame: Stigma and the Fat Body in American Culture*. New York: New York University Press.

Feagin, J. and Sikes, M.P. 1995. *Living with Racism: The Black Middle Class Experience*. New York: Beacon Press.

Fitzpatrick S. and Godwin, M.R. 1990. *The Guide to Black Washington*. New York: Hippocrene Books.

Frank, S. 2005. *If We Own the Story, We Own the Place: Cultural Heritage, Historical Preservation and Gentrification on U Street*. Master's Thesis, American Studies, The University of Maryland, College Park.

Franke-Ruta, G. 2012. The Politics of the Urban Comeback: Politics and Gentrification in Washington, D.C. *The Atlantic Monthly*, August.

Freeman, L. 2006. *There Goes the 'Hood: Views of Gentrification from the Ground Up*. Philadelphia: Temple University Press.

Freeman, L. and Branconi, F. 2004. Gentrification and Displacement: New York City in the 1990s. *Journal of the American Planning Association* 70: 39–53.

Freund, D.M.P. 2007. *Colored Property: State Policy and White Racial Politics in Suburban America*. Chicago: University of Chicago Press.

Gatewood, W. 1990. *Aristocrats of Color: The Black Elite, 1880–1920*. Bloomington: Indiana University Press.

Giddings, P. 1984. *When and Where I Enter: The Impact of Black Women on Race and Sex in America*. New York: William Morrow.

Gilbert, M.A. 2006. Race, Location, and Education: The Election of Black Mayors in the 1990s. *Journal of Black Studies* 36 (3): 318–33.

Glass, R. 1964. Introduction: Aspects of Change, In London: Aspects of Change, Centre for Urban Studies, editors. London: MacKibben and Kee, xiii–xlii.

Goode, J. and Maskovsky, J. (Eds.). 2001. *The New Poverty Studies: The Ethnography of Power, Politics, and Impoverished People in the United States*. New York: New York University Press.

Gould, S.J. 1981. *The Mismeasure of Man*. New York: W.W. Norton Company.

Gregory, S. 1998. *Black Corona: Race and the Politics of Place in an Urban Community*. Princeton: Princeton University Press.

Hackworth, J. 2007. *The Neoliberal City: Governance, Ideology, and Development in American Urbanism*. Ithaca: Cornell University Press.

Hannerz, U. 1969. *Soulside: Inquiries into Ghetto Culture and Community*. New York and London: Columbia University Press.

Harrell, E. August 2007. *Black Victims of Violent Crime*, U.S. Department of Justice.

Harris-Lacewell, M. 2006. *Barbershops, Bibles, and BET: Everyday Talk and Black Political Thought*. Princeton: Princeton University Press.

Harrison, F. 1995. The Persistent Power of 'Race' in the Cultural and Political Economy of Racism, *Annual Review of Anthropology* 24: 47–74.

Harrold, S. 2003. *Subversives: Antislavery Community in Washington, D.C., 1928–1865*. Baton Rouge: Louisiana State University.

Hartigan, J. 2010. *Race in the 21st Century: Ethnographic Approaches*. New York: Oxford University Press.

Hartigan, J. 2005. *Odd Tribes: Toward a Cultural Analysis of White People*. Durham: Duke University Press.

Hartigan, J. 1999. *Racial Situations: Class Predicaments of Whiteness in Detroit*. Princeton: Princeton University Press.

Harvey, D. 2005. *A Brief History of Neoliberalism*. London and Oxford: Oxford University Press.

Hathaway, D. and Ho, S. 2003. Small but Resilient: Washington's Chinatown over the Years. *Washington History* 15(1): 42–61.

Higginbotham, E. 1993. *Righteous Discontent: The Women's Movement in the Black Baptist Church, 1880–1920*. Cambridge: Harvard University Press.

Hill-Collins, P. 1990. *Black Feminist Thought: Knowledge, Consciousness and the Politics of Empowerment*. New York: Harper Collins.

Hochschild, J.I. and Herk, M. 1990. Yes, but....", in *Principles and Caveats in American Racial Attitudes in Majorities and Minorities*, edited by J.W. Chappman and A. Werthemer. New York: New York University Press.

hooks, b. 1998. Representations of Whiteness in the Black Imagination, in *Black on White: Black Writers on What it Means to Be White*, edited by D. Roediger. New York: Shocken Books.

Huchzermeyer, M. 2011. *Cities with 'Slums': From Informal Settlement Eradication to a Right to the City in Africa*. Claremont: UCT Press.

Humphrey, R.L. and Chambers, M.E. 1977. *Ancient Washington: American Indian Cultures of the Potomac Valley*. Washington, D.C.: George Washington University.

Ignatiev, N. 1995. *How the Irish Became White*. New York: Routledge.

Institute on Assets and Social Policy. May 2010. The Racial Wealth Gap Increases Four-Fold. Brandies University.

Jackson, J.L. 2005. *Real Black: Adventures in Racial Sincerity*. Chicago: University of Chicago Press.

Jackson, J.L. 2001. *Harlem World: Doing Race and Class in Contemporary Black America*. Chicago: University of Chicago Press.

Jaffe, H.S. and Sherwood, T. 1994. *Dream City: Race, Power and the Decline of Washington, D.C.*. New York: Simon & Shuster.

Johnson, K.E. 2007. "Trouble Won't Last": Black Church Activism in Postwar Philadelphia, in *African American Urban History Since World War II*, edited by K.L. Kusmer and J.W. Trotter. Chicago: University of Chicago Press.

Jones, W. 1929. *The Housing of Negroes in Washington, D.C.* Washington, D.C.: Howard University Press.

Joseph, M., Chaskin, R.J. and Webber, H.S. January 2007. The Theoretical Basis for Addressing Poverty through Mixed-Income Development, *Urban Affairs Review* 42(3): 369–409.

Kain, J. 1968. Housing Segregation, Negro Unemployment, and Metropolitan Decentralization. *Quarterly Journal of Economics* 82: 175–97.

Kanaaneh, R. 2002. *Birthing the Nation: Strategies of Palestinian Women in Israel*. Berkeley: University of California Press.

Keckley, E. 1988. *Behind the Scenes. Or, Thirty Years a Slave, and Four Years in the White House*. New York: Oxford University Press (originally published 1868 New York: G.W. Carlton).

Kerstetter, K., Reed, J. and Lazere, E. 2009. *New Census Data Reveal Growing Income Gaps in the District*. Washington, D.C.: D.C. Fiscal Policy Institute.

Kofie, N.F. 1999. *Race, Class and the Struggle for Neighborhood in Washington, D.C.* New York: Routledge.

Koppel, N. Are Your Jeans Sagging? Go Directly to Jail. *The New York Times*, 31 August 2007.

Kraft, B. May 2004. Ivy City: Washington's First Railroad Suburb. Washington, D.C: D.C. North (46).

Krase, J. 2012. *Seeing Cities: Local Culture and Class*. Farnham: Ashgate.

Landry, B. 1987. *The New Black Middle Class*. Berkeley: University of California Press.

Lazare, E. 2010. No *Where To Go: As D.C. Housing Costs Rise, Residents are Left With Fewer Affordable Housing Options*, D.C. Fiscal Policy Institute, 5 February 2010.

Lazare, E. 2006. *Income Inequality Grew Dramatically in D.C. Over the Past Two Decades*, D.C. Fiscal Policy Institute, 26 January.

Lazare, E. and Tallent, C. 2006. *Not Enough to Live Off: D.C. TANF's Benefits Are Among the Least Adequate in the Nation*, D.C. Fiscal Policy Institute, 14 March.

Leap, W. 2009. Professional Baseball, Urban Restructuring, and (Changing) Gay Geographies in Washington, D.C., in *Out in Public: Reinventing Lesbian/Gay Anthropology in a Globalizing World*, edited by E. Lewin and W.L. Leap. Malden: Wiley-Blackwell.

Lewis, C. 2010. East of the River or 'River East'? Gentrification is heading across the Anacostia. *The Washington City Paper*.

Liebow, E. 1967. *Tally's Corner: A Study of Negro Streetcorner Men.* Boston: Little, Brown and Co.

Lees, L., Slater, T. and Wyly, E. 2008. *Gentrification.* London and New York: Routeledge.

Lesko, K., Babb, V. and Gibbs, C. 1991. *Black Georgetown Remembered.* Washington, D.C.: Georgetown University Press.

Lopez, G.P. 2008. Rebelling against the War on Low income, of Color, Immigrant Communities, in *After the War on Crime: Race, Democracy and a New Reconstruction,* edited by M.L. Frampton, I. Haney Lopez, and J. Simon. New York: New York University Press.

Lusane, C. 2010. *The Black History of the White House.* San Francisco: City Lights Publishers.

Lutz, H., Herrera Vivar, M.T. and Supik, L. 2010. *Framing Intersectionality: Debates on a Multi-Faceted Concept in Gender Studies.* Farnham: Ashgate.

MacLean, N. 2008. Southern Dominance in Borrowed Language: The Regional Origins of American Neoliberalism, in *New Landscapes of Inequality: Neoliberalism and the Erosion of Democracy in America.* Santa Fe: School of American Research Press.

Mahmud, T. 2010. Slums, Slumdogs, and Resistance. *Journal of Gender, Social Policy & the Law* 18(3): 685–710.

Mahon, M. 2004. *The Right to Rock: The Black Rock Coalition and the Cultural Politics of Race.* Durham: Duke University Press.

Mahoney, M.R.M. 1995. Segregation, Whiteness and Transformation. *University of Pennsylvania Law Review* 143(5): 1659–84.

Manning, R. 1998. Multicultural Washington, D.C.: The Changing Social and Economic Landscape of a Post-Industrial Metropolis, *Ethnic and Racial Studies* 21(2): 328–55.

Marcus, H.R. and Moya P.M.L., editors. 2010. *Doing Race: 21 Essays for the 21st Century.* New York: W.W. Norton.

Martinez, E. and Garcia, A. 2001. What is Neoliberalism? A Brief Definition for Activists. *CorpWatch,* 22 March.

Massey, D. and Denton, N. 1998. *American Apartheid: Segregation and the Making of the Underclass.* Cambridge: Harvard University Press.

Mauer, M. and King, R.S. 2007. *Uneven Justice: State Rates of Incarceration by Race and Ethnicity,* The Sentencing Project.

McQuirter, M. 2009. *Ending Slavery in the Nation's Capital: The District of Columbia's Compensated Emancipation Act.* Washington, D.C.: The Government of the District of Columbia.

Meyer, E.M. 1996. *Public Opinion and the Political Future of the Nation's Capital.* Washington, D.C.: Georgetown University Press.

Modan, G. 2007. *Turf Wars: Discourse, Diversity and the Politics of Place.* Malden: Blackwell Publishing.

Moore, J.M. 1999. *Leading the Race: The Transformation of the Black Elite in the Nation's Capital, 1880–1920.* Charlottesville: The University Press of Virginia.

Morrison, T., editor. 1992. *Playing in the Dark: Whiteness and the Literary Imagination*. New York: Vintage Books.

Mullings, L. 2005. Interrogating Racism: Toward an Anti-Racist Anthropology, *Annual Review of Anthropology* 34: 667–93.

Mundy, L. 2010. Neighborhood of Slaves and Presidents. *The Washington Post*, 15 February.

NeighborhoodInfo DC. December 2011. Changes in Prince Georges County 2000–2010. http://www.neighborhoodinfodc.org/PrinceGeorges/ChangesinPrinceGeorgesCounty20002010.p df, Washington, D.C.: The Urban Institute.

NeighborhoodInfo DC. Winter 2011. Washington, D.C. Metropolitan Area Foreclosure Monitor. Washington, D.C.: The Urban Institute.

Nelson, D. and Ojha, H. 2012. Redistributing Up: The Unequal States of America, A Reuters Series. Washington, D.C. http://www.reuters.com/subjects/income-inequality/Washington.

Oliver, M. and Shapiro, T. 1996. *Black* Wealth/*White Wealth: A New Perspective on Racial Inequality*. New York: Routledge.

Orfield, G. 2001. *Schools More Separate Consequences of a Decade of Re-segregation.* Cambridge: Civil Rights Project, Harvard University.

Orfield, M. 1999. *Washington Metropolitics: A Regional Agenda for Community and Stability.* Washington, D.C.: Metropolitan Area Research Corporation.

Pardo, I. and Prato, G.B. editors. 2012. *Anthropology in the City: Methodology and Theory*. Farnham: Ashgate.

Pattillo, M. 2007. *Black on the Block: The Politics of Race and Class in the City.* Chicago: The University of Chicago Press.

Pew Research Center. 2007. A Social and Demographic Trends Report, Optimism About Black Progress Declines: Blacks See Growing Values Gap Between Poor and Middle Class, http://www.pewsocialtrends.org/files/2010/10/Race-2007.pdf.

Primus, R. 2004. Bolling Alone. *Columbia Law Review* 104(4): 975–1041.

Prince, S.R. Spring 2002. Changing Places: Race, Class, and Belonging in the "New" Harlem. *Urban Anthropology and Studies of Cultural Systems and World Economic Development* 31(1): 5–25.

Prince, S.R. 2004. *Constructing Belonging and Negotiating Difference: Class, Race and Harlem's Professional Workers*. New York: Routledge.

Prince, S.R. 2005. Race, Class, and the Packaging of Harlem. *Identities: Global Studies in Culture and Power* 12: 383–404.

Rasmussen, B.B., Klinenberg, E., Nexica, I.J. and Wray, M. (Eds.). 2001. *The Making and Unmaking of Whiteness*. Durham: Duke University Press.

Reed, J. 2012. *Disappearing Act: Affordable Housing in DC is Vanishing amid Sharply Rising Housing Costs*. Washington, D.C. D.C. Fiscal Policy Institute.

Rigsby, G.U. 1987. *Alexander Crummell: Pioneer in the Nineteenth-Century Pan-African Thought*. New York: Greenwood Press.

Richland, B. June 2009. On Neoliberalism and Other Social Diseases. The 2008 Sociocultural Anthropology Year in Review, *American Anthropologist* 111(2): 170–76.

Rios, V.M. 2011. *Punished: Policing the Lives of Black and Latino Boys*. New York: New York University Press.

Rivera, A., Juezo, J., Kasica, C. and Muhammad, D. 2009. *State of the Dream 2009: The Silent Depression*, Institute for Policy Studies.

Roediger, D. 2007. The Retreat from Race and Class, in *More Unequal; Aspects of Class in the United States*, edited by M.D. Yates. New York: Monthly Review Press.

Roediger, D. (Ed.). 1998. *Black on White: Black Writers on What it Means to be White*. New York: Shocken.

Roediger, D. 1994. *Toward the Abolition of Whiteness: Essays on Race, Politics and the Working Class*. London: Verso.

Roediger, D. 1991. *The Wages of Whiteness: Race and the Making of the American Working Class*. London: Verso.

Rolland, S. 2006. *Disparities in the District: Poverty is Major Cause of Social Problems in the District of Columbia*. Washington, D.C.: D.C. Fiscal Policy Institute.

Rosenbaum, J. and Popkin, S. 1991. Employment and Earnings of Low-Income Blacks Who Move to Middle-Class Suburbs, in *The Urban Underclass*, edited by C. Jencks and P.E. Peterson. Washington, D.C.: The Brookings Institution, pp. 342–56.

Royster, D.A. 2003. *Race and the Invisible Hand: How White Networks Exclude Black Men from Blue-Collar Jobs*. Berkeley: University of California Press.

Ruben, M. 2001. Suburbanization and Urban Poverty Under Neoliberalism, in *The New Poverty Studies: The Ethnography of Power, Politics, and Impoverished People in the United States*, edited by J. Goode and J. Maskovsky. New York: New York University Press.

Ruble, B.A. 2010. *Washington's U Street: A Biography*. Baltimore: Johns Hopkins University Press.

Ruiz Switzky, B. 2012. Former D.C. Mayor Anthony Williams Joins Board at Bank of Georgetown. *Washington Business Journal*, 21 June.

Sanjek, R. 1998. *The Future of Us All: Race and Neighborhood Politics in New York City*. Ithaca: Cornell University Press.

Sawyer, N. and Tatian, P. 2003. *Segregation Patterns in the District of Columbia: 1980 to 2000*. Washington, D.C.: The Urban Institute and D.C. Agenda.

Schaffer, D.L. 2003/2004. The 1968 Riots in History and Memory. *Washington History* 15(2): 4–33.

Schein, R. (Ed.). 2006. *Landscape and Race in the United States*. New York: Routledge.

Schwartzman, P. and Jenkins, C.L. 2010. How D.C. Mayor Fenty Lost the Black Vote and His Job. *The Washington Post*, 18 September.

Schwartzman, P. 2006. Whose H Street Is It, Anyway? *The Washington Post*, 4 April.

Schwartzman, P. 2005. Renewal Takes Root in D.C.'s Blighted Ivy City: Real Estate Investors Betting on Neighborhood, Washingtonpost.com

Segrest, M. 2001. The Souls of White Folks, in *The Making and Unmaking of Whiteness*, edited by Rasmussen, B.B., Klinenberg, E., Nexica, I.J. and Wray, M. Durham: Duke University Press.

Shao, Q. 2013. *Shanghai Gone: Domicide and Defiance in a Chinese Megacity*. Lanham: Rowan and Littlefield.

Simmons, K. 2001. Passion for Sameness: Encountering a Black Feminist Self in Fieldwork, in *The Dominican Republic, in Black Feminist Anthropology: Theory, Politics, Praxis and Poetics*, edited by I. McClaurin. New Brunswick: Rutgers University Press.

Slater, T. June-September 2009. Missing Marcuse: On Gentrification and Displacement. *City* 13: 292–311.

Slocum, K. 2001. Negotiating Identity and Black Feminist Politics in Caribbean Research, in *Black Feminist Anthropology: Theory, Politics, Praxis and Poetics*, edited by I. McClaurin. New Brunswick: Rutgers University Press.

Smith, N. 1996. *The New Urban Frontier: Gentrifiction and the Revanchist City*. New York: Routledge.

Smith, N. and LeFaivre, M. 1984. A Class Analysis of Gentrification in Gentrification, Displacement and Neighborhood Revitalization. J. John Palen and Bruce London, editors. Albany: State University of New York Press.

Social Compact, Washington, D.C. Drill Down. Washington, D.C.: Social Compact. 2008

Soss, J., Fording, R.C. and Schram, S.F. 2011. *Disciplining the Poor: Neoliberal Paternalism and the Persistent Power of Race*. Chicago: University of Chicago.

Swarns, R. 2006. The Nation's Capital Struggles to Lure Residents to the City. *The New York Times*, 1 January.

Swinney, D.D. 1938. Alley Dwellings and Housing Reform in the District of Columbia. M.A. Thesis, University of Chicago (as cited in Borchert).

Taylor, P., Kochhar, R., Fry, R., Velasco, G. and Motel, S. 2011. *Wealth Gaps Rise to Record Highs Between Whites, Blacks and Hispanics*. Washington, D.C.: Pew Research Center.

The Urban Institute. 2008. *State of Washington, D.C.'s Neighborhoods*. Washington, D.C.: The Urban Institute, The Office of Planning and the Government of the District of Columbia.

Tye, L. 2004. *Rising from the Rails: Pullman Porters and the Making of the Black Middle Class*. New York: Henry Holt & Co.

Vigdor, J. Does Gentrification Harm the Poor? 2002. *Brookings-Wharton Papers on Urban Affairs,*: 133–73. William Gale and Janet Rothenberg Park, editors. Washington, D.C.: Brookings Institution.

Washington, A. 2009. *Reading, Writing and Racialization: The Social Construction of Blackness for Middle School Students and Educators in Prince George's*

County Public Schools. Unpublished Doctoral Dissertation, Department of Anthropology, American University, Washington, D.C.

Weinberger, J. 4 November 2011. Gentrifying Washington, D.C.: The Nation's Capital City is Becoming Friendlier and More Diverse. City Journal.http://www.city-journal.org/2011/eon1104jw.html.

Wiggins, O. 2010. Fewer D.C. Affordable Housing Options Left as City Rents Rise. *The Washington Post*, 6 February.

Williams, B. 2004. *Debt for Sale: A Social History of the Credit Trap*. Philadelphia: University of Pennsylvania Press.

Williams, B. 2001. A River Runs Through Us. *American Anthropologist* 103(2):409–31.

Williams, B. Spring 2002. Gentrifying Water and Selling Jim Crow. *Urban Anthropology & Studies of Cultural Systems and World Economic Development* 31(1): 93–121.

Williams, B. 1988. *Upscaling Downtown: Stalled Gentrification in Washington, D.C.* Ithaca: Cornell University Press.

Williams, J. 2006. *Enough: The Phony Leaders, Dead-End Movements and Culture of Failure that are Undermining Black America and What We Can Do About It*. New York: Random House.

Winant, H. 2004. *The New Politics of Race: Globalism, Difference, Justice*. Minneapolis: University of Minnesota Press.

Wilson, D. 2007. *Cities and Race: America's New Black Ghetto*. New York: Routledge.

Wilson J.M. 1989. *Alexander Crummell: A Study of Civilization and Discontent*. New York: Oxford University Press.

Wise, T. 2009. *Between Barack and Hard Place: Racism and White Denial in the Age of Obama*. San Francisco: City Lights Books.

Yancy, G., editor. 2004. *What White Looks Like: African American Philosophers on the Whiteness Question*. New York: Routledge.

Zukin, S. 1993. *New Landscapes of Power: From Detroit to Disney*. Berkeley: University of California Press.

Index

Schram, S.F. 140–41
segregation and desegregation 42–5,
    161–2
Shallal, Andy 159
Shaw neighborhood 9, 11, 42, 48, 93–4,
    115–16
Sherwood, T. 47
Sikes, M.P. 13
Sindab, Jean 21
slavery 37–40
slum removal 41
Smith, Damu 21
Smith, N. 12, 46
social justice 26, 35–6, 128, 145, 151, 153,
    156, 163
socioeconomic differentiation 125, 128
Soss, J. 140–41
Stewart, Ami 84
Stewart, Maria 40
Stitt, Katea 159
Stokes, Carl B. 46
Street, Paul 15
Studdard, Marie 56, 58, 68–70
Sumner, Charles 148–9
The Sumner School 148–9
Swanson-Canty, Alicia 155
Sweet Honey in the Rock 141

Taylor, Billy 60
Tea Party movement 28
Temporary Assistance for Needy Families
    (TANF) program 51
Terrell, Mary Church 44, 60
Terrell, Robert 44
Thomas, D.A. 35
Till, Emmitt 30

Toure, Kwame 84
trickle-down economic policies 19
Truth, Sojourner 40
Truxton Circle 48
Tucker, Sterling 104–6, 114
Ture, Kalfani 122–3, 148

Ulaby, Neda 81
Union Station Redevelopment Corporation
    (USRC) 155
urban renewal projects 105–6, 119, 161

vagrancy laws 33–4

Washington, Booker T. 44
Washington, Walter 46
Washington City Council 46–7
Washington Metropolitan Police
    Department 106–7
The Washington Post 48, 116
Whitelaw Hotel 77
Whiteness 13, 34, 98, 122
    normalization of 29
Wiggins, Lillian 103
Wilkerson, Isabel 64
Williams, Anthony 100, 109–10, 151
Wilson, Henry 40
Wilson, Woodrow 43
Wise, Sheila 165
Wise, T. 15, 27–8
Woodson, Carter G. 60

Yes food stores 118
Young, Coleman 95

Zukin, S. 12

Made in the USA
Middletown, DE
03 October 2022

11806318R00108